Ireland: a voice among the nations

First published 2019
Royal Irish Academy, 19 Dawson Street, Dublin 2
www.ria.ie

ISBN 978-1-908997-96-8 (HB)
ISBN 978-1-908997-97-5 (pdf)
ISBN 978-1-908997-98-2 (epub)
ISBN 978-1-908997-99-9 (mobi)

British Library Cataloguing in Publication Data. A CIP catalogue record
for this book is available from the British Library.

Editor: Helena King
Design: Fidelma Slattery
Index: Lisa Scholey
Printed in Poland by L&C Printing Group

Royal Irish Academy is a member of Publishing Ireland, the Irish book publishers' association

5 4 3 2

Image on following pages: A depiction of the *Irish Poplar* by Kenneth King. This was the first vessel
commissioned by the state-owned company Irish Shipping, originally established in 1941 to guarantee
Ireland's overseas supply lines during the 'Emergency'.

Illustration on cover and throughout is a detail from a logo designed in the 1950s for the Cultural
Relations Committee's publications.

Ireland
A voice among the nations

John Gibney, Michael Kennedy, Kate O'Malley

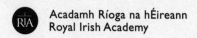
Acadamh Ríoga na hÉireann
Royal Irish Academy

An Chartlann Náisiúnta
National Archives

An Roinn Gnóthaí
Eachtracha agus Trádála
Department of
Foreign Affairs and Trade

Acknowledgments

The authors would like to thank a number of people for their help in completing this book. At the Department of Foreign Affairs and Trade, we are grateful for the assistance provided by Fiona Flood, Patrick McDonagh, Ralph Victory and Aidan O'Hara, and would like to acknowledge the wholehearted support of Secretary General Niall Burgess for this project. We also thank those current and former members, and relatives of members, of the department who commented on the text or who shared their experiences, insights and personal collections with us: Frank Aiken, Frank Cogan, Jill Corish, Marie Cross, Donal Denham, Noel Dorr, Padraig Francis, Gerard Keown, Orla McBreen, Bobby McDonagh, Rory Montgomery, Orla O'Hanrahan, and the family of the late Denis Holmes.

We are grateful to the staff of the various archives and repositories who assisted us in researching and writing this book: Hugh Beckett, Lisa Dolan and Noelle Grothier (Military Archives); James Harte (National Library of Ireland); Barry Houlihan (Hardiman Library, NUI Galway); Deirdre McParland (ESB Archives); Kate Manning (UCD Archives); Brendan Teeling (Dublin Public Libraries); and, at the National Archives of Ireland, former director John McDonough and Zoë Reid.

Finally, we would like to thank Eoin Kinsella at Documents on Irish Foreign Policy, our colleagues in the Publications Office of the Royal Irish Academy, and the anonymous reviewers who commented on the text. Any remaining mistakes or omissions are our own.

A note on conventions

Acronyms are commonly used in diplomacy, but for clarity in the text we have given the full names of institutions when they are first mentioned, with acronyms directly following in parentheses and used thereafter. Some important terminology has evolved over time. For example, the Department of External Affairs is now the Department of Foreign Affairs and Trade; the former position of 'secretary' to the department is now termed 'secretary general'; the European Economic Community has become the European Union; and, since the Good Friday Agreement of 1998, the traditional means of describing relations between Britain and Ireland as 'Anglo-Irish' has largely been replaced by 'British-Irish'. Changes in terminology and designation (such as titles of official positions and institutions) have been integrated into the text as required. We have opted for the most commonly used contemporary place names and personal names in the text; with regard to place names, we have indicated modern versions in parentheses, and we have retained individuals' preferences for spelling of their personal names (for example, Seán/Sean). The names of capital cities—Dublin, London, etc.—are sometimes used as shorthand for governments and institutions based in those cities.

A common misnomer is to call the independent Irish state the 'Republic of Ireland'. Whereas independent Ireland is a parliamentary republic, the name of the state (in English) is 'Ireland'. Throughout the text, therefore, 'Ireland' is taken to mean both the island of Ireland and, unless otherwise indicated, the independent state that existed after 1922 (including the Irish Free State). 'Northern Ireland' is the official name for the six counties retained within the United Kingdom after 1920 and is used accordingly.

PAS.   PASSPORT.

·SAORSTÁC ÉIREANN·
·IRISH FREE STATE·

Mrs Paule SLOWEY

Introduction

The passport is often the most direct connection between the Irish public and the Department of Foreign Affairs and Trade. The Irish passport is almost as old as the Irish state itself. In 1924 Ireland, then known as the Irish Free State, was the first dominion in the British Commonwealth to issue its own passport. Thus, the Irish passport became both a symbol of Irish independence and an essential travel document. The passport pictured was issued at Paris on 22 December 1930.

Ireland has the unusual distinction of having had a foreign policy and a diplomatic service before there was an internationally recognised independent Irish state. The roots of both lie in the turmoil of the Irish revolution and the remoulding of the international order in the aftermath of the First World War. The origins of the modern Department of Foreign Affairs and Trade lie in the Ministry of Foreign Affairs established as one of the first four government departments of the first Dáil in January 1919. Since before the Easter Rising of 1916 republicans had anticipated Ireland making a claim for the recognition of its independence at a post-First World War peace conference, and the new foreign affairs ministry was intended to do that. Thus, a mission was established in Paris.

Despite the best efforts of the independence movement, however, the Irish Free State that legally came into existence in December 1922 was a dominion within the British Commonwealth. As a result of Britain's partition of Ireland in 1920 and the creation of Northern Ireland, the Irish Free State comprised only 26 of Ireland's 32 counties.

Independent Ireland sought to carve out an international identity; nevertheless, a key theme that ran through the first three decades of Irish independence was the British-Irish relationship, and the efforts of successive Irish governments to build upon the measure of sovereignty obtained in 1922 against the unstable backdrop of the interwar period.

The Second World War—the 'Emergency'—was, and remains, the greatest international challenge faced by independent Ireland. The state sought to navigate a path between the belligerent powers, ensuring in the process that neutrality would become enshrined as a core principle of Irish foreign policy. The post-war era brought attempts to grapple with new realities, along with efforts to highlight the partition of Ireland to an international audience preoccupied with the Cold War; 'cultural' diplomacy increasingly became part of the state's diplomatic repertoire. The change of government in 1948 opened the door to the severing of Ireland's remaining links to the Commonwealth, and, in April 1949, brought the declaration of Ireland as a republic.

Yet Ireland remained relatively isolated internationally in the first decade of the Cold War. This would change from 1955 onwards, however, following admission to the United Nations. With increased involvement in the UN—such as participation in peacekeeping missions and service on the Security Council at times of great international tension—and the expansion of Ireland's diplomatic footprint into Asia, the 1950s and 1960s could be seen to mark a shift from Ireland's traditional focus on the Anglo-American axis.

By the early 1970s, however, three developments had redefined the scope of Ireland's foreign policy: an official commitment to overseas aid; membership of the European Economic Community (the forerunner of the modern European Union); and the outbreak of conflict—the 'Troubles'—in Northern Ireland in 1969, which brought Anglo-Irish relations back to the fore. After 50 years of independence, the key preoccupations of Ireland's foreign policy were redefined in the 1970s, with a renewed emphasis on multilateralism, in particular via the United Nations; attempts at brokering a peace settlement on the island of Ireland; a commitment to the provision of aid to developing countries; and a commitment to the long-term project of

European integration. In the twenty-first century, these remain core planks of Ireland's foreign policy.

This book examines how a small European state has, in the century since its foundation, engaged with the wider world. It is conceived of as an official history of Irish foreign policy, presented through text and images, rather than as an institutional history of the Department of Foreign Affairs and Trade and its predecessors (though the two obviously go hand in hand). The text broadly follows a chronological approach, with some key themes ranging more widely in time; the profound changes of the late 1960s and early 1970s have required that a thematic approach is taken within some of the later chapters. Yet the book is also intended to be a visual essay, in which the diverse range of images and documents reproduced reveal the story of Ireland's engagement with the world since independence. In short, this is a book with a straightforward purpose. It is intended to explore, in a broad sense, how Irish diplomats and politicians responded to the challenges presented by the upheavals of the twentieth century and beyond, from the Paris peace conference of 1919 to the globalisation of the twenty-first century.

PASSPORTS

Passports are the most tangible link between citizens and the modern Department of Foreign Affairs and Trade.

The first Irish passport was issued in 1923 to the Irish delegation to the League of Nations. They were issued to the general public from 3 April 1924, when the Irish Free State became the first dominion to issue its own passports. Irish passports, therefore, became a symbol of independence as well as an essential travel document. In time the wording used to describe passport holders changed from 'Citizen of the Irish Free State and the British Commonwealth of Nations' to 'Citizen of Ireland'.

The size of passport books has remained constant, though the format and colour have changed over time. The current format, introduced in 2013, incorporated a range of motifs relating to Ireland's culture and geography into its security features. Passport Cards, a credit-card sized passport for travel within the EU, were introduced in 2015. The Irish passport continues to be one of the global passports least likely to be affected by visa restrictions.

In 2018 there were over 855,000 applications for Irish passports. This high demand arose from a general increase in the number of Irish citizens travelling abroad and a growing population. In the context of the UK's decision to leave the EU in 2016, however, there was also a significant rise in applications for Irish passports from United Kingdom citizens of Irish origin or ancestry.

1919–
1922

Revolutionary diplomats

A future member of the Irish diplomatic service: Michael MacWhite (L) serving as a member of the French Foreign Legion, guarding a German prisoner at an unidentified location during the First World War. Born in Cork, MacWhite was a journalist before enlisting in the Foreign Legion. He was decorated for gallantry on three occasions. He became one of Sinn Féin's representatives in France after Ireland's declaration of independence in 1919. He enjoyed a lengthy career as a diplomat—serving as Ireland's representative to the League of Nations, and as minister to the US and then Italy—before retiring in 1950. MacWhite's career path is indicative of those of the first generation of the Irish foreign service, from diverse backgrounds, all of whom drifted into their careers as diplomats amidst the upheaval of the post-war world.

On 22 February 1919, Seán T. Ó Ceallaigh wrote a letter to French premier Georges Clemenceau from the Grand Hotel in Paris. Ó Ceallaigh was from Dublin and had been an activist in a wide range of Irish nationalist organisations. He had also fought in the unsuccessful Easter Rising of April 1916 in pursuit of Irish independence from Britain, and was imprisoned by the British in the aftermath before resuming his involvement in the increasingly popular independence movement.

His presence in Paris three years later was in a very different role. Now he was a de facto diplomat, and, with the title 'Delegate of the Provisional Government of the Irish Republic', was one of the first members of what would become the Irish diplomatic service. His letter to Clemenceau sought, as he put it, 'international recognition of the independence of Ireland' from the international peace conference convened in the French capital in the aftermath of the First World War.

Ó Ceallaigh was the first diplomatic representative of an Irish government that had, as yet, no international standing. Ireland had been ruled since the twelfth century by the English and later the British monarchy, and since 1801 had formally been part of the United Kingdom of Great Britain and Ireland. Movements demanding Irish independence from Britain, usually couched in terms of a 'republic' of some kind, had existed since the 1790s. Virtually all of these movements sought to exploit the balance of international affairs in pursuit of that objective. The eighteenth-century Society of United Irishmen, founded by a diverse coalition of Catholic and Protestant radicals in 1791, had concluded that Ireland's socio-economic and political problems could best be resolved by a complete separation from Britain. Their objective was a secular state modelled on the French revolutionary republic. They also sought French military assistance for the rebellion that they staged in pursuit of that objective in 1798.

This failed, but other 'republican' organisations in the nineteenth century sought to exploit international circumstances and the emergence of Irish emigrant communities overseas, especially after the Great Famine of the 1840s. In the 1860s, for example, the Irish Republican Brotherhood (IRB) or 'Fenians' sought to tap into the fact that large numbers of Irish emigrants had fought in the Union and Confederate armies during the American civil war, in order to seek experienced recruits for a prospective rebellion at home. International tensions could be exploited to put pressure on the British—as a popular nineteenth-century nationalist slogan would have it, England's difficulty was to be Ireland's opportunity. Irish communities overseas, most especially in the United States, could offer material support to Irish nationalists of all types, who were acutely aware of Ireland's position in the wider world, and especially within the British Empire. As with Ó Ceallaigh in Paris in 1919, an awareness of foreign relations, international affairs and the global balance of power was, and would remain, integral to Ireland's struggle for independence.

●

Yet on the eve of the First World War itself there had been every indication that Ireland's future was to remain an internal matter within the United Kingdom. In the first decades of the twentieth century, much of Ireland remained an overwhelmingly Catholic and agricultural society. The north-east was distinctively different, with a predominantly Protestant population (the legacy of British colonisation in previous centuries) and Ireland's only significant industrial heartlands. In 1914 Ireland was firmly located within the British Empire—thousands of Irish people served as administrators and military personnel for the empire—and was in a political and economic union with Britain. This situation favoured the larger country and was seen to be the major political cause of chronic social and economic problems in Ireland, such as poverty and endemic emigration.

In political terms, Ireland was represented within the British parliament by 105 members of parliament (MPs). The majority were nationalists, and supporters of 'Home Rule': a form of devolution that was intended to secure an autonomous local legislature for the island of Ireland within the United Kingdom. The predominantly Protestant north-east of Ireland was unionist in political orientation, and unionism favoured the maintenance of the status quo of government from London. The prospect of Home Rule being granted to Ireland in 1912 by the British Liberal government of Prime Minister Herbert Asquith had sparked a stand-off between nationalists and Ulster unionists; the latter feared discrimination on religious and cultural grounds by a potential Catholic-dominated parliament in Dublin. They also feared that their livelihoods would suffer, as the industrialised economy of the north-east would be marginalised by agricultural interests and could be exploited to subsidise the rest of the island. Genuine fears that this would lead to civil war were defused by the outbreak of the First World War, but the war also provided an opportunity for a new generation of separatists to stage a rebellion at Easter 1916; indeed, in the circumstances they had even sought military assistance from Britain's German enemies.

The idea of seeking recognition for Irish independence from a post-war peace conference was held by many of the leaders of the Easter Rising. The rebellion was defeated militarily, but the heavy-handed British response that followed, along with widespread disillusionment in Ireland with the war effort and the Home Rule movement, bred support for the fringe nationalist Sinn Féin party, originally founded in 1905 and reorganised as a separatist party after being incorrectly blamed for the 1916 rising. It won 73 seats in the United Kingdom parliament in the post-war general election of December 1918 (most of the remaining Irish seats were won by unionist candidates in the north-east).

Instead of taking their seats in London, however, those of the new Irish MPs who were at liberty (many were in prison or at risk of arrest) assembled in Dublin on 21 January 1919 as Dáil Éireann (loosely meaning 'Assembly of Ireland') and declared

SINN FEIN.

TO EACH ELECTOR OF THE

Stephen's Green Division

A General Election is expected before the end of this year. Sinn Fein means, through it, to let the world know the **REAL NATURE OF IRELAND'S DEMAND.**

All the belligerents in the world war claim to stand for the principle of **THE FREEDOM OF NATIONALITIES, GREAT AND SMALL.** That principle will be the **TEST OF THEIR SINCERITY WHEN PEACE IS DISCUSSED.**

The enemies of Ireland are trying, and will try, to represent the Irish Claim, not as **A NATIONAL CLAIM FOR INDEPENDENCE, BUT** as a **DOMESTIC PROBLEM WITHIN THE BRITISH EMPIRE.**

These enemies will point to the participation of Irish representatives in Westminster politics as a proof that the question is a domestic one.

SINN FEIN IS GOING TO REMOVE THAT ARGUMENT AT THE COMING ELECTION by giving Nationalists in every constituency, yours included, an opportunity **TO CAST THEIR VOTES FOR NATIONAL INDEPENDENCE, AND NOTHING LESS.**

In order to gain this great object it asks your help. **ELECTIONS ARE EXPENSIVE,** but if every Nationalist vote be not cast for Independence we lose **THE GREATEST CHANCE OF CENTURIES FOR WINNING IRISH FREEDOM.**

Therefore we appeal to you, when you are asked by **SINN FEIN** Collectors (who will, if required, produce their authority), to subscribe towards the cost of **FIGHTING THE ELECTION IN STEPHEN'S GREEN DIVISION** as generously as your means will permit, and thus, as well as by your vote and influence, to enable **SINN FEIN**

TO PUT YOUR COUNTRY'S REAL CASE BEFORE THE WORLD.

OPENING OF FIRST SESSION DAIL EIREANN,
at the Mansion House, Dublin, Tuesday, January 21st, 1919.

The Message of Dail Eireann to the Free Nations.

Below is the English Translation of the Message

"To the Nations of the World : Greeting.

"The Nation of Ireland having proclaimed her national independence, calls, through her elected representatives in Parliament assembled in the Irish Capital on January 21st. 1919, upon every free nation to support the Irish Republic by recognising Ireland's national status and her right to its vindication of the Peace Congress

"Nationally, the race, the language, the customs and traditions of Ireland are radically distinct from the English : Ireland is one of the most ancient nations of Europe, and she has preserved her national integrity vigorous and intact, through seven centuries of foreign oppression. she has never relinquished her national rights and throughout the long era of English usurpation she has in every generation defiantly proclaimed her inalienable right of nationhood down to her last glorious resort to arms in 1916.

"Internationally. Ireland is the gateway to the Atlantic. Ireland is the last outpost of Europe towards the West. Ireland is the point upon which great trade routes between East and West converge : **her independence is demanded by the Freedom of the Seas: her great harbours must be open to all nations, instead of being the monopoly of England.**
To-day these harbours are empty and idle solely because English policy is determined to retain Ireland as a barren bulwark for English aggrandisement, and the unique geographical position of this island, far from being a benefit and safeguard to Europe and America, is subjected to the purposes of England's policy of world dominion.

HISTORIC NATIONHOOD.

"Ireland to-day re-asserts her historic, nationhood the more confidently before the new world emerging from the war, because she believes in freedom and justice as the fundamental principles of international law, because she believes in a frank co-operation between the peoples for equal rights against the vested privileges of ancient tyrannies, because the permanent peace of Europe can never be secured by perpetuating military dominion for the profit of empire, but only by establishing the control of government in every land upon the basis of the free will of a free people, and the existing state of war, between Ireland and England, can never be ended until Ireland is definitely evacuated by the armed forces of England.

"For these. among other reasons, Ireland—resolutely and irrevocably determined at the dawn of the promised era of self-determination and liberty, that she will suffer foreign dominion no longer—calls upon every free nation to uphold her—

national claim to complete independence as an Irish Republic—

against the arrogant pretensions of England founded in fraud and sustained only by an overwhelming military occupation, and demands to be confronted publicly with England at the Congress of the Nations, that the civilised world having judged between English wrong and Irish right may guarantee to Ireland its permanent support for the maintenance of her national independence.

Below: L–R: George Gavan Duffy, Seán T. Ó Ceallaigh and Margaret Gavan Duffy leaving the Grand Hotel in Paris, May 1919, en route to present French premier Georges Clemenceau with a memorandum setting out the case for recognising Irish independence. The Grand Hotel was the headquarters of the Irish delegation in Paris. Note the tricolour flag on the car.

Opposite: Official acknowledgement of Seán T. Ó Ceallaigh's application for an identity card as a foreigner in France; his nationality is listed here as 'Britannique'.

RÉPUBLIQUE FRANÇAISE

RÉCÉPISSÉ

DE

DEMANDE DE CARTE D'IDENTITE

Le (Maire ou Commissaire) *Le Préfet de Police* de

la commune de _____

a reçu les déclarations destinées à l'obtention de la

carte d'identité d'étranger formulées par

Monsieur *O Ceallaigh Sean T*

de nationalité *S Britannique*

résidant à *Paris*

Adresse: *2 Rue Scribe*

Paris, le *15 9* 19*19*

Timbre de la Mairie
ou du Commissariat:

La carte d'identité devra être retirée auprès des autorités qui lui auront délivré le présent récépissé et en échange de celui-ci

Dans le cas où l'étranger se serait déplacé avant la délivrance de la carte d'identité, il demandera cette pièce au Préfet du département de sa nouvelle résidence en lui faisant connaître son adresse actuelle et la mairie (ou commissariat) où il a fait sa déclaration

Ce récépissé tient lieu provisoirement de sauf-conduit. L'étranger ne peut aller s'établir dans une autre localité sans l'avoir fait viser au départ par les mêmes autorités qui l'ont délivré. Chaque déplacement doit, de même, être revêtu d'un visa à l'arrivée et au départ.

Tout étranger qui ne se conformerait pas à ces prescriptions serait passible des sanctions prévues au décret du 2 avril 1917.

(texte vertical, marge gauche) Ce récépissé est provisoire et ne saurait en aucun cas servir de carte d'identité.

La guerra contro l'Irlanda

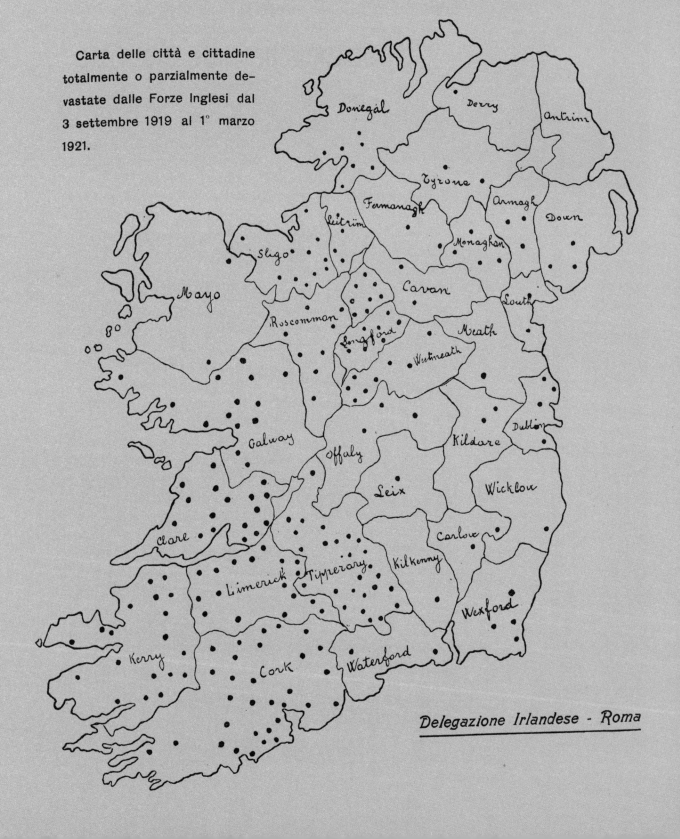

Carta delle città e cittadine totalmente o parzialmente devastate dalle Forze Inglesi dal 3 settembre 1919 al 1° marzo 1921.

Delegazione Irlandese - Roma

Opposite: A key function of the Dáil Éireann diplomatic service was the distribution of propaganda in favour of Irish independence, in the hope of bringing international pressure to bear on the British. It reached a surprisingly wide range of countries. This map of engagements in the Irish War of Independence (1919–21) was intended for an Italian audience; the conflict is described here as the 'war against Ireland'.

Ireland to be an independent republic. (Members of the Dáil did not describe themselves as MPs but used the equivalent Irish-language term 'Teachta Dála', abbreviated as TD). The Dáil's 'message to the free nations of the world' emphasised Ireland's unique cultural and racial characteristics, Ireland's geographic location as the 'gateway of the Atlantic', its domination by Britain, and called upon 'every free nation to support the Irish Republic by recognising Ireland's national status and her right to its vindication at the Peace Congress'.

It was one thing to demand independence and international recognition. It was quite another to achieve it, which is why a delegation was despatched to Paris in early 1919 to seek recognition for Dáil Éireann and Ireland's independence. The two principals who made up what was, to all intents and purposes, Ireland's first diplomatic mission, were Ó Ceallaigh, who was also a TD for Dublin, and the English-born solicitor and his fellow Dublin TD George Gavan Duffy, whose legal background and fluency in French and Italian qualified him for the role.

The overall strategy of Dáil Éireann was to construct an alternative government in Ireland, one that would hopefully undermine the British administration and also prove to the world that it commanded the legitimate support of the Irish people. In January 1919 it had created four 'ministries' to give credibility to this claim; the Ministry of Foreign Affairs was one of them. Count George Plunkett, the former director of the National Museum of Ireland, whose son Joseph was one of the executed leaders of the Easter Rising and who was himself a Sinn Féin TD, was appointed the Dáil's Minister for Foreign Affairs.

The bulk of the administrative work in Ireland was done by two more veterans of the independence movement: the Cork-born clerk of the Dáil, Diarmaid O'Hegarty, and the Wexford journalist Robert Brennan, who in 1921 was appointed 'Under-secretary for Foreign Affairs' (in essence, the first secretary general of the department). The activities of the Dáil and its assertion of Irish independence were a propaganda exercise as well as a practical measure, and one that had to be communicated to as wide an audience as possible. What better venue to do this than in Paris to the leaders of the post-war world?

The idea of sending emissaries to Paris was inspired by the wartime rhetoric of self-determination, as articulated by US

President Woodrow Wilson in his famous 'Fourteen Points'—the statement of principles for peace that was to form the basis for the negotiations in Paris. If the war had indeed been fought for the rights of small nations, surely Ireland was one of those nations? The Irish were by no means alone in directing their attention to Paris. Many other nationalities did the same as the European empires began to fragment and collapse in the wake of the war. The Dáil's embryonic Ministry of Foreign Affairs worked closely with its Ministry of Publicity, which over the coming years assiduously distributed multilingual propaganda recounting British atrocities and repression during the Irish War of Independence—the guerrilla conflict fought, as Dáil Éireann was establishing its authority as Ireland's alternative government, between British forces and the paramilitary Irish Republican Army (IRA) between 1919 and 1921.

There were, however, some figures in the independence movement who were sceptical of the chances of success in Paris. Senior figures such as Michael Collins (the Dáil's Minister for Finance who also held senior positions in the IRA and IRB) were

A Sinn Féin postcard showing 'Uncle Sam' ushering Ireland, in the form of a uniformed member of the Irish Volunteers (the forerunner of the Irish Republican Army), to a seat at the head of the Paris peace conference. Hopes that the United States would support Irish independence in this manner were, however, wildly optimistic.

wary lest the focus on Paris cause the movement to forget that London was the key to its objective of Irish independence. And this was the greatest obstacle faced by the embryonic Irish diplomatic service: the other countries looking for independence after the war were often seeking it from the Austro-Hungarian, German and Ottoman empires, which had all been defeated, or from the Russian empire, which had collapsed into revolution. Ireland, on the other hand, was seeking independence from one of the victor powers. Due to the alignment of Irish republicans with Germany in the early years of the war, sympathy for the Irish cause was in short supply amongst the victorious allies in Paris in 1919. Conscious of the need to preserve their empire in a world of rising demands for self-determination and independence, Britain, with the United States, ensured that Ó Ceallaigh and his fellow Sinn Féin representatives in Paris did not receive a hearing at the peace conference.

●

If direct approaches to the world's leaders did not work, there was another possibility: the mobilisation of public support in favour of Irish independence, especially within the large Irish

Members of the delegation that accompanied Dáil Éireann president Éamon de Valera on his publicity and fundraising tour to the US in 1919–20 pose with the veteran (and extremely influential) Irish republican émigré John Devoy. Of those pictured, Harry Boland and Liam Mellows both fought in the Easter Rising of 1916 and were killed in the Irish civil war of 1922–23. Patrick McCartan was the Sinn Féin representative to the US from 1917 and in 1920 became the Dáil's emissary to Bolshevik Russia. Diarmaid Lynch, another 1916 veteran, had been deported to the US by the British in 1918 and became the secretary of the Irish-American 'Friends of Irish Freedom'.

H. BOLAND, T.D.   L. MELLOWS, T.D.   E. DE VALERA, T.D.   JOHN DEVOY.   Dr. Mac CARTAN, T.D.   D. LYNCH, T.D.

communities of the United States. The Friends of Irish Freedom was founded in the United States in early 1916 as a public alternative to the secret and conspiratorial Irish-American group Clan na Gael. It was set up to lobby for popular and ultimately Congressional support for Irish independence and also to counter British influence in the United States prior to its entry into the war in 1917.

The Friends of Irish Freedom also helped to pay for Éamon de Valera, the American-born maths teacher who, as one the most senior survivors of the Easter Rising, had become president of the Dáil and thus the public leader of Ireland's independence movement, to embark on an eighteen-month, coast-to-coast fund-raising and publicity tour of the United States in 1919–20. The tour was marred by squabbling between the major Irish-American organisations, though Harry Boland (another 1916 veteran) continued to represent Ireland in the United States after de Valera returned home in

The substantial Irish and Irish-American population of the United States was a crucial constituency wooed by the independence movement for both financial and political support. This image depicts a vast crowd in Boston's Fenway Park (home of the Red Sox baseball team) attending a pro-Irish independence rally being addressed by Éamon de Valera in 1919.

A bond certificate issued by Dáil Éireann in the US. One of the objectives of de Valera's American tour of 1919–20 was to raise additional funds for the independence struggle. This copy was signed by de Valera's secretary Sean Nunan, who had a lengthy career as an Irish diplomat in the US (1932–50) and was then secretary of the Department of External Affairs (1950–55). This bond certificate was posted to Seán T. Ó Ceallaigh in 1958 when the latter visited the US as President of Ireland. It was sent to Ó Ceallaigh by the daughter of its original subscriber; presumably, it had never been redeemed.

December 1920. Irish-American emissaries continued to lobby unsuccessfully for Ireland's independence at the Paris peace conference.

With the direct approach to the peace conference in Paris failing, the Dáil and its emerging foreign service began to focus their limited resources on maintaining a high international profile to ensure that overseas attention remained fixed on the situation in Ireland. Propaganda activity continued in Paris, and a global web of envoys and agitators was created, which stretched from Argentina and Chile to Australia and New Zealand and back to the old and new states of Europe. In Britain, groups such as the Irish Self-Determination League sought to keep the Irish question firmly in the public eye, particularly amongst the large Irish diaspora in London and many of Britain's larger cities. The key figure here was the electrical engineer Art O'Brien; born in London to an Irish father and an English mother, he had joined the Gaelic League (founded to promote the Irish language) in 1899, and became politically radicalised during the First World War.

OBJECTS.

1. To secure the application of the principle of Self-Determination to Ireland

2. To secure the release of all Irish Political Prisoners.

MEMBERSHIP.

Membership of The Irish Self-Determination League of Great Britain is confined to people of Irish birth or descent, and resident in Great Britain, and who shall undertake to support the determination of the people of Ireland as to the Government of their country.

MEMBERSHIP SUBSCRIPTION.

The subscription for each Member shall be a minimum of 2/- for Executive purposes, in addition to a local subscription to be paid by each Branch.

IRISH SELF-DETERMINATION LEAGUE OF GREAT BRITAIN

Member's Name

....

Address

....

In time, Ó Ceallaigh decamped from Paris to Rome, Gavan Duffy departed for Brussels, and there was even an attempt to reach out to the Bolshevik government via the Tyrone-born doctor Patrick McCartan, who spent an unsuccessful six-month sojourn in Russia from December 1920 to July 1921.

The publicity-raising activities of these roving Irish envoys became intertwined with propaganda; the *Irish Bulletin*, issued from Dublin under the direction of Robert Brennan, was crucial in this regard. This propaganda newsletter contained extensive accounts of British atrocities and repression in Ireland, which were intended to foster international sympathy to the cause of Irish independence. The Dáil's campaign to bring international pressure to bear upon the British was driven by a network of official and unofficial emissaries around the world, such as Eamon Bulfin and Laurence Ginnell in South America, Donal Hales in Genoa, Art O'Brien in Britain, Máire

A membership card for the Irish Self-Determination League of Great Britain. This was a lobbying and propaganda group that organised major demonstrations and campaigns in support of Irish separatism. It was apparently the largest Irish organisation of any kind ever founded in Great Britain.

Arthur Griffith and Michael Collins emerge from 10 Downing Street during the Anglo-Irish Treaty negotiations, with Emmet Dalton visible on the far left. Dalton had served in the British Army during the First World War and subsequently joined the IRA; he had organised some of the logistics for the Irish delegation, including the provision of an aircraft to fly Collins out of London should the talks break down. He was later one of the founders of Ardmore Film Studios in Wicklow.

O'Brien in Madrid, Nancy Wyse-Power in Berlin, and many others. The pressure of international opinion, especially from the United States, played a role in bringing about the truce that ended the War of Independence.

Negotiations followed between the British coalition government led by David Lloyd George and the 'representatives' of the Irish people (the British never officially recognised the Dáil). The treaty eventually signed on 6 December 1921 established the Irish Free State as a dominion within the British Empire; the constitutional status of this state was to be modelled on Canada. Irish parliamentarians were to recognise the British monarch as head of state, and, in terms of Anglo-Irish relations, the treaty incorporated clauses dealing with fiscal legacies, restrictions on an Irish military and the maintenance of three British naval bases on the Atlantic seaboard of Ireland.

The treaty was influenced by the prevailing climate in international affairs exemplified by Wilson's fourteen points. It was also rooted in British self-interest, which did not envision Ireland becoming fully detached from Britain's sphere of influence. British concerns over domestic defence, in particular the defence of the Atlantic sea lanes off Ireland's west coast, and with the integrity of the empire, guaranteed this.

IRISH PEACE CONFERENCE, JULY, 1921. Delegates leaving Dun Laoghaire.

A postcard of (L–R) Arthur Griffith, Erskine Childers, Éamon de Valera, Count George Plunkett and Éamonn Duggan, pictured at Kingstown (Dún Laoghaire) prior to departing for London for preliminary talks with the British government following the truce of July 1921. Originally a journalist, Griffith was the founder of Sinn Féin. Childers was a former British naval officer who had become sympathetic to Irish nationalism. Duggan was a solicitor who had fought in the Easter Rising and became Sinn Féin's principal liaison officer with the British after the truce. All three were later part of the official delegation that negotiated the Anglo-Irish Treaty of December 1921; de Valera, controversially, was not. Plunkett was officially the Dail's foreign minister, but his hands-on involvement in foreign policy was minimal.

Members of the Treaty delegation at their headquarters in Hans Place, Knightsbridge. Back row (L–R): Michael Knightly, John Chartres, George Gavan Duffy, Robert Barton, Éamonn Duggan, Arthur Griffith, Erskine Childers. Seated, far left: Joseph McGrath, D.L. Robinson. Leaning forward, far right: Fionán Lynch. Front (L–R): Lily O'Brennan, Ellie Lyons, May Duggan, Bridget Lynch, Kathleen Napoli-McKenna, Alice Lyons.

Opposite: The credentials issued to Michael Collins by Éamon de Valera for the Anglo-Irish Treaty negotiations; it was later claimed that Collins and his fellow envoys did not have the authority to conclude the negotiations without recourse to Dublin.

(28)

SAORSTAT EIREANN

OFFICE OF THE PRESIDENT

DUBLIN

DO CHUM GACH A BHFEICFIDH NO A GCLUINFIDH E SEO, BEATHA AGUS SLAINTE:

De bhrigh an ard-churaim ata curtha ormsa ag DAIL EIREANN, ainmnighim trid seo

Art O Griobhtha, T.D., Aire um Ghnothai Coigcriche, Cathaoirleach.

Micheal O Coileain, T.D., Aire Airgid,

Riobard Bartun, T.D., Aire um Ghnothai Tionnscail,

Eamon O Dugain, T.D.

Seoirse Gabhanach O Dubhthaigh, T.D.

mar Theachtai Lán-fheidhme o Riaghaltas Toghtha SAORSTAIT EIREANN chum a dheanamh agus a thabhairt chum criche ar son na hEireann le n-a Shoillse, SEOIRSE V. na Breataine, Connradh no Connartha Socruighthe, Comh-bhainte agus Comh-oireamhna idir Eire agus an saor-chumann naisiun ar a nglaodhtar Impreacht Shasana.

DA CHOMHARTHA SAN ag seo mo shighin mar Uachtaran.

I gCathair Bhaile Atha Cliath dhom an 7adh. la de Deire Foghmhair i mbliain d'aois ar dTighearna 1921 agus deanta i gcuig macasamhla bunusacha.

Éamon de Valéra

2 - M.C

BY APPOINTMENT

TO HER MAJESTY
THE QUEEN.

AS DRAPERS &
FURNISHERS.

Telephones
WESTERN ONE (101 LINES)
(DAY & NIGHT)
Telegrams:
"EVERYTHING, HARRODS, LONDON."

REG. Nº I 82

PAGE Who.

The Irish Delegation Office,

22, Hans Place,

S.W.

BY APPOINTMENT

TO H.M. QUEEN ALEXANDRA
AS GOLDSMITHS, SILVERSMITHS &
SILK MERCERS.

IN ACCOUNT WITH

HARRODS LTD

LONDON,
S.W.1.

BY APPOINTMENT

TO H.M. THE QUEEN OF NORWAY
AS FURNISHING DRAPERS.

WEEK ENDING November 19 21   CHEQUES SHOULD BE CROSSED BARCLAYS BANK LIMITED.

Nov. 8th								
1 bx	Crackers				9	0		
1 bx	Do				10	3		
1	Fancy Baskets		2	1	0		
1 lb	J. Bonbons			3	6		
1 lb	Peppermints Lumps			2	8		
1 bx	E. Sweets			6	9		
1 bx	Assorted Sweets			3	6		
1 bx	M. Brazils			4	6		
1 lb	Peppermint Liquers			3	0		
3 lbs	Assorted Chocolates 4/6			13	6		
1	Serviettes			1	6		
1 doz	Do				7		
1	D. O'yleys			1	3		
1, doz	Do			1	1		
1 doz	Do				10		
1 doz	Ice Cases			6	9		
6	Fancy Baskets 9/6		2	17	0		
1 bx	Fruits			8	6		
2	Baskets 18/6		1	17	0		
	c.f.					10	12	2

			£	s	d	£	s	d
I 82 Who		Brought Forward				10	12	2
Nov. 8th		To Hire of Candilabra	1	2	6			
		Candlestick		18	0			
	12	Bon Bon Dishes		4	0			
						2	4	6
Nov. 9th		Boors		3	6			
	2	Blowouts		1	0			
	2	Streamers		2	6			
	3	Blowouts		1	0			
	1	C. Joke			5			
	1	Joke			2			
	2	Balloon		1	0			
	1	Raifle			6			
	1	Flag			4½			
	1	Clapper			4			
	1	Bag Ball			9			
	3	Tambor 1/6		4	6			
	2	Blowouts		1	4			
	2	Cigars @ 3d			6			
	3 yds	Muslin @ 1/0½		3	1½			
	3 yds	Do @ 1/0½		3	1½			
		Cards		1	4			
						1	5	5½
Nov. 10yh	6	Trumpet		1	0			
	3	Rattles		1	0			
	1	Fish		1	0			
	3	Blowouts			9			
	4	Clappers		1	0			
		Ball Room Powder		4	6			
	1 doz	Menus		4	6			
							11	0
						14	13	1½

The new Irish Free State would ultimately cover 26 of Ireland's 32 counties. In 1920 Ireland had been partitioned by Britain into two jurisdictions, with six north-eastern counties remaining within the United Kingdom under a devolved assembly. Irish unionist opposition to being governed from Dublin, which predominated in these six counties, had not abated. Partition was intended to create a mainly Protestant enclave in the north-east to cater for the wishes of most of Ireland's Protestant and unionist population. This was, to put it mildly, a contentious issue for Irish nationalists, but the existence of Northern Ireland was nominally addressed within the terms of the 1921 treaty by the creation of a boundary commission that would adjudicate on a new border between the two jurisdictions in Ireland. Many nationalists expected that the new Northern Ireland would soon wither and collapse.

The new constitutional status of the Irish Free State as a dominion in the British Empire was, however, a far more controversial matter. That Ireland's elected representatives would have to swear an oath of fidelity to the British crown led to civil war within seven months. Though divisive and far from ideal to those who supported the goal of an Irish republic, the treaty commanded majority political and public support in what was to become the Irish Free State. Many supported it simply on the grounds that it was not automatically a final settlement. But for those who espoused a fully independent Irish republic, what the British offered in 1921 fell far short of what they and their colleagues had fought and died for.

When the independence movement split over the terms of the treaty, the infant diplomatic service was also torn apart. Its head, Robert Brennan, opposed the treaty and resigned in January 1922. In doing so he joined such prominent figures as Boland and Ó Ceallaigh, and their ranks were later swelled by Leopold Kerney (Paris), Máire O'Brien (Madrid) and Mary MacSwiney (United States), who formed part of an anti-treaty diplomatic and propaganda service that sought every opportunity to counter the international legitimacy of the nascent Irish Free State.

Brennan had managed to impose some administrative order on the Dáil's foreign service, and before he resigned had as good as handpicked his successor. Joseph P. Walshe was a former

Previous pages: An invoice from Harrods for goods purchased by the Irish treaty delegation, at least some of whom had a sweet tooth.

The split over the 1921 treaty was reflected in the Dáil Éireann diplomatic service. Here, anti-treaty diplomats are pictured with Éamon de Valera; note the prominent position of the tricolour. Also of note (on de Valera's right) is Art O'Brien, Dáil Éireann's representative in Britain, who opposed the treaty and was removed from the Dáil's diplomatic service as a result. He later served as the Irish Free State's minister to France (1935–38).

Jesuit seminarian and a Francophile lawyer and linguist who had also been a teacher at the exclusive Clongowes Wood College in Co. Kildare. In 1920 Walshe had joined the Irish delegation in Paris, and in early 1922 he took over the pro-treaty elements of the Ministry of Foreign Affairs from Brennan. Beginning under the Dáil's Minister for Foreign Affairs, George Gavan Duffy, Walshe essentially built a new Irish foreign service in the wake of the treaty split and remained in charge of the department from 1922 until 1946, when he became Ireland's first diplomat to hold the rank of ambassador, in this case to the Vatican. He was, without exaggeration, the founding father of independent Ireland's diplomatic service and a key foreign policy strategist for the first three decades of Irish independence.

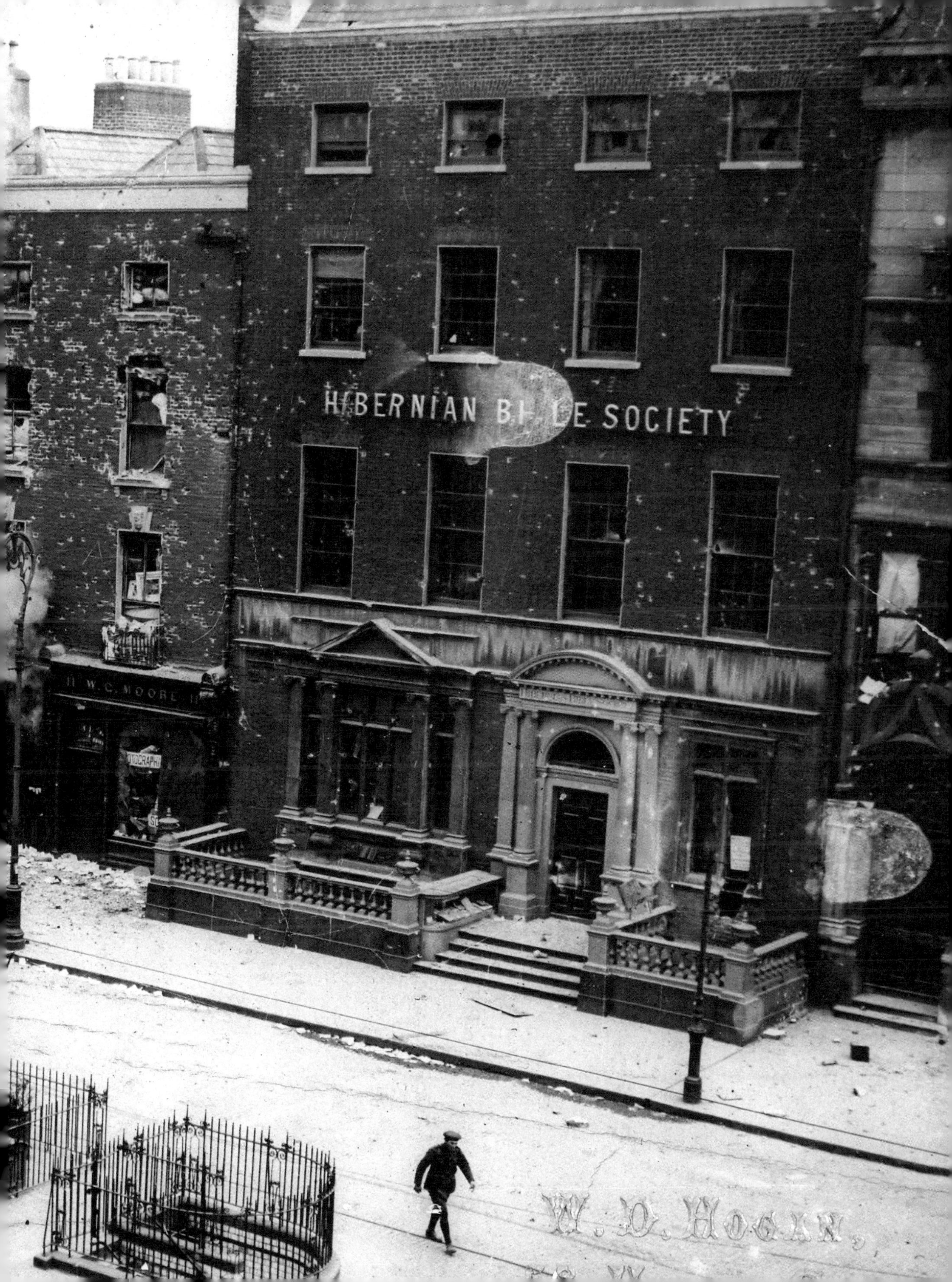
HIBERNIAN BI LE SOCIETY
W. C. MOORE
W. D. HOGAN,

The Provisional Government of the Irish Free State led by Michael Collins was established on 14 January 1922 to prepare for the inauguration of the Irish Free State on 6 December 1922. It had no international status, however, and until December 1922 Irish diplomats could not be accredited to foreign countries, sign treaties or join international organisations. As a result, the Dáil Éireann administration and the Provisional Government worked side by side where foreign relations were concerned. Walshe pulled together remaining pro-treaty diplomats such as Michael MacWhite, Charles Bewley, Sheila Murphy, John Chartres and Seán Murphy and added to them a publicity staff—Rosita Austin, Seán Lester and Francis Cremins—to form the core of his small department; temporary diplomats were recruited for specific tasks as they arose. Many of these were at the beginning of what would prove to be lengthy diplomatic careers.

This first generation of post-independence Irish diplomats who coalesced around Gavan Duffy and Walshe had drifted into the service by accident or by virtue of their linguistic or legal skills. After 1922, a preference for legal training was in accord with the requirements of Irish foreign policy within the British Commonwealth and the League of Nations, as international law and establishing legal precedents were central to Irish policy in both. The emphasis on legal training, however, ensured that women were essentially forced out of the Irish Free State's diplomatic service, as it increasingly drew from a male-dominated profession. The absence of female diplomats after 1922 also reflected the prevailing chauvinism of the period. Joseph Walshe, for instance, was unwilling to countenance women serving as diplomats in the new Irish foreign service; thus, the preference for men was also in accord with Walshe's personal wishes.

In 1922 achieving international recognition of the Irish Free State and founding a foreign policy independent of Britain were George Gavan Duffy's primary goals. This defined the national interest of independent Ireland, and its pursuit would continue to underpin Irish foreign policy until after the Second World War. The outbreak of civil war in June 1922 over the terms of the 1921 treaty meant that Gavan Duffy also had to deal with an international dimension to the conflict: countering anti-treaty propaganda in Europe and America and trying to regain influence over the fractious Irish-American community. Gavan

Previous pages: The consequences of the treaty split were very real. Despite attempts at compromise, civil war broke out in June 1922 between the pro- and anti-treaty factions. Here, a pro-treaty armoured car sits outside republican positions on O'Connell Street in Dublin during the fighting at the start of the conflict.

The 'Irish Race Convention', held in Paris in early 1922, was intended to foster links between Ireland and its diaspora. Instead, it became a last-ditch attempt at maintaining unity in face of the deepening split over the 1921 treaty. In this photograph, Éamon de Valera is clearly visible in the front row.

Duffy resigned in July 1922, in protest at the approach of the Irish Free State government to the prosecution of the civil war. He was succeeded in September by Desmond FitzGerald, an internationally-minded linguist, journalist and philosopher, who became the Irish Free State's first Minister for External Affairs in December 1922.

From late 1922 FitzGerald, Walshe and a small group of diplomats moved quickly to create the foreign policy of the Irish Free State. Amidst civil war and some uncertainty as to whether the new state could continue to survive as a self-governing entity or would be dragged down by conflict and an uncertain birth, they began to seek international recognition for the Irish Free State and carve out Ireland's place amongst the nations in the 1920s.

EXHIBITION OF CONTEMPORARY IRISH PAINTING

ORGANIZED BY THE CULTURAL RELATIONS COMMITTEE OF IRELAND

NORTH AMERICA
1950

The cover of the catalogue accompanying a travelling exhibition of 'contemporary
Irish painting', organised by the Cultural Relations Committee of the Department of
External Affairs. The exhibition was hosted in Providence, Boston and Ottawa between
March and June 1950. The cover motif is based upon Edward Smyth's keystone
personifying the River Liffey on Dublin's eighteenth-century Customs House.

CULTURAL DIPLOMACY

The use of Irish artistic output and cultural heritage to promote Ireland overseas can be traced back to the 1920s, but it was not until after the Second World War that Thomas J. Kiernan, the Irish minister to the Holy See, proposed that the promotion of Irish culture be incorporated into the mission of the then Department of External Affairs. He suggested, amongst other things, that literary works originally written in Irish be translated into English, French, Italian and Spanish, and that 'an hour of music and prose and poetry' should be prepared for international broadcast on St Patrick's Day. The deployment of Irish culture as a diplomatic tool was formalised from the 1940s onwards, with the establishment of the department's Cultural Relations Committee in 1949.

Literature, drama, music, and increasingly the visual arts, continue to be an important part of Ireland's diplomatic repertoire. Embassies and consulates fund and engage with Irish cultural activity abroad. Over time such activity, along with academic, Irish language and sporting initiatives, has come to encompass broader links with the Irish diaspora—and with the so-called affinity diaspora of foreigners who feel a strong connection to Irish culture. As such, the definition of Irish culture and its role in Irish diplomacy is now, in the twenty-first century, far broader than originally envisaged by Kiernan in 1945.

1922–
1932

The Irish Free State

Joseph P. Walshe, aged 36 (standing, centre), and 26-year-old Seán Murphy (standing, right) built the Irish Free State's Department of External Affairs out of the remnants of the Dáil Éireann foreign service. The secretive and enigmatic Walshe can rightly be described as the founder of today's Department of Foreign Affairs and Trade. Walshe would head External Affairs from 1922 to 1946, with Murphy as his second-in-command to 1938. They are photographed here in 1922 with Minister for External Affairs Desmond FitzGerald (sitting) and the Marquis MacSwiney, who was then Ireland's unofficial representative to the Holy See.

The Irish Free State was legally established on 6 December 1922. An immediate foreign policy goal of W.T. Cosgrave, the president of the new state's Executive Council, and of his pro-treaty Cumann na nGaedheal (literally 'Society of the Irish') government, which emerged from the pro-treaty faction of the Sinn Féin party, was to secure the international position of the Irish Free State as a sovereign, independent state.

The split over the treaty resonated through Irish foreign policy in the early 1920s.

Anti-treaty propagandists remained active overseas, including some former members of the Dáil Éireann diplomatic service based in Britain, France and particularly the United States. In December 1922 the consular offices in New York had even been occupied by anti-treaty republicans seeking to gain control of the enormous sums raised in the United States by Sinn Féin in 1919–20. International support for the anti-treaty side dwindled, however, as the Irish Free State government consolidated its domestic and international position after the civil war officially ended in May 1923.

From early 1922 the Cork-born academic and economist Timothy A. Smiddy had represented the Dáil in Washington, in order to counteract anti-treaty propaganda and to secure recognition for the Irish Free State from the US administration of Warren Harding. This did not mean, however, that Smiddy was

recognised as Ireland's official representative. The US position was that the component parts of the British Empire—and the Irish Free State was a dominion within the empire—were to be represented by the British. The Irish government sought to press home the case that it should have a separate representative and found the US authorities open to the suggestion. The British themselves reluctantly conceded the point, and so in October 1924 Smiddy became Ireland's minister plenipotentiary in Washington. Not only was he Ireland's first accredited diplomatic agent, but the Irish Free State was the first dominion to appoint a diplomatic representative independently of Britain. This was a major milestone for the Irish Free State, and indeed for the other dominions.

The Irish Free State also sought to assert its sovereignty through membership of the League of Nations, which it joined on 10 September 1923. Cosgrave led a delegation to the League's seat at Geneva, and Michael MacWhite (a former member of the French Foreign Legion who had been part of Ó Ceallaigh's team

Timothy Smiddy (left) at a reception at the White House in January 1925. Smiddy was an economist and had been sent to the US in March 1922 as the representative of the Provisional Government. On 7 October 1924 he became the first diplomatic representative appointed by the Free State, when he became Ireland's envoy extraordinary and minister plenipotentiary to the United States. This gave the Irish Free State a distinct voice in the US, one that was not channelled via the British embassy, as was the case with other dominions.

On 10 September 1923 the Irish Free State joined the League of Nations in Geneva. Pictured are the delegates to the 1923 League Assembly. Front: Hugh Kennedy (Attorney General), William T. Cosgrave (President of the Executive Council) and Eoin MacNeill (Minister for Education); standing (L–R): Michael MacWhite (Irish Free State Permanent Delegate to the League of Nations), Desmond FitzGerald (Minister for External Affairs), the Marquis MacSwiney (Delegate), Kevin O'Sheil (Delegate), Ormonde Grattan Esmonde (Delegate), Diarmaid O'Hegarty (Cabinet Secretary) and Joseph O'Reilly (aide-de-camp to Cosgrave).

in Paris) took up the post of Ireland's permanent delegate to the League. League membership allowed Irish diplomats to engage with the representatives of over fifty states in an international forum through one diplomatic mission in Geneva. For a small state with limited resources, such international organisations offered value for money. Ireland would otherwise have had no relations with many states with which it had much in common.

Ireland's stance at Geneva sought to emphasise Irish sovereignty and a belief in the League's ideal of a peaceful international system. Despite British protests, the lodging of the 1921 treaty as an international treaty at Geneva in July 1924 achieved the first objective. While the Irish Free State was not hugely active in the early years of its League membership, in 1926 it stood for election to the League's governing council (the equivalent of the modern United Nations Security Council), in protest at the rotating of council seats among informal groups after the admission of Germany to the League (though Ireland did not object to German membership). Ireland also stood for election on this occasion to assert the right of the dominions to stand, as none had yet done so. While the effort was unsuccessful, the experience showed Dublin what Irish diplomats could do at Geneva with just a little effort and some international goodwill. From 1927 Dublin also made active support for the League of Nations a key plank of its foreign policy, signing League social and economic conventions, embracing its codification of international law and supporting League-sponsored moves for international disarmament.

With such visible support for the League to hand, in 1929 the Department of External Affairs began seeking international support for Ireland's election to the Council in 1930. Ireland stood as an independent member of the League, as a representative of small and powerless members against the Great Powers. It worked. In September 1930 the Irish Free State, a League member since only 1923, was elected to the top table by its international peers. This was a vindication of the active stance taken by Ireland at Geneva after 1926.

•

Anti-treaty sympathisers outside the US Capitol building, holding placards protesting against the visit of Richard Mulcahy to the US, October 1925. Mulcahy had been chief of staff of the IRA during the War of Independence and later headed the pro-treaty National Army during the civil war before serving as Minister for Defence. The placards highlight his role in overseeing the Free State's campaign against the IRA (including executions) during the civil war and his support for the 1921 treaty; as such he was a hate figure for republicans opposed to the treaty.

In the first half of the 1920s, Anglo-Irish relations were dominated by the issue of the boundary between the Irish Free State and Northern Ireland. Before the outbreak of the civil war the Provisional Government under Collins had sought some kind of accommodation with the Northern Ireland prime minister, James Craig, whose own preference had been to keep Dublin at arm's length. From late 1922 the Irish Free State had adopted a policy of peaceful co-existence with Northern Ireland, as it developed its case for maximum border changes to transfer territory south under the 'Boundary Commission' proposed by the 1921 treaty. (The treaty had also contained proposals for a 'Council of Ireland', to address matters of mutual concern, but it was not convened).

The Boundary Commission did not finally meet until 1924, but the leaking of its report in November 1925 showed that the commission proposed only minor alterations to the boundary as it stood between the Irish Free State and Northern Ireland, and that it envisaged land transfers to Northern Ireland. Given the composition of the three-man commission, such minor alterations were unsurprising. The Irish Free State was

Above: A border checkpoint between Northern Ireland and the Irish Free State, *circa* 1922. Northern Ireland had been created in 1920, before the negotiations that led to the creation of the Irish Free State. Irish nationalists of all types were, in principle at least, in favour of Irish unity but the treaty had proposed a 'boundary commission' to adjudicate on redrawing the border. The assumption held by many at the time was that this would result in major transfers of territory to the Irish Free State and would undermine the viability of Northern Ireland's continued existence.

Opposite: William T. Cosgrave, British prime minister Ramsay MacDonald and prime minister of Northern Ireland Sir James Craig at Chequers, the country residence of the British prime minister, for discussions on the appointment of the members of the Boundary Commission, 31 May 1924. The leaking of the Commission's report in November 1925 led to crisis talks between the three leaders and the suppressing of the report. The Irish border remained unchanged.

The Irish Free State maintained a small number of honorary consuls across the globe. The role was generally undertaken by members of the Irish diaspora with significant business concerns; the example shown here is William Craig Martin's insurance office, which maintained an Irish presence in Shanghai in the inter-war years.

The Irish Free State maintained an active role at Imperial Conferences in the 1920s. At the 1926 conference Irish delegates were central in negotiating the Balfour Declaration, which led to the 1931 Statute of Westminster giving the dominions greater autonomy within the Commonwealth. The Irish delegation was led by W.T. Cosgrave, shown here (front row, extreme left) at Lancaster House, London with British prime minister Stanley Baldwin (front, in centre), dominion prime ministers and other officials, including Winston Churchill (back row, second from right).

represented by former minister for education Eoin MacNeill, and the Northern Ireland government by the unionist former newspaper editor J.R. Fisher. The chairman, appointed by the British government, was the English-born South African judge Richard Feetham, whose narrow definition of the criteria for altering the border ensured that the proposed changes were minimal; arguably, this was why he had been appointed. Crisis talks between the Irish, British and Northern Ireland governments led to an agreement on 3 December 1925 to suppress the commission's report, to retain the existing boundary and to cancel certain Irish debts owed to Britain under the treaty. After 1925 cross-border co-operation was limited to technical affairs, and the two prime ministers of partitioned Ireland would not meet again until 1965.

Between 1922 and 1949 Ireland was a reluctant member of the British Commonwealth, which had evolved from the British Empire. Cosgrave's government did, however, hope to

Previous pages: The commemoration of the dead of the First World War was contentious in independent Ireland. Military service by Irish soldiers in the 'Great War' had generally taken place in the British armed services; this was problematic for a state that had recently emerged from a political and military conflict with the British. In this image of the London cenotaph on Armistice Day, 11 November 1926, Irish Free State Minister for Justice Kevin O'Higgins is present, second from the right in the back row to the right of the cenotaph.

Left: The governor-general of the Irish Free State was the official representative of the British monarch. The post was first occupied by the veteran former Home Rule MP Tim Healy. He is pictured here *circa* 1930 with the two young daughters of Kevin O'Higgins, Una and Maev, in his official residence in the old Viceregal Lodge in Dublin's Phoenix Park, which would later become the Irish presidential residence, Áras an Uachtaráin.

Opposite: An October 1927 memorandum on rates of subsistence and travel for Irish diplomats, signed in Irish by Joseph P. Walshe (Seosamh P. Breathnach). The black border is presumably official mourning protocol, as a result of the assassination of Minister for External Affairs Kevin O'Higgins by the IRA in July 1927, less than a month after he had taken up the post.

move the Commonwealth away from its role as an imperial body towards a grouping of like-minded independent sovereign states, and this became a hallmark of Cumann na nGaedheal foreign policy.

As early as the 1923 Imperial Conference Irish diplomats began developing plans to reform the status of the dominions, and these efforts bore fruit in the 1926 Balfour Declaration, which declared each dominion internationally equal to Britain. The Irish Free State Minister for Justice, Kevin O'Higgins, played a key role alongside Cosgrave and the Minister for External Affairs, Desmond FitzGerald, at these conferences. Further reforms diminishing Britain's role as the controlling force over the Commonwealth followed in the later 1920s and led to the

SAORSTÁT ÉIREANN
(IRISH FREE STATE).

Uimh. Eagartha
(Reference No.)

ROINN GNÓTHAÍ COIGRÍCHE
(DEPARTMENT OF EXTERNAL AFFAIRS).

A.98/112.

BAILE ÁTHA CLIATH
(DUBLIN).

5th October, 1927:

Vaughan B. Dempsey Esq.,
   7 Rue Georges Ville,
     Paris.

      I am directed by the Minister to refer to my circular of the 4th July last (A.98/1927) and my circular letter of the 8th December 1924 (A.98/200) relative to subsistence rates for travel on the Continent and to say that the Minister for Finance has sanctioned the following rates in lieu of those specified in paragraph 2 of my circular letter of the 8th December, 1924 for absences in the countries and cities given, viz:-

United States of America,	.... £2
Canada,	.... £2
Sweden,	.... ~~35/~~ 30/-
Holland,	.... ~~35/~~ 30/-
Paris,	.... 30/-(rest of France £1)
Rome or Milan,	.... 30/-(rest of Italy £1)
Brussels,	.... 25/-(rest of Belgium £1)
Norway,	.... 25/-
Denmark,	.... 25/-
Spain,	.... 25/-
Berlin,	.... 30/-(rest of Germany 25/-
Poland,	.... 30/-
Switzerland.	.... 25/-

              S.P. Breathnach
            Rúnaidhe.

Statute of Westminster (1931), which ensured the domestic sovereignty of the dominions and allowed a dominion to repeal legislation passed for it by Westminster. This opened the way both for the eventual revision of the Anglo-Irish Treaty of 1921 and, more significantly, the replacement of the 1922 Irish Free State Constitution.

Such activities illustrated the ongoing necessity for a dedicated Irish diplomatic service. The scope of Ireland's international interests and activities widened in the 1920s, but the resources at the disposal of the small Department of External Affairs were limited. It had perhaps 50 members of staff at home and overseas in 1927. The post-civil war Irish Free State was relatively impoverished, and its lack of financial resources was reflected not just by an inability to tackle pressing social and economic problems at home, but also in the way in which it presented itself to the world.

The Irish Free State's diplomatic service in the early 1920s was restricted to the posts in Washington, London and Geneva,

W.T. Cosgrave and William Hale ('Big Bill') Thompson, the Mayor of Chicago, in January 1928. Cosgrave arrived in New York, and visited Chicago, Philadelphia and Washington, DC, where he paid a visit to President Calvin Coolidge and addressed the senate. The visit was intended to bolster support for the Irish Free State in the United States, in response to growing support there for Éamon de Valera's Fianna Fáil party. Cosgrave also visited Canada; this was the first official state visit overseas by the leader of independent Ireland.

The signing of the Kellogg-Briand pact at the Quai d'Orsay in Paris, 27 August 1928. Officially 'The international treaty for the renunciation of war as an instrument of national policy', it was sponsored by French foreign minister Aristide Briand and US Secretary of State Frank Kellogg. This was the first international treaty signed by the Irish Free State. W.T. Cosgrave is seated on the far right; this seating arrangement, with Ireland on the periphery, reflects the junior status of the Irish Free State as the youngest state present.

along with two trade and general offices in Paris and Brussels (the missions in Rome and Berlin were closed in 1923 and 1924 respectively). Indeed, the very existence of the Department of External Affairs as a separate entity remained uncertain as late as 1927. In the early 1920s Irish foreign policy had been narrowly defined as little more than an extension of Anglo-Irish relations. By the late 1920s there was a broadened foreign policy remit through activities in both the League of Nations and the Commonwealth. This naturally made the case for the maintenance of a dedicated government department. Any lingering uncertainty over the future of External Affairs as a separate department of state was dispelled in August 1927 when the post of secretary of the department was officially confirmed (this was the equivalent of the modern position of 'secretary general'); Walshe was now given a rank commensurate with the other administrative heads of the Irish Free State's government departments.

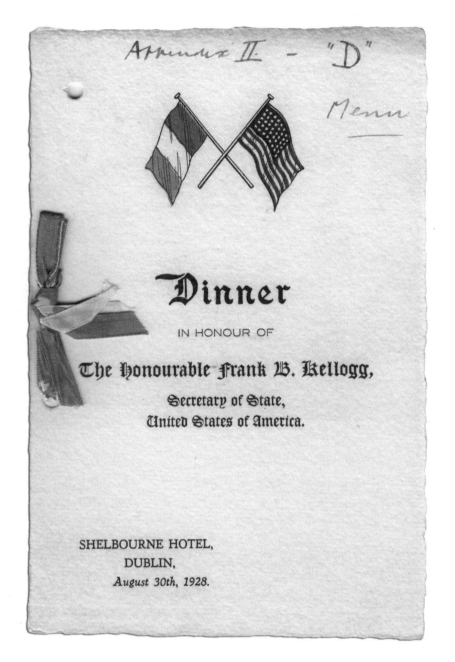

Appendix II - "D"

Menu

Dinner

IN HONOUR OF

The Honourable Frank B. Kellogg,

Secretary of State,
United States of America.

SHELBOURNE HOTEL,
DUBLIN,
August 30th, 1928.

The cover of the menu for the state banquet held for Kellogg in Dublin's Shelbourne Hotel; the menu itself was deeply influenced by French cuisine. The protocol for Irish diplomatic dining evolved from these origins. By the twenty-first century, such events could be held on premises owned by the state, and very consciously made use of bespoke tableware and ingredients of exclusively Irish origin, with an emphasis on domestic cuisine.

Secretary of State Frank Kellogg arriving at Dún Laoghaire on his return journey to the US following the signing of the Kellogg-Briand Pact; the funnels of the USS *Detroit*, the destroyer on which he travelled, are visible in the distance. Cosgrave returned to Ireland with Kellogg, who was, at this stage, the highest-ranking foreign dignitary to have visited the Irish Free State. The brief visit did present some difficulties in relation to protocol: plans for a champagne reception on the quayside had to be abandoned due to the US policy of 'Prohibition' on alcohol in the 1920s.

Kevin O'Higgins replaced Desmond FitzGerald as Minister for External Affairs in June 1927 but was assassinated by the IRA the following month. He had been a hate-figure for republicans, who blamed him for the Free State's execution of 77 republican prisoners during the civil war. His replacement was the Coleraine-born lawyer and academic Patrick McGilligan, who also held the Industry and Commerce portfolio in Cosgrave's cabinet. Under McGilligan, the Irish Free State took its first steps towards developing a practical foreign economic policy. It sought trade agreements with both France and Germany and pleaded the case at the League of Nations for tariffs to support under-industrialised and under-developed states when other states sought the removal of all trade restrictions. McGilligan also oversaw the opening in 1929 of three new foreign missions—at the Vatican, Paris and Berlin—thus doubling the Irish Free State's overseas representation.

•

By the early 1930s Cosgrave's government had definitively placed Ireland on the international stage. The young state now had diplomatic representatives in London, Geneva, Washington, Paris, Berlin and the Holy See, along with consulates in Boston and New York. It had secured Ireland's place as an active member of the League of Nations, for which, as already noted, Ireland's peers elected the state to the League Council in 1930. In the Commonwealth, the Cumann na nGaedheal government's actions had ensured that the dominions were well on the way to achieving ultimate international sovereignty. It had shown that the 1921 treaty could indeed, as Michael Collins famously observed, provide the freedom to achieve freedom. Ironically, the beneficiary of these achievements was not Cosgrave's Cumann na nGaedheal but a new political party—Fianna Fáil—created by Éamon de Valera in 1926. This new party provided republicans hostile to the treaty of 1921 with another political outlet for their ambitions. When they came to power in 1932 Irish foreign policy would shift in a new, and more radical, direction.

The hydro-electric power station at Ardnacrusha, on the River Shannon, pictured at night. This massive infrastructural project was undertaken by Siemens-Schukert in the 1920s and was the largest of its kind undertaken by the Irish Free State in the first decade of its existence. The 'Shannon Scheme' was consciously promoted at home and abroad as a symbol of modernity in a newly independent state that, emerging from civil war, could run its affairs with competence.

The 'Geneva Window'. In November 1926 Irish artist Harry Clarke received a commission from the Cosgrave government to create an artwork that could be gifted to the League of Nations. The concept was for a stained-glass window to be located in the offices of the International Labour Organisation in Geneva, consisting of vignettes from Irish literature. Cosgrave was concerned that some elements of the window would be offensive. The main cause of this concern was the sixth panel, which featured two nudes: a dancing woman from Liam O'Flaherty's novel *Mr Gilhooley*, and a reclining woman from George Russell's play *Deirdre*. Clarke died of tuberculosis in Switzerland in January 1931 before the window could be amended, and it was never presented.

LAUNCHING THEIR BOATS

Minister for Industry and Commerce Patrick McGilligan also became Minister for External Affairs after the assassination of Kevin O'Higgins. It was feared that External Affairs would be downgraded, but McGilligan, an international lawyer by training, reinvigorated Ireland's approach to the League of Nations. He oversaw the first expansion of Ireland's diplomatic service, opening missions at the Vatican, Paris and Berlin in 1929, and Ireland's successful election to the Council of the League of Nations in 1930. His years in office also saw the successful negotiation of a number of trade treaties, including with France. The cartoon depicts McGilligan and French minister to Ireland M. Charles Alphand.

Daniel Binchy in Berlin, October 1929, having presented his credentials as the first Irish envoy extraordinary and minister plenipotentiary to Germany. Binchy had studied in Munich and his grasp of German proved to be a rare asset as Ireland's diplomatic footprint expanded. As a student he had witnessed Adolf Hitler speak in public, and harboured deep concerns over the rise of Nazism. He later reported to Dublin on the collapse of the Weimar Republic. Binchy remained in the post in Berlin until 1932. He resigned after Fianna Fáil entered government and later became a distinguished historian of early medieval Ireland.

1932–
1939

External affairs under de Valera

The new president of the Executive Council of the Irish Free State, Éamon de Valera and his vice-president, Seán T. Ó Ceallaigh leave government buildings in March 1932 followed by, on the right, Joseph Walshe. In March 1932 the Fianna Fáil electoral victory over Cumann na nGaedheal brought about the first change of government since the creation of the Irish Free State. In addition to being president of the Executive Council, de Valera became Minister for External Affairs. Walshe was worried lest his association with the outgoing Cosgrave administration would lead to his dismissal, and moved to convince de Valera of his loyalty, including, it was rumoured, by attending the same church for daily mass. Walshe became a crucial foreign policy adviser to de Valera in his recasting of Anglo-Irish relations throughout the 1930s.

The first change of government in Dublin following independence took place in 1932 when Fianna Fáil (roughly translated as 'Soldiers of destiny') came to power. The party was founded by Éamon de Valera in the years following the civil war. The majority of anti-treaty republicans who had been defeated militarily split from Sinn Féin and regrouped under his leadership. Fianna Fáil had loudly proclaimed its hostility to both the Cosgrave government and the Anglo-Irish Treaty and had boycotted the Irish Free State parliament.

The party had been forced to enter the Dáil in 1927, however, following new legislation passed after the killing of Kevin O'Higgins that obliged elected TDs to take their seats or forfeit them. This meant taking the oath of fidelity to the British crown, which de Valera and his colleagues did while simultaneously denouncing it as meaningless. This stance left no doubt that when Fianna Fáil finally came to power the Anglo-Irish Treaty would be one of its principal targets. In addition to becoming president of the Irish Free State Executive Council (the post was renamed 'Taoiseach' after 1937), de Valera took the External Affairs portfolio.

International relations mattered to de Valera and he saw the pursuit of an independent foreign policy as the ultimate expression of Ireland's independence. He remained President of the Executive Council/Taoiseach and Minister for External

An Irish Free State passport, issued to Paule Slowey in Paris in 1930 by Ireland's minister to France, Count Gerald O'Kelly de Gallagh. Along with achieving membership of the League of Nations, appointing ministers to foreign states and signing treaties in its own right, the government's issuing of Irish passports was another assertion of the Irish Free State's international sovereignty. The front cover of this passport features on p. viii.

Affairs from 1932 to 1948. De Valera was to become the dominant intellectual force behind Irish foreign policy from the 1930s to the late 1940s, though he built his vision of Ireland acting independently upon the achievements of Cumann na nGaedheal in world affairs in both the Commonwealth and the League of Nations.

De Valera's immediate priorities, however, lay much closer to home. He laid down new guidelines for Anglo-Irish relations based on detailed advice from three key diplomats: Walshe; the legal adviser at the Department of External Affairs, John Hearne; and the Irish High Commissioner in London, John Dulanty. Walshe and Dulanty had good working relationships with senior officials at the Dominions Office in London, and de

Valera gave the three men considerable latitude, though he kept outright control of the strategic direction of Irish foreign policy.

On taking office in the spring of 1932, Fianna Fáil immediately began to attack the existing framework of Anglo-Irish relations, by removing the oath of fidelity and deliberately downgrading the status of the representative of the British monarch in Ireland, the governor-general, by treating the office with contempt. The de Valera government also began to withhold land annuities—repayments for loans granted to Irish farmers by the British exchequer under the reforming Land Acts of the late nineteenth and early twentieth century. London retaliated by placing tariffs on Irish exports to Britain, triggering a trade conflict that lasted until 1938 and became known as the 'Economic War'. While Cumann na nGaedheal had broadly favoured free trade, the aftermath of the Wall Street Crash of 1929 ensured that many countries would shift towards protectionism in the 1930s. A small economy such as Ireland's was not ultimately suited to protectionism, and economic self-sufficiency was a key objective for de Valera's government. Irish officials investigated new markets in continental Europe and North America in order to compensate for the exports to Britain lost through the Economic War, but their efforts were ultimately unsuccessful.

Fianna Fáil's return to power with a majority government following a snap general election in January 1933 indicated clearly to the British that de Valera was a force to be reckoned with, and one who would hold power for the foreseeable future. In 1934 there was a small improvement in British-Irish relations with the negotiation of the 'coal-cattle pact'. British imports of Irish livestock were increased in exchange for a parallel increase in the Irish importation of British coal. Nevertheless, the broader questions of Ireland's relationship with the Commonwealth and a settlement of the annuities dispute still stood in the way of harmonious relations between Dublin and London. The death of King George V, the accession of King Edward VIII and attempts to renegotiate the 'coal-cattle pact' dominated British-Irish relations through the first months of 1936. In November of that year the constitutional crisis arising from King Edward VIII's relationship with the American divorcée Mrs Wallis Simpson and his subsequent abdication also impinged upon British-Irish relations.

John W. Dulanty buying shamrock from a street vendor in London, 1933. Born in Liverpool to Irish parents, Dulanty had been a former Whitehall insider until 1918, and an election agent to Winston Churchill before the First World War. Giving his allegiance to Dáil Éireann and the Irish Free State, Dulanty served as Ireland's trade commissioner in the UK from 1926, and Irish high commissioner in London from 1930, a role that was elevated to the status of ambassador in 1950. Dulanty had an unrivalled understanding of how to negotiate the highest political circles in London and across Britain.

De Valera had previously indicated to London his intention to introduce legislation to abolish the functions of the monarchy in Irish domestic affairs, as a prelude to introducing his anticipated new constitution, which was being drafted primarily by John Hearne. De Valera now used the abdication to legislate to end the functions of the British crown in relation to internal affairs in the Irish Free State. This did not imply a complete break, however: the Executive Authority (External Relations) Act of 1936 allowed for the continued exercise by the monarch, on the advice of the Irish government, of functions relating to Ireland's external relations (the British monarch continued to accredit Irish diplomatic representatives overseas). That act made possible the continued association of Ireland with the Commonwealth, though Irish ministers ceased to attend Imperial Conferences or their equivalent. The swift enactment of the new constitution of Ireland, Bunreacht na hÉireann, on 29 December 1937 was one of the major milestones in the peaceful evolution of the Irish Free State into another legal entity; as the new constitution specified, the English-language name of the state was now officially Ireland.

•

The years from 1930 to 1935 were Ireland's heyday at the League of Nations. De Valera, in contrast to his austere image in Ireland, enjoyed the cosmopolitan atmosphere of Geneva and was a popular and respected international statesman in 1930s Europe. He addressed the League's Assembly yearly and often represented Ireland on its Council during the state's three-year membership of that body from 1930 to 1933.

Membership of the Council, the League's highest body, gave Irish diplomats opportunities to engage with global problems that rarely otherwise involved Ireland—from the operation of the League's mandates in Africa, to public health issues in less developed countries, to the 1931 Japanese invasion of Manchuria in China. Ireland's permanent delegate to the League of Nations, Seán Lester, supported efforts to penalise Japan for invading Manchuria despite instructions from Dublin that, notwithstanding its actions, Japan was to be supported as a bastion of anti-Communist stability in the East.

M. CLARKE.

EVERY TIME YOU B
YOU HELP THE EMP

B.S.3.—Issued by the Empire Marketing Board.

EMPIRE PRODUCE
TO BUY FROM US.

Printed for H.M. Stationary Office by Waterlow & Sons Limited, London, Dunstable & Watford.

Ireland's term on the League's Council ended in September 1933, but by the middle of the decade Ireland was marked out as a League supporter. Indeed, in 1934 when the League sought to oversee a plebiscite in the Saarland, a League-run territory between France and Germany, de Valera was approached to see if Irish military personnel could be deployed to join an international force policing the vote. He agreed, even though the Irish troops would be under British command. Ultimately, Dutch troops were called upon instead, but this was a ground-breaking call on the still relatively new Irish state's armed forces. Both this and Seán Lester's secondment to the League's secretariat as high commissioner in the 'free city' of Danzig in 1934 illustrated Ireland's potential and actual role as a 'middle power' in

Éamon de Valera is greeted in London by Secretary of State for Dominion Affairs Malcolm MacDonald. MacDonald's appointment in 1935, replacing J.H. Thomas, paved the way for an improvement in Anglo-Irish relations, which ultimately led to the April 1938 Anglo-Irish agreements on finance, trade and defence, including the return of the 'Treaty Ports' to Irish control.

the League (the contested city was ruled under the jurisdiction of the League from 1920 to 1939). Lester offered those who would listen evidence of what Nazism ultimately would lead to in Europe. Few took more than cursory notice of his warnings.

●

While the League of Nations gave Irish diplomats an international stage and access to an international network, Ireland's only diplomatic representation outside Europe in the 1930s was in the US, where Michael MacWhite had sought to assure the State Department that it should not fear an upsurge in anti-British activity in Irish-America following de Valera's election victory in 1932.

MacWhite's remit was divided between maintaining traditional contacts with the Irish-American community and enhancing Irish interests within the wider American political system. He tried unsuccessfully to use a personal relationship with US president Franklin Roosevelt, which dated back to 1918, to open negotiations for an Irish-American trade agreement. In developing Irish interests throughout America, MacWhite had the support of a chain of consular posts at New York, Boston, Chicago and San Francisco, which also served as publicity and promotional bureaux for Ireland.

With regard to diplomatic missions in continental Europe, the establishment of the Irish legation to the Holy See and the appointment of a Papal Nuncio in Dublin in 1929 and 1930, ensured that relations with the Vatican remained a significant feature in Irish foreign policy in the early 1930s. Although the Holy See had reacted with some unease to Fianna Fáil's election victory in 1932, de Valera and his government demonstrated their attachment to Catholic values at the international Eucharistic Congress held in Dublin in the summer of 1932; this was strengthened by visits to Rome and the Vatican by de Valera and his vice-president Seán T. Ó Ceallaigh in 1933 (Joseph Walshe, a staunch Catholic, attached particular importance to establishing good relations with the Vatican). De Valera made sure to sound out the Holy See in relation to foreign policy issues that were of interest to Catholics, such as the admission of the Soviet Union to the League of Nations in 1934, or the political tensions that

preceded the outbreak in 1936 of the Spanish civil war. In doing so he could appear to remain loyal to the Vatican, which helped to counter criticism of and opposition to his foreign policy from the Irish Catholic hierarchy, and indeed the wider public.

By the mid-1930s the hopes for international order encapsulated by the League were fracturing. Italian forces invaded Abyssinia on 3 October 1935, and the League's inability to counter Italy's military aggression against a fellow member showed that its system of collective security had failed. De Valera's view was that the League's fate would be decided by its response to Italy's actions. There was at the time no Irish diplomatic representative in Italy. It was through reports from William J.B. Macaulay, Irish Minister to the Holy See, that Dublin was informed on Italian perspectives on the international response to Mussolini's invasion of Abyssinia and on the domestic situation in Italy.

Ireland loyally implemented League of Nations sanctions against Italy, despite considerable Irish public and parliamentary sympathy towards a Catholic country supposedly bringing civilisation to what was perceived in some quarters to be a backward

O'Connell Street in Dublin, illuminated during the June 1932 Eucharistic Congress, marking the 1,500th anniversary of the missionary Patrick's arrival in Ireland. The congress was organised by the Catholic Church and supported by the newly elected Fianna Fáil government, as it permitted a very public association with the Catholic Church (note the temporary altar on the left). An international gathering attracting large numbers of pilgrims, it was also promoted to bolster Ireland's international image. The Eucharistic Congress was used by de Valera to deliver a very public snub to the incumbent governor-general, James McNeill, who was deliberately not invited to the state reception for the papal legate.

Seán T. Ó Ceallaigh, and John J. Hearne (far right), legal adviser at the Department of External Affairs, lead a group from the Irish delegation to the Commonwealth Economic Conference held in Ottawa in July 1932.

and pagan country (despite Abyssinia's long Christian tradition). There were public criticisms that Ireland was supporting Britain by placing sanctions on Italy. This was a misinterpretation: the sanctions had been initiated by the League, not Britain, and given that Ireland's trade with Italy was minimal in the mid-1930s, its implementation of the sanctions was a political statement in support of the League rather than an economic weapon against Italy. The League's ineffectual response to the Italian invasion of Abyssinia did, however, give rise to a quiet, but nonetheless perceptible, feeling in the Department of External Affairs that the League of Nations had failed outright in its essential task. The aftermath of the Abyssinian crisis saw a noticeable lessening of the Irish commitment to Geneva.

Ireland's small network of bilateral relations with continental Europe had been augmented slightly in September 1935 when a legation was opened at Madrid, with Leopold Kerney (a veteran of the original Dáil diplomatic service who had been reinstated by de Valera after he came to power) being appointed as Ireland's minister plenipotentiary and envoy extraordinary.

Telephone
Nº 100. (3 Lines.)

ESTD 1791

TRADE MARK
P

POT STILL ONLY.

Telegraphic Address
"POWER, DUBLIN".
A.B.C. CODE.

JOHN POWER & SON, LTD.

John's Lane Distillery,
DUBLIN, 4th July   19 32

Sean T. O'Kelly Esq.

Dear Sir,

    We have pleasure to inform you
that we have placed on board S.S
"Laurentic" a case of our "Three Swallow
Whiskey" for use of Irish Delegation on
board this vessel on the journey to
Ottawa.

    We hope you will accept it with our
compliments and good wishes.

    May we mention that this whiskey is
stocked by the Liquor Control Board of
Ontario and is procurable in Ottawa.

    We are,

      Faithfully yours,

        John Power & Son Ltd.

        per.

Ireland was elected to a three-year term on the Council of the League of Nations in 1930 by the members of the League's Assembly. Ireland's election was an illustration of the active role the state and its diplomats had played at Geneva since the mid-1920s. Here, Éamon de Valera is sitting at the centre of the Council's famous horseshoe shaped table, as he chairs a Council session in 1932.

Opposite: A letter to Seán T. Ó Ceallaigh from the Power's whiskey distillery in Dublin sent prior to his departure for Ottawa to represent Ireland at the 1932 Commonwealth Economic Conference. The distillery assured him that the Irish delegation would travel with some creature comforts.

When civil war finally broke out in Spain in July 1936 Kerney found himself cut off from Madrid, so he established an Irish mission at St Jean de Luz on the Spanish-French border, where he remained until the end of the conflict in 1939. In Ireland, de Valera faced considerable domestic political discontent over the conflict in Spain; significant elements of popular opinion, along with the Catholic Church, supported General Franco's nationalist forces, which were perceived as standing against the atheistic Communism of the elected republican government. Despite this, Ireland supported the Anglo-French sponsored Non-Intervention Committee from its inception in August 1936 and sought to restrict Irish volunteers travelling to Spain to fight on either side in the civil war. But by November 1936, with the victory of the nationalists looking increasingly inevitable, External Affairs was turning its attention to the likelihood that Dublin would soon have to recognise a de facto change of government in Spain.

De Valera remained a supporter of the League of Nations despite its failure in Abyssinia. But after 1936, as the European powers used the civil war in Spain as a proxy conflict, Ireland began quietly to shift towards greater self-reliance in international

affairs. Indeed, de Valera had given a very strong hint that Ireland might do this in a debate on the Abyssinian crisis in the League assembly in July 1936, when he had warned that

> Ten years ago, a Norwegian representative reminded you that you must deal in time with situations that might one day become acute. Two miles above Niagara, he said, it is possible to land, but wait until you are a hundred feet from the falls and you are lost. How much more necessary is this advice now than then? How much nearer is Europe to the falls? Will it be said, when the array of tombs which stretch from end to end of Europe has been multiplied, that there

Éamon de Valera in attendance at the League of Nations Assembly, Geneva in the mid-1930s. Like his predecessors in government Cumann na nGaedheal, de Valera regarded engagement with the League of Nations as a central pillar of an independent Irish foreign policy. De Valera was a respected figure at the Assembly and remained a supporter of the League's Covenant and ideals even after the outbreak of the Second World War.

A candid shot of Éamon de Valera and a number of Irish diplomats, including Michael Rynne, the head of the department's League of Nations' section (profile to camera) and John J. Hearne (looking towards de Valera) near Geneva while taking time off from attending a meeting of the League of Nations in 1938.

had been plenty of time to land, but that the statesmen waited too long and the soldiers took control?...Despite our juridicial equality here, in matters such as European peace the small states are powerless...All the small states can do, if the statesmen of the greater states fail in their duty, is resolutely to determine that they will not become the tools of any great power, and that they will resist with whatever strength they may possess every attempt to force them into a war against their will.

By the late 1930s a European war was on the horizon; the League had failed. Geneva nevertheless continued to serve as

Seán Lester, with cigarette in hand, in the Palais des Nations, Geneva, in 1946, speaking to Swiss delegate Paul Ruegger. Born in Antrim, Lester had a successful career as a journalist before becoming a diplomat. In 1929 he became Ireland's permanent representative to the League of Nations, and in 1933 became the first Irish diplomat to serve an international institution directly when he was seconded to the League's Secretariat as high commissioner to Danzig. A firm believer in the value of such institutions, Lester became the League's last secretary-general. He prevented the League being handed over to pro-Axis elements in the Secretariat led by his predecessor, Joseph Avenol. On Avenol's resignation, Lester maintained a lonely vigil in Geneva and ultimately oversaw the dissolution of the League in 1947, before retiring to the west of Ireland.

Dublin's continent-wide listening-post. Reports by Lester's successor in Geneva, Francis Cremins, identified the expansionist and militaristic intentions of a resurgent Germany under the Nazis as potentially the greatest destabilising force in Europe.

Irish diplomats witnessed the rise of German fascism at first hand. Ireland had opened a legation in Berlin in 1929, and throughout 1933 the young chargé d'affaires at Berlin, Leo McCauley, witnessed the Nazi takeover. McCauley was moved to New York to take up the post of consul general in the summer of 1933, to be replaced in Berlin by Charles Bewley, formerly the minister to the Holy See. Bewley had served in Berlin in the early 1920s as Sinn Féin envoy with mixed and troubled results. He was known to have a deep admiration for Germany, not to mention being strongly anti-Semitic. On returning to Berlin in 1933 Bewley's fascination with the Nazis was evident, though he was not yet an uncritical admirer.

This soon changed. Bewley swiftly became intoxicated with the rhetoric of the Nazi regime. This, along with an ongoing

A postcard of Danzig (Gdansk) collected by Seán Lester whilst serving as League high commissioner to the 'Free City' from 1934 to 1937. The contested 'Free City' was ruled under the jurisdiction of the League of Nations from 1920 to 1939. Attempting to mediate between Nazi and local political forces, Lester saw at first-hand what the ideology and actions of the Nazis meant for Europe, but his warnings that Danzig's fate would be Europe's fate went unheeded.

The Spanish civil war (1936–9) divided public opinion in Ireland and led to strong calls for de Valera to support the nationalist forces of Francisco Franco against the republican government in Madrid. Significant numbers of Irish travelled to Spain to fight on either side. De Valera's policy was that Ireland would support League of Nations-sponsored Anglo-French attempts at non-intervention in Spain, as evidenced by this donation forwarded by Dulanty. A small number of Irish nationals served on monitoring bodies supported by the non-intervention council.

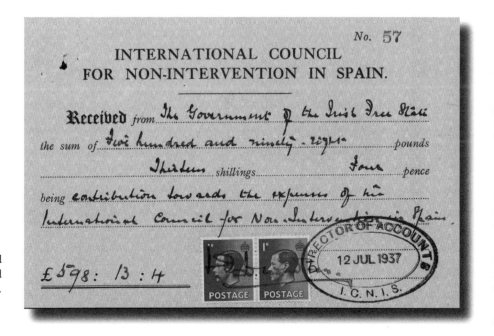

CÓMHARTHAÍ SÓIRT — PERSONAL DESCRIPTION — SIGNALEMENT.

		A Bhean Chéile—Wife—Femme
Gairm ... ... Profession ... ... Profession	Nuadhachtánach Journaliste	
Áit agus dáta beireatais Place and date of birth Lieu et date de naissance	Baile Átha Cliath, 12 Iúl, 1888. Dublin, le 12 juillet, 1888	
Áit chómhnaithe ... ... Domicile Domicile	Éire Irlande	
Aoirde ... ... Height ... ... Taille	5' 11"	
Dath na súl ... ... Colour of eyes Couleur des yeux	Donn Brun	
Dath na gruaige ... Colour of hair ... Couleur des cheveux ...	Donn Brun	
Aghaidh ... ... Face ... ... Visage	Fada Long	
Cómharthaí fé leith ... Special peculiarities Signes particuliers ...		

Sighniú an tSealbhóra.
Signature of Bearer.
Signature du Porteur.

(PHOTO)

Sighniú a Mhná Céile
Signature of Wife
Signature de la Femme.

Joseph Walshe pictured outside the tomb of the Mahdi in Omdurman, Khartoum, whilst on holiday, 9 May 1938. Having travelled south from Cairo by flying boat and crossing the desert in an old Ford car, Walshe wrote to de Valera from Khartoum that, 'Of course, I found Omdurman very interesting. I met some old warriors there who had fought against the British (under Kitchener) in 1898.' Walshe died in Cairo in 1956, while travelling through Egypt after his retirement, and is buried there.

Opposite: Charles Bewley's diplomatic passport. Born in Dublin and a barrister by profession, Bewley had served in the Dáil Éireann diplomatic service from 1921 to 1923. He rejoined the Department of External Affairs in 1929, becoming the Irish Free State's first minister to the Holy See and was posted to Germany in 1933. Bewley's anti-Semitism, which had been noted as early as 1922, then reasserted itself. He became infatuated with Nazi Germany and as a result was removed from his post in Berlin in 1939. During the Second World War he seems to have provided information on Ireland to Nazi Germany's intelligence agencies, and he was interned by the Allies at the end of the war. Bewley moved to Rome and later wrote a sympathetic, and best-selling, biography of Herman Goering.

dispute with Walshe over the direction of Ireland's policy at the League of Nations (Bewley disagreed with Irish support for sanctions against Italy), reduced the usefulness of Ireland's troublesome envoy in Berlin. With Bewley's reports becoming less reliable, Cremins's reports from Geneva on the shifting European balance of power came to have an increased importance. Following his report on Kristallnacht in November 1938, in which he had sought to minimise the grossly anti-Semitic excesses that characterised the Nazi regime, Bewley was sidelined by Walshe. His pro-Nazi views were unacceptable to his superiors in Dublin and he was removed from his post in 1939.

•

The future relationship between Britain and Ireland in the European war that was widely assumed to be on the horizon by the late 1930s was the spur that produced the April 1938 Anglo-Irish Agreements. These covered defence, finance and

Éamon de Valera arriving at Spike Island, Cork, 11 July 1938, for the handover of one of the three 'Treaty Ports' retained by Britain as naval bases in Ireland after 1922. Photographed here immediately prior to the handover by the British is Minister for Defence (and future Minister for External Affairs) Frank Aiken; also visible, in uniform, is de Valera's son Vivion. The return of these ports enabled Ireland's successful neutrality in the Second World War.

trade and during their negotiation de Valera had vainly hoped for movement on ending partition. The trade element of these agreements ended the Economic War and the financial arrangements resolved British-Irish debts arising out of the 1921 treaty.

The trade and financial agreements concerned events in the past; for the future of British-Irish relations in wartime, the defence agreement was paramount. By handing over to Ireland British naval facilities in the ports of Cobh and Berehaven in Co. Cork, and Lough Swilly in Co. Donegal, the defence agreement ended the remaining British military presence in Ireland outside Northern Ireland. The return of these 'Treaty Ports' finally gave Dublin sole control of all the state's territory, and this in turn would enable Dublin to declare meaningful neutrality should war break out.

The probability of a major European war grew during 1938. The Irish government and administration seriously anticipated the outbreak of conflict from the time of the Sudeten crisis of August-September that year. The likelihood of war increased over the next twelve months and Irish missions continually reported rumours of imminent conflict. By August 1939 most missions were reporting that the outbreak of war was only a matter of days away. Irish military preparations had commenced too late, and as a result the state was almost defenceless when the Second World War finally began. Despite crippling deficiencies in equipment, weapons and organisation, Ireland might have to defend itself against invaders, but the principal strategy for avoiding the horrors of war was to be a political decision: Ireland would adopt a policy of neutrality.

Patrick Brennan, son of Robert Brennan, Ireland's minister to the United States (1938–47), and an unidentified cat. Patrick's elder sister, the novelist and author Maeve Brennan, remained in the US after the Brennans returned to Ireland and became a long-standing columnist at *The New Yorker*.

Opposite: Cultural diplomacy: one of Robert Brennan's personalised (and hand-coloured) Christmas cards, sent whilst he served as Ireland's minister to the United States. The card is one of a series created by the Cuala Press, the firm co-founded and managed by Elizabeth Yeats, sister of the poet W.B. Yeats and the painter Jack Yeats. The mountain in the image is perhaps based on Croagh Patrick, an important Christian pilgrimage site in Co. Mayo.

Following pages: Members of the staff of the Irish pavilion at the 1939 World's Fair relaxing on the deck of the *SS Manhattan* en route to New York, April 1939. The Irish attendance at the fair was overseen by Seán Lemass's Department of Industry and Commerce. Seated (R-L): future secretary of the Department of External Affairs Hugh McCann (Aodh Mac Canna), Caitlín de Bhaldraithe, Domnall Ó Súilleabháin, Cáit Ní Chróinín, Fintín Ó Cuidighthe.

CUALA PRESS

Should strangers walk abroad to-night,
  Where'er their footsteps turn,
In every cottage window, bright
  The Christmas candles burn;
And every door stands open wide
  Lest Two there be would come inside.

The exterior of Michael Scott's modernist Irish pavilion at the 1939 World's Fair in Flushing Meadows, New York. Given the theme of the fair on 'the world of tomorrow', the plan of the main building was intended to resemble a shamrock to make it visible (in principle) to those travelling by air; the design and the contents were, however, intended to emphasise Ireland's modernity. The Irish government insisted that it be separate from the British pavilion, which also incorporated the pavilions of the various dominions. This was the first time that Ireland had been represented as a distinct entity at such an event. The Irish Pavilion was selected as the best pavilion at the fair; Scott went on to become one of the leading Irish architects of the twentieth century.

Opposite: An interior shot of the Irish pavilion, May 1939, with a huge mural by Seán Keating of the 'Shannon Basin' looming above the staff at the bureau. In keeping with the intention to present a modern and innovative version of Ireland, artists such as Keating, Evie Hone, Oliver Sheppard and Mainie Jellett all contributed works to the design of the pavilion.

Ireland's Permanent Representative to the UN, Geraldine Byrne Nason (centre), as chair of the Commission on the Status of Women (CSW), speaks at the opening meeting of the CSW 63rd session, 11 March 2019. She is flanked by UN Secretary-General António Guterres, and Under-Secretary-General for General Assembly and Conference Management Catherine Pollard.

WOMEN IN THE DIPLOMATIC SERVICE

Women became de facto diplomats in the Dáil's foreign service from its inception. In the post-independence period, however, Ireland's diplomatic service became an almost completely male preserve, as was the case in other foreign ministries and at senior levels in the Irish civil service generally at the time. Diplomatic spouses did play an important, though always unpaid, unofficial and often unrecognised role in Irish missions.

From the 1920s onwards legal restrictions on the employment of women in the Irish civil service, including a ban on employing married women, further ensured that women did not, for the most part, serve as Irish diplomats until after the Second World War. The marriage bar remained a major obstacle that forced women who had entered the diplomatic service to choose between the personal and the political. It was only after its removal in 1973, when Ireland joined the then EEC, that women could opt for a full career in the Irish public service. At that point, the number of women serving in diplomatic ranks increased steadily, despite continuing challenges posed by social attitudes and traditional family patterns.

Women can now be found in the highest echelons of the Irish diplomatic service and occupy some of the most important posts, and in 2013 almost two-thirds of third secretaries (and those at equivalent ranks) were women. The modern Department of Foreign Affairs and Trade is officially committed to gender equality, as part of a broader commitment to equality and diversity in the workplace.

1939–
1948

ESTERO,
    DUBLIN.

33.   PERSONAL.   GERMAN GOVERNMENT HAS INFORMED ME OFFICIALLY THAT NEUTRAL COUNTRIES ARE REQUESTED TO ADVISE SHIPS AND AIRCRAFT TO AVOID POLAND, DANZIG, GDYNIA BLOCKADED - HOSTILITIES EXPECTED IMMEDIATELY.

                              EIREANN.

<u>S. G. M.</u>

The 'Emergency'

This telegram from the Irish legation in Berlin is how the Department of External Affairs in Dublin learned of the outbreak of the Second World War in Europe. Sent by Chargé d'affaires William Warnock on the morning of 1 September 1939 in his 'Personal Code', it was addressed to 'Estero' the telegraphic address of the Department of External Affairs from 'Eireann', the telegraphic address of the Berlin Legation.

On 2 September 1939, in response to the outbreak of what became the Second World War, the Dáil declared a state of emergency. Ireland remained neutral during the war. This stance, as developed principally by the External Affairs department's legal adviser Michael Rynne, was strongly influenced by de Valera's belief that as a small and relatively powerless state, Ireland's interests were best served by avoiding involvement in wars between the major powers that might place Irish independence in jeopardy (de Valera's July 1936 speech in Geneva had said as much).

A very real concern for the Irish government was that participation in a European war, particularly at Britain's instigation, would enhance support for the IRA and even lead to renewed civil war in Ireland, not to mention the prospect of making Ireland a target for the Axis and Allied powers. Ireland's first generation of diplomats had personal memories of British forces on the streets of Irish cities and towns. Rynne himself had served in the IRA during the War of Independence before embarking on his legal studies on the continent. Others had experience of military service during the struggle for independence, and even in the First World War. All knew that Ireland had to avoid involvement in a world war unless, as a result of invasion, Ireland had no option but to fight.

Throughout the war the control of Irish foreign policy remained in the hands of a small group of senior officials in

Dublin: Walshe, his deputy Frederick Boland, legal adviser Rynne, and Walshe's private secretary, Sheila Murphy. They worked directly under de Valera, but not always with his hands-on involvement. Neutrality had wide public support, and the policy enabled the government to keep Ireland out of the almost five years of global conflict—the 'Emergency'—that would follow.

The use of the term 'Emergency' for the period of the Second World War in neutral Ireland lies in wartime emergency planning, whereby a state of 'Emergency' would precede the state's invasion or declaration of war. Ireland would remain neutral until it was invaded, at which point the 'Emergency' would end. The fear of invasion and war encroaching on Ireland's territory remained very real from 1939 to 1945, and in particular from 1939 to the summer of 1941, before Germany's priorities shifted away from Britain and Ireland and turned east towards its invasion of Russia. The Nazi regime had plans to invade Ireland as part of its proposed invasion of Great Britain; Ireland was spared this prospect by the defeat of the Luftwaffe in the Battle of Britain and the postponement of the invasion. The de Valera government was,

Below: The outbreak of the Second World War had an immediate, if indirect, impact on neutral Ireland. On 1 September 1939 the passenger liner *Athenia* was sunk by the German U-boat *U-30* close to the Rockall Bank off north-west Ireland. Survivors, picked up by the Norwegian vessel *Knut Nelson*, are shown here being landed at Galway docks on Ireland's west coast.

Following pages: Though Ireland declared its neutrality in September 1939, the fear of invasion, whether by Allied or Axis forces, remained a real threat. This memorandum issued from the Department of the Taoiseach to government departments hints at the steps Éamon de Valera's government was prepared to take in order to avoid, or prepare for, a possible invasion.

however, also concerned about the prospect of a British military incursion into Ireland, whether in response to a German landing or to seize strategic assets such as the former 'Treaty Ports'.

On the outbreak of the war, de Valera's government had moved to secure Ireland's neutrality as best it could. On 12 September 1939 an *aide mémoire* on restrictions on the use of Irish territorial waters was communicated to belligerent governments, including the British. Ten days later, on 22 September, Dublin and London agreed to the appointment of a British diplomatic representative—Sir John Maffey—in Dublin. There had been no British diplomatic presence in Ireland up to this point, and with tensions rising between Dublin and London over Ireland's neutrality—especially over the refusal to allow the Royal Navy use of naval facilities on Irish territory—a direct assertion of neutrality alongside a British diplomatic presence in Dublin were deemed necessary. While the British retained military facilities in Northern Ireland, the return of the 'Treaty Ports' by Neville Chamberlain's government was bitterly resented by his successor Winston Churchill, who felt they could have been of value to Britain in the Battle of the Atlantic.

The League of Nations was effectively abandoned after war broke out. The Irish office at Geneva was closed in 1940 and Frank Cremins was transferred to Berne as Ireland's first representative to neutral Switzerland. Still seconded from External Affairs to the League of Nations, Seán Lester remained in Geneva through the Second World War and held together the remnants of the League Secretariat. He served as the organisation's last secretary-general in 1946 and oversaw its dissolution. Other Irish diplomatic representatives remained posted to belligerent and neutral states through the war. In Berlin, however, where Charles Bewley had yet to be replaced, the vacancy for a minister plenipotentiary was filled by a chargé d'affaires. Under the terms of the External Relations Act, King George VI still signed the credentials of Irish diplomats. As head of a state at war with Germany he could not sign credentials of a diplomat posted to the capital of the Reich.

The capitals of the powers at war in Ireland's immediate vicinity and posing the greatest threat to Ireland—London, Washington and Berlin—became the overseas missions of most significance to Dublin during World War Two, followed

ROINN AN TAOISIGH
(Department of the Taoiseach)

21adh Meán Fhomhair, 1939.

To........ Rúnai,
Roinn Gnóthai Eachtracha,
      "   Cosanta.
Rúnai Priobh;aideach,
   Aire Cóimhriartha Cosantais.

      I am directed by the Taoiseach to inform you that
he proposes when the Dail meets on Wednesday to deal in a
comprehensive survey with the special problems of this
country arising out of the present situation with special
reference to such matters as neutrality, finance, essential
commodities, &c., military preparedness, unemployment, &c.,
and to indicate the steps which have been taken or which
are contemplated by the Government to deal with the problems
which have arisen.

      For this purpose he wishes to be supplied at a
very early date with a statement from your Department
covering the various matters with which it is or will be
dealing and in particular the following -

1. Problems that arise in preserving our neutrality as
    a relatively small country while powerful neighbouring
    States are at war.

2. The necessity for being prepared to deal with any
    demands from belligerents on any side, the acceptance
    of which would involve infringement of our neutrality.

3. Illustrations by reference to problems presented to
    neutral countries (a) in the war 1914-1918 and (b) in
    the present war.

4. The necessity for avoiding any action which by giving
    assistance to belligerents on either side in their war-
    like operations could reasonably be interpreted as a

                      breach/

To each member of the Government.

ROINN AN TAOISIGH
(Department of the Taoiseach)

To...

2.

breach of neutrality.

5. The necessity for being prepared as far as practicable
against the danger, however remote, of attack from any
quarter.

6. The censorship of communications and Press censorship
with reference to 4 above.

7. Light restrictions with reference to 4 and 5 above.

8. The necessity for certain minimum military preparations
within our resources.

I am also to request that you will be good enough
to enumerate in detail the special emergency measures which
it has been found necessary to take in your Department by
way of (a) Government orders and (b) ministerial and
subsidiary orders, and to indicate in each case the reasons
which have rendered such measures necessary.

Rúnaí.

ECH

To each member of the Government.

Uimh. ~~~agartha
(Reference No.)

ROINN GNÓTHAÍ EACHTRACHA

Department of External Affairs,

BAILE ÁTHA CLIATH
Dublin.

éιτε

13 Bealtaine, 1941.

An tÁire Lán Chómhachtach,
Quirinal.

    I am to state, for your
information that as from Wednesday,
the 14th May, 1941, the address of
the Department will be Iveagh House,
80, St. Stephens Green, Dublin.

    The new telephone number
of the Department will be 21681.

John A. Belton

    <u>Rúnaídhe.</u>

A note from Dublin to the Irish legation in Rome informing it of the change of address from Government Buildings to the Department of External Affairs' new headquarters at Iveagh House on St Stephen's Green. The buildings that became Iveagh House date back to the early eighteenth century but were combined and extensively remodelled after the Guinness family purchased them in 1856. The house was used as the central Dublin residence of the family, who donated it to the state in 1939. It was renamed Iveagh House after the aristocratic title held by the Guinness family from 1919 onwards.

in importance by those in Ottawa, Madrid, the Holy See and Lisbon. Diplomatic postings in some of these cities offered direct access to some of the warring powers. The same was true of the missions in Vichy (the capital of the pro-German regime headed by Philippe Pétain, ruling the south and west of France), Berne and Rome, which provided Dublin with important streams of information on the global conflict. That said, communications were challenging, and it became increasingly difficult for diplomats to take up new postings and for Dublin to fill vacancies.

The hardships facing Irish diplomats serving overseas in wartime were considerable: the discomforts of rationing, the physical and mental dislocation of wartime life, not to mention the very real danger of death. Irish diplomats witnessed the war at first-hand, from the London Blitz to the Allied bombing of Germany. The Irish legation in Berlin was destroyed in an air raid in November 1943; according to the chargé d'affaires, William Warnock, little more than a single typewriter survived.

•

Throughout the early years of the war British propaganda, supported by the United States, attacked Ireland for remaining neutral and called on Dublin to enter the war effort on the Allied side. Germany wished Ireland to remain neutral, but still occasionally dropped bombs on Irish territory and launched unsuccessful intelligence operations in Ireland. While Ireland's political and military leaders remained wary of the prospect of a British military incursion, ultimately their greatest fear was a devastating German invasion along the south coast. Dublin attempted to act even-handedly towards both parties, but by 1941 the vicissitudes of war ensured that, despite de Valera's poor relations with Winston Churchill, Irish neutrality could accommodate limited and discreet co-operation, in particular on intelligence matters, with Britain on war-related matters.

Dublin did not view this as covert involvement in the war effort. Neutrality was deemed a flexible policy that took into account geopolitical realities as well as Ireland's international interests, one of which was ensuring that Britain did not seriously entertain the possibility of invading Ireland. London never accepted Ireland's right to remain neutral, and for Dublin,

Opposite: The Hook Peninsula in Co. Wexford in the 1940s. The word 'Eire' can be seen clearly, denoting Irish territory to any belligerent pilots passing through Irish airspace from 1943 onwards; a small Defence Forces Coastwatching Service lookout post can be seen to the right of the picture, on the edge of the rocks. These posts, which were continually manned throughout the war to provide a means of alerting the Defence Forces to possible invaders, also functioned as an observer corps following the progress of the Second World War in Ireland's seas and skies. The number '16' denotes that the post was that at Hook Head. Each of the 83 'Eire' signs located around the coast (they were constructed without the *fada* above the initial letter 'E', although in some Gaeltacht areas it was added in) was marked on a numbered map given to Allied pilots crossing the Atlantic from the United States. This enabled them to plot their European landfall by the location of each sign should they be passing over neutral Irish territory.

German military plans and maps that were to be used in 'Operation Green', a proposed German invasion of Ireland.

partition remained a real concern during wartime, as Northern Ireland was now at war as part of the United Kingdom.

Irish–American relations were another matter entirely. The Roosevelt White House was uninterested in Ireland, except in so far as it could assist the British in the war effort. Ireland's minister in Washington, Robert Brennan, found little open support for Ireland's neutral stance on Capitol Hill and within the State Department. The United States minister in Dublin, David Gray, viewed Ireland's neutrality with disdain, and his relationship with de Valera and Walshe was often poor. Due to his close personal relationship with the Roosevelts, Gray's anti-Irish opinions circulated through the White House and the State Department and onwards into the United States media, further complicating Brennan's task; his protests that the stationing of United States forces in Northern Ireland amounted to American approval of partition were met with incredulity. High-level US opinion hardened even further in 1941, when Frank Aiken, as the Minister for the Co-ordination of Defensive Measures, visited the United States in search of arms and supplies. Nothing came of this: a tetchy interview between Aiken and President Franklin D. Roosevelt saw Roosevelt angrily scattering cutlery on the floor of the Oval Office after Aiken repeatedly told him he was concerned with British as well as German aggression.

The US was not prepared to entertain such a stance towards its key ally in Western Europe, and the provision of vital supplies to a neutral such as Ireland was simply not a priority. As formal US entry into the war became likely, wider Irish-American opinion also turned against Irish neutrality.

Dublin remained fearful of German intentions toward Ireland. Germany's official position was that it expected Ireland to remain neutral, which carried an implicit threat. These fears became more pronounced as German air attacks on Irish territory started in the summer of 1940. After the Luftwaffe bombing of the North Strand neighbourhood of Dublin in May 1941, it was suggested to the German government that should a similar raid to occur in the future, Ireland's neutrality might be strained to breaking point. By the summer of 1941 German attacks on Irish shipping had also become a serious concern for

The wreck of a crash-landed German Heinkel bomber at Ballywristeen, Co. Waterford on 1 April 1941. The crew of five was interned in the Curragh Camp.

The aftermath of the German Luftwaffe bombing of Dublin's North Strand on the Bank Holiday weekend 30–31 May 1941. This was almost certainly an accident, but it was the most destructive of numerous Luftwaffe bombings of Irish territory during the Second World War: 28 people were killed, over 90 were injured, and over 300 houses were destroyed in this densely populated area of Dublin's north inner city.

Dublin, though Irish merchant vessels remained unarmed, lest this provoke further German attacks which could drag Ireland into the war.

The most difficult aspects of Irish–German relations concerned German intelligence operations in Ireland and the use of the radio transmitter at the German legation by the German envoy, Eduard Hempel, and his colleagues. Though all German spies in Ireland were ultimately rounded up and held in custody and the legation transmitter was impounded, such activities remained a continuing problem for Dublin until the end of the war.

The chance of an Axis invasion of Ireland declined in the months after the Battle of Britain and the German invasion of the Soviet Union in June 1941. The chance of a British invasion also lessened as the war turned eastward and the Battle of the Atlantic moved away from Irish shores. Ireland was removed from the physical centre of the storm. The final occasion when overt British pressure was placed on Ireland to abandon neutrality came in December 1941, when, in the immediate aftermath of the US entry into the war, Churchill called on Ireland to join the war, apparently in exchange for the ending of partition. It was not seriously entertained by de Valera.

By early 1942 neutral Ireland retained little geo-strategic value for the Allies. Demands for the use of Irish ports evaporated as modern naval facilities were built at Derry on the River Foyle in Northern Ireland, and new airbases in Northern Ireland allowed long-range aircraft to patrol far over the Atlantic to counter German U-boats. From January 1942 to February 1944 the Allies often simply ignored Ireland, though limited co-operation with the Allies continued. Such links could bring sensitive matters to Dublin's attention. In 1942 the Department of External Affairs learned via British intelligence channels that Leopold Kerney, Ireland's minister in Madrid, was meeting German agents. Kerney later held that he was acting with Dublin's approval and that by meeting representatives of the different belligerents he was simply doing what any diplomat should do. Kerney's actions, regardless of his motives, did have the potential to cause further damage to Ireland's relations with the Allies. Ireland kept its representative in Berlin, William Warnock, in place, and his reports offer a unique English-language perspective on the prosecution and conduct of the war as seen from the German capital. Warnock and, from 1943, his successor Con Cremin, witnessed the defeat of the Third Reich and reported on its collapse in detail to Dublin.

Franco–Irish relations remained low-key until the Allied invasion of North Africa in November 1942. Seán Murphy's confidential dispatches from Vichy show the anti-Semitic policies undertaken in both German-occupied and Vichy France. By early 1943 de Valera was receiving telegrams from his friend Rabbi Isaac Herzog in Jerusalem, and appeals from prominent Dublin Jewish families and Jewish organisations in London, urging representations in Berlin on behalf of Jews in danger or already incarcerated in occupied Europe. These representations were invariably ignored by the German government.

While the level of detail now known about the treatment of Jews in wartime Europe was unclear (the destruction of the

Irish legation in Berlin in 1943 limits the surviving record of Warnock's insights into wartime Germany), general knowledge of the dispossession, deportation and incarceration of European Jews in specific concentration camps in Nazi-occupied Poland and the east of Europe is clear from Irish diplomatic traffic: the names Bergen-Belsen, Birkenau and Auschwitz appear in telegrams between Dublin and the Irish legation in Berlin. In October 1944 Dublin asked Cremin to investigate information received that the extermination of all Jews in Auschwitz was planned by German forces should they be forced to retreat. In January 1945 Brennan wrote from Washington to Walshe about the German policy of 'exterminating' the surviving Jewish population of Hungary.

If the means of extermination were not referred to, German intentions were certainly known to Dublin. Prior to the war, at the 1938 Évian-les-Bains refugee conference, Ireland had declined to offer assistance to German-Jewish refugees on the grounds, it was claimed, that it could not accommodate them. During the war, External Affairs intervened on behalf of a small number of Jews in Germany and France to get them visas or exit permits to leave occupied or German territory, but to no avail; the Irish legation in Berlin was told that this was an internal matter for the German government. Another attempt agreed by de Valera in 1944–5, to bring a group of German Jewish children to Ireland for subsequent travel to the United States also came to nothing.

•

The Irish desire to follow an independent outlook in international affairs meant that, even as an Allied victory in the Second World War became more likely, Ireland did not automatically comply with Allied demands. But by spring 1944, with the invasion of Europe imminent, the Allies were concerned that Ireland could become a centre for German intelligence activities that might impede the invasion, and equally that Ireland would not co-operate in preventing such an outcome occurring.

Consequently, the Allies sought to isolate Ireland in the prelude to the proposed invasion ('D-Day') in June 1944. On 21 February 1944 Gray, at the behest of his superiors, wrote to de Valera calling for the expulsion of the German, Italian and Japanese diplomatic representatives from Dublin. To de

Valera and Walshe this was unwelcome interference. Dublin interpreted Gray's so-called American Note as the pretext for a possible Allied invasion of Ireland through Northern Ireland. The State Department assured Brennan that no invasion of Ireland was planned, but if any intelligence leak concerning the invasion of Europe was traced to Ireland, the responsibility for the leak—and with it the potential endangering of the invasion—would lie with Dublin.

Preventing such leaks now became a top priority for the de Valera government. To this end, between March and June 1944 the Allies and Ireland co-operated closely to shut down travel and communication links with the outside world. The weather report from the Atlantic coast from which US General Dwight Eisenhower judged the conditions favourable for the invasion to begin came from Blacksod Bay, in Co. Mayo. This, like much of Ireland's covert co-operation with the Allies, would remain classified and unknown until the 1980s.

In the months after D-Day efforts were made to repair and improve relations with the Allies as the Irish government began to deal with various matters arising from the liberation of Western Europe (the ongoing war in the Far East against Japan was not a central concern for Irish foreign policy-makers). The impending conclusion of the war in Europe brought two issues to the fore: whether or not Ireland would give asylum to Axis war criminals, and how it would dispose of any German property and assets in Ireland.

The response was that Ireland, following the rules of international law, would not give asylum to persons whose presence in Ireland was contrary to Ireland's interests and those of friendly states, and would not permit Irish territory to be used to hide unlawful assets. Ireland would keep only those lawful assets it was due by way of compensation for German wartime actions against Ireland. The underlying issue here, however, was not the status of war criminals or of German assets, but David Gray's attempts to use both matters to exert Allied influence over Ireland.

The most notorious event in Ireland's wartime history took place on 2 May 1945, when de Valera visited Hempel's residence and signed the book of condolences opened on the death of Adolf Hitler. De Valera never publicly explained the rationale behind

Opposite: A page from Joseph Walshe's notebook recording in delicate terms that Eduard Hempel's mission as the German minister to Ireland in Dublin had been 'terminated' by 'events' in 1945.

Dr Hempel the German Minister called on The Minister for External affairs ~~today at~~ This morning and informed him that in view of the events which had occurred he regarded his mission as terminated, ~~and~~ wished to hand over ~~the custody of~~ The Dr Hempel Minister stated that he was vacating the Legation premises and that he wished ~~the Govt~~ to take charge of them ~~of them~~ of the German Govt property contained therein. The ~~return~~ Irish Govt will retain the custody of the property [until] the definite assumption ~~try~~ of the ~~control~~ Govt of the Reich by new authorities.

this but, writing to Brennan in Washington three weeks later, he stated that it was done out of respect for Hempel and the need to honour formal protocol. There is, however, another possible explanation. The US State Department feared the destruction of the archives at the German legation in Dublin and sought an assurance that the building would be handed over to the Allies before the cessation of hostilities. De Valera refused to accede to this demand, and on 1–2 May both he and Walshe told Gray that Ireland would co-operate with the Allies over custody of the legation only after Germany had formally surrendered. External Affairs felt that Gray had been mischievous in his handling of the request and de Valera was clearly displeased. It was only after this that he signed the book of condolences. The German legation was finally handed over to the Irish authorities on the morning of 10 May 1945; the Allies took over the premises that afternoon.

Reports soon arrived in Dublin of the international outcry at de Valera's signing Hitler's book of condolences, and External Affairs had to deal with fallout from small but vocal pro- and anti-Allied protests in Dublin on 'Victory in Europe' (VE) Day, 8 May 1945. Such protests had apparently involved Trinity College Dublin students attempting to burn a tricolour and the breaking of windows at both the British Representative's office and the United States Consulate General.

Churchill criticised Ireland's neutrality in his VE Day speech from London. Shortly afterwards came de Valera's reply, through a radio broadcast in which he stated that a world in which small powers were to be subordinate to the requirements of larger powers was a world doomed to war. Reports to Dublin about the speech stressed the maturity and dignity of the taoiseach's response to Churchill, but added that it was almost immediately old news compared to the problems of building peace.

•

As Europe returned to peace, Dublin began to adjust to the challenges of the post-war world. In September 1945 senior diplomats, and officials from other key departments, met in Dublin at the headquarters of the Department of External Affairs, Iveagh House on St Stephen's Green, for an unprecedented four days of discussions on the future direction of Irish foreign policy.

An informal shot of Éamon de Valera, Joseph Walshe and John W. Dulanty at the heads of mission conference, Iveagh House, Dublin, September 1945. The photograph was most likely taken by Michael Rynne.

After the critical interlude of the 'Emergency', many crucial pre-war issues, such as Anglo–Irish relations, participation in international institutions and the maintenance of international sovereignty, resumed their places as the central concerns of Irish foreign policy. De Valera stressed the need to redouble efforts to end the partition of Ireland and secure Ireland's national identity in an increasingly Anglo-American dominated world. He accepted that the legacy of neutrality would make relations with Britain and the United States difficult in the short to medium term.

Ireland's immediate post-war foreign policy was concerned not with these idealistic plans, however, but with specific technical and legal legacies of the war. This included explaining to the Allies that there were no significant German assets in Ireland, seeking compensation for bombing of Irish territory, dealing with German internees in Ireland and former Axis diplomats in Dublin, ensuring the removal of British minefields off the southeast coast, and addressing the position of Irish nationals who had fought in the Allied forces; especially those Defence Forces deserters who had joined the Allied armies. External Affairs did ask its overseas missions to stress that legislative action against these men was taken because they had deserted the Irish Defence Forces and not because they had fought with the Allies. Dublin

would not do anything overt to alienate the victorious Allies, but this was a small attempt to demonstrate that as a sovereign state Ireland would not automatically accede to what appeared to be unilateral demands from the victors of the war.

A more pressing issue, which provoked considerable disagreement between the departments of External Affairs, Justice and Industry and Commerce, was the post-war immigration of displaced persons from Europe to Ireland. The three departments were aware of the need to guard against the arrival in Ireland of individuals sought by the Allies. But the Department of Justice remained opposed generally to opening up immigration to Ireland, particularly for Jews, the arrival of significant numbers of whom, it was argued, would stir up anti-Semitic feeling. In addition, the Minister for Industry and Commerce, Seán Lemass, was opposed in principle to allowing refugees into Ireland purely on humanitarian grounds. For Lemass, refugees had to have the specific skills and resources that Ireland needed for economic modernisation (a stance that dated from before the Second World War).

The more open views of the Department of External Affairs won the argument, at least in theory. De Valera himself favoured the admission of at least 10,000 refugees to Ireland, though no such numbers were actually admitted. Ireland did not adopt a welcoming attitude to refugees in the post-war years. Immigration of all kinds, but particularly that of displaced families without resources, continued to be viewed largely in terms of the alleged burden it placed on the taxpayer, and the associated risk of public resentment, rather than of wider humanitarian and other considerations.

Maintaining Anglo–Irish relations remained vital to independent Ireland. In July 1945 Churchill's wartime coalition was replaced in the first post-war British election by a Labour government led by Clement Attlee. It was expected by External Affairs, without any solid evidence, to adopt a warmer attitude to Ireland than its predecessor. Although British resentment of Irish neutrality endured, the Anglo–Irish relationship was moving on because of economic and geopolitical necessity and the practicalities of the close connections between the two jurisdictions. The United Kingdom, faced with the massive challenges of post-war reconstruction at home and in Europe, needed Irish food and Irish labour. Ireland, equally, needed outlets for her produce and for her emigrants.

Attlee's government was also expected by Dublin to display less commitment to Northern Ireland, and even to be well disposed towards ending partition by negotiation. Northern Ireland's strategic wartime role in the Allied victory had, however, augmented Belfast's standing in London and the new Attlee government, many of whom had served in Churchill's wartime coalition, displayed no interest at all in moving to end partition or even to put pressure on the unionist administration in Belfast to take a more accommodating approach towards the Catholic minority population in Northern Ireland. Cross-border relations remained frozen. The differing paths taken by Dublin and Belfast during the Second World War ensured that the two Irish jurisdictions were, if anything, further apart in 1945 than had been the case in 1939. Northern Ireland did not receive a great deal of attention in Dublin in the immediate post-war years.

DONO IRLANDESE
SITUAZIONE DELLA DISTRIBUZIONE AL 30-6-1946

Legenda:

- ● ZUCCHERO AGLI ISTITUTI DI ASSIST. E BENEFICENZA
- ● " CON TESSERA AI CONSUMATORI DA 0 A 18 ANNI
- ● LATTE CONDENSATO O IN POLVERE
- ● BURRO
- ● BACON
- ● FORMAGGIO
- ● COPERTE, FILATI E INDUMENTI DI LANA

An unidentified but nonetheless delighted Italian girl with a packet of Irish sugar distributed as food aid after the Second World War; the inscription in Italian says, 'A gift from the people and government of Ireland to Milan'.

Opposite: A map indicating the locations at which Irish emergency relief aid to Italy was distributed in the post-war years.

Aid distribution in post-war France, with Irish minister plenipotentiary to France Seán Murphy, a future secretary general of the department, taking a hands-on role.

Dublin felt that one of the legacies of neutrality was that London and Washington purposely ignored Ireland's post-war relief programme to Europe. Using food and materials stockpiled for domestic use during the war, Ireland made aid available to Europe through 1945 and into 1946. The initial focus was the Netherlands, Belgium, France, Germany and Italy, but aid was redirected to central Europe in 1946, and consignments of food and living materials were sent to Poland, Yugoslavia and Hungary.

External Affairs had a particular interest in post-war developments in Eastern European countries with significant Catholic populations, specifically Poland and Yugoslavia. The threat posed by the Soviet Union to these countries became a recurrent theme in Irish foreign policy after 1945. The commencement of the Cold War called a halt to plans to initiate formal diplomatic relations with the states of Eastern Europe for over a

Aid distribution in post-war Berlin. Note the gender and age profiles of those pictured; presumably, the younger men had been killed or captured during the war.

generation. Walshe, as ambassador to the Holy See from 1946, and the vastly experienced Michael MacWhite in Rome were External Affairs' most active commentators on the development of the Cold War in Europe. The legations in Paris, Madrid and Lisbon, on the other hand, were often quiet places during the immediate post-war years.

The Irish diplomatic network did begin to expand, both inside and outside Europe, as peace returned. New offices were opened in Canberra (1946), Stockholm (1947), and Buenos Aires (1947). Ireland's presence in Canberra was initially focussed on the Irish community in Australia and Ireland's links with Australia as a dominion, but the mission provided Dublin with its first insight into post-war Asia. The chargé d'affaires in Buenos Aires had the short-term goal of ensuring wheat supplies for post-war Ireland, but was mainly concerned with the large Irish community in Argentina. The opening of this mission, along

Dankschreiben.

Im Namen meiner erholungsbedürftigen Heim-
kameraden, schreibe ich dem irischen Volke
Dank für die schöne Spielzeugspende. Sie
wurde uns durch das Schweizer-Rote-Kreuz
über die Volkssolidarität Potsdam übermittelt.

Wir haben uns sehr über die schönen Sachen
aus Irland gefreut. Beim Spielen werden wir
stets der irischen Kameraden gedenken.

Horst König

Kinderheim Kampehl über Neustadt-Dosse.

with that in Canberra, indicated a growing concern for the wider Irish diaspora. The legation in Stockholm gave Ireland its first formal diplomatic contacts with Scandinavia, and this along with the mission in Berne became extremely important in developing Dublin's understanding of the outlook of fellow European neutrals.

Ireland remained a member of the League of Nations until its dissolution in April 1946. It was not a founding member of the new United Nations in 1945, having neither sought nor received an invitation to attend the San Francisco conference that established the organisation. On 2 August 1946, Éamon de Valera informed the UN's first secretary-general, Trygve Lie, that Ireland was applying for membership and was prepared to accept the obligations contained in the UN Charter. But on 29 August the Soviet Union vetoed Ireland's admission, citing the country's wartime neutrality and its lack of diplomatic relations with Moscow (Ireland was one of a number of Western states whose admission was vetoed by the Soviets). There was an element of Cold War politics in the Soviet action, as Ireland was seen as a natural ally of the Western powers. In fact, all other members of the Security Council, including Poland, supported Ireland's bid for UN membership. Irish hopes were repeatedly dashed over the next nine years by the Soviet stance. Lie's successor as UN secretary-general, Dag Hammarskjöld, noted in 1954 that half the states of Europe, including Ireland, remained absent from the General Assembly.

An Anglo-French invitation to participate in the Conference on European Economic Co-operation (CEEC) in July 1947 gave a new impetus to Irish foreign policy. In 1946 Frederick Boland replaced Walshe as secretary of the Department of External Affairs, and he guided Ireland through its first steps in multilateral economic and financial diplomacy via involvement in the United States' move to reconstruct Europe's devastated economies through the European Recovery Programme (the Marshall Plan). The international conferences and committees Boland attended from the summer of 1947 gave External Affairs a much greater insight into the challenges of European reconstruction and recovery, and especially the question of how to rebuild Germany as the engine of European growth. Boland began to establish informal alliances with the Swiss and the Swedes,

Mr. Holloy c.c. 19/10

ROINN AN TAOISIGH
DEPARTMENT OF THE TAOISEACH

Mr. _____
you will note
that there is to be
no publication
HS
19/10.

BAILE ÁTHA CLIATH
DUBLIN

An Rúnaí Príobháideach,
An tAire Gnóthaí Eachtracha.

      I am to transmit herewith,
for the information of your
Minister, the attached copy of
a telegram recently received
by the Taoiseach from Chief Rabbi
Herzog, Jerusalem.

Mr Sheullbury.
For file, please.

₰m
21/10

Séamus Nachige
ₕ RÚNAÍ PRÍOBHÁIDEACH
7ú D.Fómhair, 1948

COPY/

JERUSALEM

2:10:1948.

Premier Irish Government Dublin.

Jewry Israel and everywhere most grateful your
magnificent gift Kosher Meat stop Your noble
act illustrative Irish kind-heartedness and
sympathy with victims of persecution irrespective
race creed. Heaven bless Irish nation whom I
shall never forget.

                    Isaac Herzog, Chief Rabbi

knowing that de Valera's preference was for Ireland to associate primarily with other European neutrals.

Though given a considerable degree of latitude, Boland, like Walshe, made sure to obtain de Valera's consent on all major decisions. He also ensured de Valera's attendance at the closing session of the CEEC in Paris. The conference was convened in order to draw up an inventory of European needs for recovery to present to the United States government, which was preparing to distribute extensive aid to post-war Europe under the Marshall Plan. The conference established the Organisation for European Economic Co-operation (OEEC), membership of which allowed Ireland to become involved once again in mainstream European multilateral relations.

Early Irish views on European unity did not go beyond advocating the primacy of the nation state in a 'Europe of the states'. Sharing or pooling sovereignty, as the 1950 European Coal and Steel Community would later propose, was not then considered. De Valera remained sceptical of the concept of a customs union, although he had no difficulty with Ireland being party to discussions on its establishment. Post-war Ireland remained tied economically and financially to Britain. The impact of this on Ireland's economy and national finances became clear in August 1947, when Sterling ceased to be convertible against the dollar and Ireland, as a member of the Sterling Area pool, was forced to negotiate with Britain to ensure that it was able to maintain a supply of dollars to buy American imports.

This economic crisis demonstrated that the Department of External Affairs and the Department of Finance had fundamentally different views of Ireland's place in the international economic system. External Affairs looked to develop a specific Irish attitude towards the international monetary and financial system, whereas Finance maintained that Ireland's international economic and financial position was best served by maintaining a close relationship with London. It was a difference of opinion that would recur as Ireland slowly shifted its foreign policy focus toward Europe and European integration. But this lay in the future: in February 1948 when, as the result of a general election defeat, de Valera and Fianna Fáil left office after sixteen years, the adjustment of Irish foreign policy to meet the challenges of the post-war world was far from complete.

A striking Fianna Fáil poster for the 1948 election, in which international turmoil from the 1930s onwards is the theme. Despite the attempt to present incumbent Taoiseach Éamon de Valera as the best 'skipper for this storm', after sixteen years in power Fianna Fáil was replaced by an 'inter-party' coalition led by Fine Gael and comprising Clann na Poblachta, the Labour Party, National Labour and Clann na Talmhan.

ISSUED BY FIANNA FAIL, 13 UPR. MOUNT ST. PRINTED BY THE FREDERICK PRESS.

1948–
1955

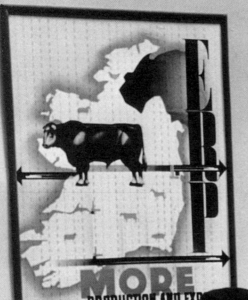

New directions

A stand publicising the US-backed European Recovery Programme (ERP, also known as the 'Marshall Plan') at the 1949 Dublin Horse Show held at the Royal Dublin Society.
The immediate post-war years saw Irish foreign policy attempting to overcome the aftermath of international isolation caused by Ireland's wartime neutrality. Involvement in the ERP was one means by which Ireland was brought back into multilateral diplomacy. The loans and grants provided by Marshall Aid contributed much needed funds to Ireland and saw a first, if rather unsuccessful, attempt at stimulating economic growth via capital expenditure and investment by the state.

In February 1948 a broadly based 'inter-party' government made up of Fine Gael (the successor party to Cumann na nGaedheal), the new radical republican party Clann na Poblachta, the Labour Party, and Clann na Talmhan (the Farmers' Party) took office in Dublin. The Fine Gael leader Richard Mulcahy had served as chief of staff of the army and as minister of defence during the civil war, and he was still blamed by many for the ruthless repression of republicans during the conflict. Clann na Poblachta refused to join any government under his leadership, so his party colleague John A. Costello became taoiseach in his stead, and Clann na Poblachta's leader, the barrister and former IRA leader Seán MacBride, was appointed Minister for External Affairs.

Costello and MacBride were from very different political parties. Fine Gael was traditionally seen as conservative, wealthier and more favourable towards the Commonwealth, while Clann na Poblachta had emerged after the Second World War with a socially radical and explicitly republican agenda. One area in which Costello and MacBride did share common ground was their Catholicism. The archbishop of Dublin, John Charles McQuaid, regularly advised Costello and MacBride, and both men regarded obedience to Catholic values as the pre-eminent guide to their political actions.

The 'Inter-party government', as the coalition became known, went to great lengths to appease the Catholic Church; its approach to foreign policy was no exception.

MacBride lacked experience in government and ran Ireland's foreign policy as he believed international relations should be run, rather than in accordance with international practice and diplomatic procedure. This lack of experience made MacBride more susceptible to alarmist reports on the progress of the Cold War in Europe and on Ireland's position in the deepening East–West struggle. Unsettled on his second day in office by a report from Joseph Walshe that the Italian press was reporting that Ireland was veering to the left under the new government in Dublin, MacBride instantly reacted by instructing, with the approval of Costello, that a message of Ireland's 'filial devotion' to the Holy See be sent by the Irish government to Pope Pius XII. In this context Walshe, who had seemed to exert less influence on policy-making in Dublin since his appointment as ambassador to the Holy See, now became a major influence on MacBride (whom he privately disdained). Walshe now found a receptive listener to his own increasingly narrow obsession with the Communist threat to Europe.

Ambassador Joseph P. Walshe hosts a garden party at the Villa Spada, the Irish embassy to the Holy See. As secretary of the Department of External Affairs from 1922 onwards, Walshe, more than any other individual, was responsible for establishing the department as a distinct entity and creating the mechanisms to pursue and develop an independent Irish foreign policy. A devout Catholic throughout his life, in May 1946 he became Ireland's ambassador to the Holy See: the first Irish diplomat to hold this rank.

Minister for External Affairs Seán MacBride signs the convention establishing the Organisation for European Economic Co-operation (OEEC) in Paris, 16 April 1948. On the extreme left, with his arms folded, Ireland's minister to France Seán Murphy looks on. Access to multilateral organisations such as the OEEC was particularly important as Ireland sought to find its place in the post-war world.

MacBride's approach to foreign policy emphasised anti-Communism, a vocal support for Christianity and democracy and an avowedly pro-Western stance, along with a strong desire to promote Ireland's independence and international sovereignty and above all the ending of the partition of Ireland. His high-handed and idiosyncratic personal style impacted on his working relationship with senior officials such as Boland, who became ambassador to Great Britain in 1950. Boland was replaced at the helm in Iveagh House by yet another veteran, this time Sean Nunan, who had spent most of his diplomatic career in the US, having begun it with de Valera on his American tour in 1919.

When it came to the appointment of officials, MacBride did oversee one landmark decision. The appointment of Josephine McNeill as Envoy Extraordinary and Minister Plenipotentiary to the Netherlands in November 1949 made her one of only two female heads of diplomatic missions in the world (the other was Clare Boothe Luce, then US ambassador to Italy). The expansion of the department in the late 1940s had led to a shortage of senior staff, and it was decided that suitable individuals should be brought directly into the diplomatic service. McNeill was the wife of former governor-general of the Irish Free State James

McNeill, a role in which, MacBride argued, she had gained a good deal of relevant experience (though she was also known to be a supporter of his party, Clann na Poblachta). The Irish legation at the Hague was seen to be one of Ireland's less important diplomatic missions; the Netherlands was deemed to be a country to which it was acceptable to send female diplomats.

MacBride also instituted structural changes in the department that he now headed. Following a suggestion originally made at the 1945 heads of missions conference, he created a 'Cultural Relations Division' to foster international appreciation of Ireland's culture and heritage. He also had great ambitions for the newly established 'Information Division', which would work with another new venture, the 'Irish News Agency', to establish an international consensus on ending partition. While the traditional hierarchy of secretary, assistant secretaries and the legal adviser remained the key senior officials in Iveagh House, MacBride's tenure in External Affairs also saw the rise of the new 'Political Division', which would, by the mid-to-late-1950s, become the core area in the department that oversaw foreign policy development.

•

In his first months in office, MacBride displayed great dynamism, most notably travelling to Washington, DC, in May 1948 to negotiate on the financial provisions earmarked for Ireland under the European Recovery Program (the Marshall Plan). Ireland eventually received $18-million of grants under the plan, in addition to $130-million of loans (the form of aid which the United States preferred to give to neutral countries).

There was, however, one major and somewhat unexpected development that essentially defined the foreign policy of the Inter-Party government. After the 1936 External Relations Act, neither Dublin nor London had sought clarification of Ireland's exact status in relation to the Commonwealth; both sides seemed willing to tolerate the status quo that had prevailed since the legislation was enacted. Ireland had continued to show considerable interest in the Commonwealth in the years after the war; it allowed Irish officials to participate in scientific, technical and trade-related conferences in an era when other

Opposite: An anti-partition pamphlet, one of a series produced by the Department of External Affairs under the direction of Seán MacBride and distributed in their thousands to Irish missions around the world; this copy was sent to the Irish mission to Argentina, which had opened in Buenos Aires in 1947. MacBride saw the ending of the partition of Ireland as a key goal of Irish foreign policy.

THE PARTITION OF IRELAND

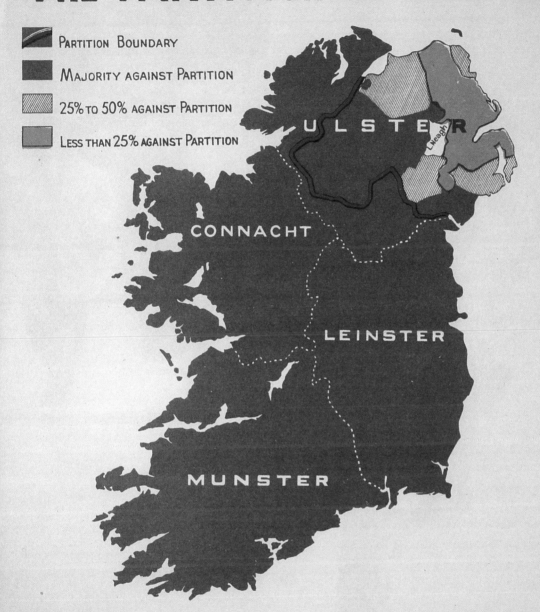

Legend:
- Partition Boundary
- Majority against Partition
- 25% to 50% against Partition
- Less than 25% against Partition

ULSTER

CONNACHT

LEINSTER

MUNSTER

L. Neagh

IRELAND WAS ONE UNIT UNTIL IN 1920 SHE WAS PARTITIONED BY BRITAIN AGAINST THE WILL OF THE OVERWHELMING MAJORITY OF THE IRISH PEOPLE. WITHIN THE PARTITIONED AREA – THE SIX COUNTIES STILL OCCUPIED BY BRITISH TROOPS – THERE IS IN A REGION COVERING MORE THAN FOUR COUNTIES, A MAJORITY AGAINST PARTITION AND IN FAVOUR OF UNITY WITH THE REST OF IRELAND.

Taoiseach John A. Costello (fourth from left in the front row) arrives in Ottawa in September 1948, commencing the official visit to Canada that saw him declare, apparently spontaneously, the repeal of the 1936 External Relations Act and that, as a result, Ireland would leave the Commonwealth. Pictured between Costello and his wife Ida (née O'Malley) is Canadian prime minister William Lyon Mackenzie King.

Opposite: An anti-partition rally in New York in 1949; MacBride explicitly sought to raise awareness of the partition of Ireland amongst the Irish diaspora.

opportunities for such multilateral engagement did not exist. Yet by 1947 it appears that plans were in hand to repeal the 1936 act and declare a republic.

De Valera may have been waiting to see how newly independent India managed its relationship with the Commonwealth before proceeding further, possibly on the grounds that a republic within the Commonwealth, as India would become in 1949, might serve as a model to emulate. But on 7 September 1948, whilst in Ottawa, Costello suddenly announced that the repeal of the External Relations Act was imminent and that Ireland's formal departure from the Commonwealth and the declaration of Ireland's status as a republic would follow.

There appears to be little truth in the story that Costello was prompted to declare a republic after taking offence at the presence of a replica of 'roaring Meg'—one of the cannon used in the defence of the besieged city of Derry in 1689 and a symbol beloved of unionists in Northern Ireland—on a table during an official dinner, despite the fact that Costello told the anecdote himself to a number of people. But the repeal of the 1936 act and the declaration of the republic was, to the Irish authorities, simply a matter of altered legal language and expression regarding the Crown. For the British, on the other hand, this was a development of the deepest political and economic significance, as the Commonwealth was evolving and decolonisation across the British Empire was accelerating. London remained more deeply affected by Costello's actions in Canada than Dublin understood, and the British explained to their Irish counterparts that there could be consequences for Ireland: citizens' rights, trade and freedom of travel now became live issues, and subject to negotiation. The British also hinted at punitive measures against Ireland, but Canada, Australia and New Zealand persuaded them to tone down their attitude. At the same time London confirmed the territorial integrity of Northern Ireland within the United Kingdom with the passing of the Ireland Act in June 1949, in a move that took Dublin by surprise. That said, this act also gave Irish citizens a special status within the UK; there was no restriction on their rights to travel to and work

Opposition to partition was shared across the Irish political spectrum. In 1948 Éamon de Valera and Frank Aiken, out of office for the first time in sixteen years, embarked on an anti-partition world tour, encompassing the United States, Australia, New Zealand and India, seeking to raise international awareness of the issue. De Valera is pictured here in Delhi with Jawaharlal Nehru, the first prime minister of India, and Lady Edwina Mountbatten, the wife of the last viceroy and subsequently governor general of India, Lord Louis Mountbatten. This was one of the last official functions Mountbatten undertook in India.

THE
PARTITION OF IRELAND

Address by

T4/1353

EAMON DE VALERA, T.D.

At THE STADIUM, LIVERPOOL
On Sunday, 10th October, 1948

Under the auspices of the

LIVERPOOL AND LANCASHIRE AREA
COUNCIL
ANTI-PARTITION OF IRELAND LEAGUE

Doors open at 2-30 p.m.   To commence at 3 p.m.

A Dia Saor Eire

 SOUVENIR PROGRAMME

IRISH NEWS, LTD., BELFAST.

within the UK, a status that became increasingly important given the mass emigration of Irish people to the UK during the 1950s.

Ending partition had always been to the fore in the rhetoric, if not in the conduct, of Irish foreign policy and it remained so for the Inter-Party government. Following de Valera's example, MacBride placed ending partition and uniting Ireland as the primary goal of Irish foreign policy. MacBride's raising of the 'sore thumb' of partition, as it was popularly dubbed, at all international opportunities won Ireland few friends and did nothing to improve already poor relations with Northern Ireland.

The Inter-Party government placed great emphasis on vocal opposition to partition, during a period in which the Ireland Act became a further political barrier between north and south. But ironically, the term in office of this government also saw the most successful developments in cross-border co-operation

Members of Liverpool's Irish community en-route to hear de Valera address an anti-partition rally in the city while he was in opposition, 10 October 1948.

Previous page: The cover of the programme for the rally addressed by de Valera in Liverpool, 10 October 1948.

Crowds throng Dublin's
O'Connell Bridge on the
evening of 17–18 April 1949
to celebrate the declaration of
the Republic of Ireland Act. At
midnight on Easter Sunday,
17 April, Ireland's last links
with the Commonwealth were
severed. Celebrations took place
across the state, with the main
official ceremonies in Dublin
corresponding with the annual
commemorations of the Easter
Rising. Events to mark the
occasion were also hosted by
Irish legations abroad.

since partition. The conclusion of an agreement to develop the
Erne Hydro-Electric scheme, the establishment of the Foyle
Fisheries Commission and a series of direct north-south ministerial meetings concerning the future of the Dublin to Belfast
railway line saw real progress in relations. But Dublin's anti-partition campaign in Britain, North America and elsewhere held
the limelight.

At no time while MacBride was minister did Dublin ever
attempt to understand the Ulster Unionist position; in essence,
cross-border co-operation was seen only as a means to short-
term technical ends. Moreover, opposition to partition was
shared across the Irish political spectrum: de Valera, whilst out
of government, embarked on a world tour to highlight the partition of Ireland. MacBride, acutely conscious of de Valera's global
presence and international impact, and knowing that many
senior Irish diplomats remained personally loyal to their former

minister, prohibited de Valera and members of the opposition from staying in Irish diplomatic residences whilst campaigning overseas.

MacBride did take an interest in one very distinctive new state: Israel. In February 1949 the Cabinet agreed *de facto* to recognise Israel, making Ireland one of the last states to do so. Ireland refused to give *de jure* recognition to Israel, however, citing Vatican concerns about the future control of the Holy Places in Jerusalem as the reason. MacBride saw strong parallels between Ireland and Israel when it came to their freedom struggles, and by mid-April 1951 MacBride envisaged Ireland's complete *de jure* recognition of Israel, but by this date the Inter-Party government was facing into a general election, and ultimately no action was taken.

In Europe, MacBride played a leading role in the drafting of the Council of Europe's European Convention on Human Rights. The country's refugee policy, however, remained ungenerous during the Inter-Party government. Despite its pro-Western outlook, Ireland was also unenthusiastic about joining the various post-war collective security pacts proposed by the Western Allies. The North Atlantic Treaty Organisation (NATO) was a specific case in point. Membership of NATO involved commitment to the mutual self-defence of all members, including the UK, and, by extension, Northern Ireland. Joining a pact of which the UK was a member would mean accepting the reality that British military forces were stationed in Northern Ireland, and thus the acceptance of partition.

In spring 1949 MacBride indicated to the American government that Ireland agreed with the terms of the alliance and would be prepared to join NATO if Washington first put pressure on London to end partition, but as NATO had access to facilities in Northern Ireland, access to bases elsewhere on the island of Ireland was deemed irrelevant. Washington was not moved by Irish arguments to do anything that might go contrary to the Anglo-American relationship. The legacy of Ireland's wartime neutrality was compounded in some American eyes (and especially those of the State Department) by Ireland's refusal to join NATO. The outbreak of the Korean War in June 1950 led to some in Washington questioning where Ireland really stood in relation to the Cold War and support for the West, though

While the movements of Irish diplomats sometimes made front-page news in the Irish press, the travels of Minister to Australia Thomas J. Kiernan (right) always came second to that of his wife, the internationally famous ballad singer Delia Murphy (left). Kiernan had been posted to the Vatican during the Second World War; whilst in Rome, Murphy actively aided Irish priest Hugh O'Flaherty's efforts to organise escape routes from Italy for refugees and Allied POWs. The couple are pictured here at a function in Sydney Town Hall in 1947 alongside Elizabeth Dryer. Elizabeth's husband, Albert Dryer, was of Irish extraction and a prominent sympathiser with Irish republicanism (especially Fianna Fáil). In 1915 he had founded the Irish National Association of New South Wales.

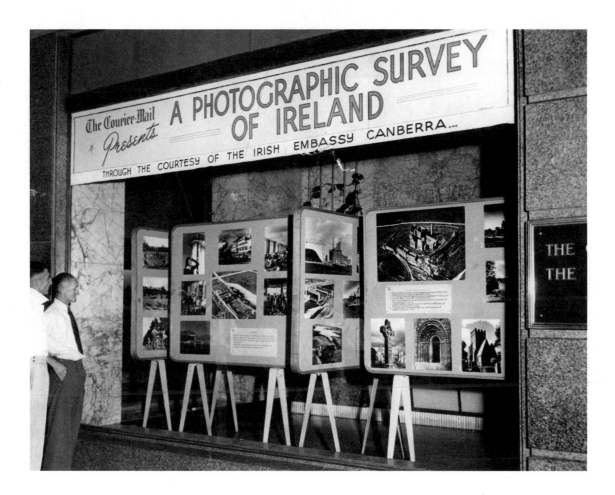

From its establishment in 1919 the Irish diplomatic service had focussed solely on the northern hemisphere. In 1946 an Irish diplomatic mission opened in Canberra, headed by Thomas J. Kiernan. Whilst focussing its attentions largely on the Irish diaspora in Australia, the mission promoted Ireland and its history and culture to a wider Australian audience, as illustrated by this photographic display at the offices of the *Courier Mail* newspaper in Brisbane, *circa* 1950.

Ireland's reputation as a staunchly Catholic society ensured that it was not seen as a country likely to turn to Communism. The Korean War further strengthened the Anglo-American alliance and highlighted the futility of trying to use the prospect of Ireland's NATO membership as a lever against ending partition.

The one notable exception to Ireland's detachment from the multilateral institutions of the post-war world was the Council of Europe. In May 1949 Ireland was one of the ten founding members of the Council, which had been established in the aftermath of the Second World War to promote democracy and human rights on the continent, and ultimately to begin to work towards European integration. While Ireland would not seek to join the latter project until the 1960s, membership of the Council of Europe allowed Irish politicians and diplomats to explore the possibilities of European integration. In that sense,

involvement was a crucial, if often overlooked, milestone in Ireland's foreign relations.

By the summer of 1951 the Inter-Party government had collapsed for a variety of domestic reasons. As MacBride prepared to leave Iveagh House, Ireland's external relations had become increasingly international in scope but remained limited in many ways. While Ireland had a definite series of international interests to enhance and protect, it now did so in an orbit somewhat removed from the major foreign relations actors of the period.

Limited in size and power, Ireland had never been as significant geopolitically in the Cold War world as MacBride had believed; it certainly never had the means and influence to direct the major international crises of the day in a manner he had hoped. The question of how Ireland could most effectively and actively play a role in the post-war international system remained unanswered.

In 1947 women entered the diplomatic ranks of the Department of External Affairs at third-secretary level. Here, Máire MacEntee (Mhac an tSaoi), the first woman appointed third secretary by open competition, walks in procession with Ireland's ambassador to Spain Leo T. McCauley as he presents his credentials to Generalissimo Francisco Franco in Madrid in 1949. MacEntee told McCauley that in order to fulfill protocol requirements, she had been obliged to exceed her dress allowance. He wrote to the secretary, Frederick Boland, seeking a special allowance for female officers to cover such occasions.

•

Ambassador John J. Hearne, his wife Monica and their young family disembark at Union Station Washington, DC, to take up his new posting as Ireland's first ambassador to the United States, 29 March 1950. The girl presenting the bouquet is Claire Brennan, the daughter of Joseph D. Brennan, counsellor in the Irish embassy. The Hearne children are (L–R) Mary Elizabeth, Justin and Daniel.

The Cold War was the backdrop to Irish foreign policy through the 1950s. The governments in power in Dublin during that decade all saw Ireland as militarily neutral but politically and intellectually Western and anti-Communist. Ireland's absence from the United Nations and her non-involvement in the Western military alliances meant that, despite the best efforts of Irish diplomats, the information they obtained on events in Asia, such as the Chinese Revolution and the Korean War, was often second-hand or diluted.

Relations with India were good, however, resting in part on Ireland's and India's connections with the British Empire and their respective independence movements. While Ireland would not join military alliances, the private and public positions of politicians and foreign policy-makers placed Ireland in the Western camp in the Cold War, even if by the time he left office in 1951 MacBride had done little to effectively build Ireland's international position within that bloc. After de Valera

returned to power in 1951, he handed the External Affairs brief to his trusted lieutenant Frank Aiken.

Aiken, originally from Armagh, was a former chief of staff of the IRA. He had reluctantly taken the anti-treaty side in the civil war and was later a founding member of Fianna Fáil. He was a hard-headed minister and was firmly republican in outlook. In 1953, for instance, he turned down the offer of seats at the coronation of Queen Elizabeth II and forbade Irish officials from attending due to the continued existence of partition and reference to 'Northern Ireland' in the new queen's royal title.

But Aiken did hope for the harmonising of British-Irish relations, and in his meetings with senior British figures he usually took a pragmatic attitude. With regard to partition itself he hoped that Britain would take a step towards ending it by issuing a declaration favouring a united Ireland which would, he suggested, influence unionists to improve relations with Dublin. Irish unity would be, Aiken argued, in the interests of London, Washington and the security of Western Europe in the Cold War. But like MacBride before him, Aiken was unable to comprehend that there was little or no British or international interest in his call to end partition.

Róisín O'Doherty, second secretary at the legation in Stockholm, speaks at a function in the Swedish capital, *circa* 1949. After MacEntee, she was the second woman to enter the Irish foreign service as a third secretary.

Equally, the lack of enthusiasm amongst the Irish diaspora for Dublin's anti-partition campaign was commented upon by Irish diplomats. The 1950s witnessed extremely high levels of emigration from Ireland, especially to the UK, where the demands of both post-war reconstruction and the expansion of the British 'welfare state' opened up significant employment opportunities across a number of sectors, from construction to the new National Health Service. The diaspora, particularly its new, younger members, was developing interests of its own and breaking its direct cultural and political links with Ireland.

This was evident in reports from the Irish embassy in London throughout the 1950s. The dwindling national cultural awareness of younger Irish migrants in the face of an increasingly multicultural modern consumer society was noted. Of particular worry were the apparent vices awaiting young Irish men, and more to the point women, in the midst of post-war British urban life. This somewhat paternalistic attitude seemed to overlook the fact that British society had attractions for younger emigrants above and beyond simply providing a wage.

As the Cold War continued, official-level Anglo-Irish discussions were underway by 1953 to develop technical co-operation between both countries in the event of a Third World War. In line with Ireland's neutrality, and building from the limited co-operation that had gone on during the Second World War, these discussions centred on civil defence, the evacuation of refugees, the monitoring of shipping, weather reporting, and fallout warnings in the event of nuclear war between the new 'superpowers' of the US and Soviet Union. Aiken ensured that the state of national emergency declared in 1939 was maintained because of the ongoing high level of global tension and the need to appear ready to counter the anticipated international crises of the 1950s.

When it came to defence and military matters, Aiken's ideas came from Ireland's experience of neutrality during the Second World War, and now refocussed to meet the threats of the Cold War. A modernised Irish Defence Forces would ensure that neutral Ireland would be a well-defended anti-Communist bastion on Europe's western seaboard. His continual reiteration of neutral Ireland's strong anti-Communism and insistence that the country could defend itself against the Soviet threat if only it were given the weapons to do so were given a polite

The McDonagh family arriving in Copenhagen, 1962. While Robert McDonagh had a long and distinguished career in the Irish diplomatic service, including as secretary general of the department, his wife Róisín O'Doherty was obliged to resign after their marriage due to a ban on married women serving in the Irish public service. This practice meant that that the upper echelons of the Department of External Affairs remained a male-only preserve for generations. Two of their sons pictured here, Philip and Bobby, also became diplomats; Bobby's future wife Mary was also a diplomat.

Opposite, top: The expansion of the Department of External Affairs under Seán MacBride led to staff shortages, and he sought to fill senior diplomatic posts from outside the department. Josephine McNeill became Ireland's first female head of mission as minister to the Netherlands from 1950 to 1955. She subsequently served as minister to Sweden, Switzerland and Austria.

Opposite, bottom: An interior view of the Aer Lingus public office at the newly refurbished Irish embassy in London in the early 1950s.

FIG 10

10 MEGATON BOMB GROUND BURST
AT CENTRE OF DUBLIN

0—3½ MILES—AREA A—TOTAL DESTRUCTION
3½—5 MILES—AREA B—IRREPARABLE DAMAGE
5—13 MILES—AREA C—SEVERE TO MODERATE DAMAGE
13—20 MILES—AREA D—MODERATE TO LIGHT DAMAGE

EA DUBLIN

SERIAL NO. 2044

FOR PSA FROM PSS

    THE AMBASSADOR HAS JUST LEFT FOR WATERVILLE AND ASKED
ME TO LOOK AFTER THE PARCEL FOR FR. O'LEARY OF MILLTOWN.
THIS HAS NOT ARRIVED AS YET/: DO YOU KNOW WHEN IT IS TO COME
AND FR. O'LEARY'S CHRISTIAN NAME? IT CONTAINS THE SKULL OF A
MARTYRED PRIEST, I THINK.

    ALSO, DID HE REMEMBER TO ASK YOU TO GET A TICKET FOR
THE TEST MATCH FOR THE WEEK COMMENCING SATURDAY, 15TH INSTANT,
WHICH HE PROMISED TO PROCURE FOR BRIAN DURNIN? SEEMINGLY,
THIS IS BRIAN'S ANNUAL LEAVE SO HE ANXIOUS TO KNOW IF THE
TICKET WILL BE FORTHCOMING. PLEASE LET ME KNOW.

MM 10/8/53. 11.55

The everyday challenges of diplomacy: two slightly incongruous issues are mentioned in this dispatch, from August 1953, by May Mooney, private secretary to the secretary of the department, Sean Nunan. It was transmitted from Iveagh House in Dublin to the Irish embassy in London via a recently installed teleprinter link.

Opposite: While Ireland was militarily neutral during the Cold War and did not join NATO, it was obvious that Ireland would be seen as being aligned with the West in the event of a conflict between the US and Soviet Union and thus could become a target of the Soviets. This map indicates the potential impact of a 10-megaton nuclear device on Dublin and its hinterland.

hearing and expressions of sympathy, but nothing else. NATO members could not understand why Aiken protested when their armed forces took part in joint NATO exercises in Northern Ireland, and they did not see the international significance Aiken attached to the matter. Dublin's turning down United States aid under the Mutual Security Assistance (MSA) programme, the successor to Marshall Plan aid, in the winter of 1951–2 again put Dublin and Washington on an uncertain footing.

Aiken had given private assurances to American diplomats that Ireland would never allow its territory to be used as a base from which the United States would be endangered, but Dublin had realistically concluded that Ireland would get no aid, military or otherwise, from the United States. Aiken was repeatedly told that NATO membership was Ireland's only option when it came to avenues for rearmament. Instead, Ireland began sourcing weapons from neutrals such as Sweden, or small European states, such as Belgium. Contrary to Aiken's hopes, however, only small amounts of modern weapons were purchased, because throughout the 1950s the Defence Forces' operational capacity was run down as a result of budgetary cutbacks.

By mid-1952 Aiken had been in office for a year and his principal goals remained unfulfilled. Ireland was no closer to being reunited and remained effectively undefended. The remaining two years of his tenure were directionless, yet he did take an important step forward in developing Dublin's contacts with Northern Ireland. In March 1953 he sent teams of diplomats to Northern Ireland to discuss political, social and economic affairs with the nationalist community and interested unionists.

These discussions gave External Affairs a greater insight into ground-level feelings in Northern Ireland in both communities and into political developments within the unionist government. They also allowed Dublin to pick up on growing nationalist discontent, which would feed into the rise of new republican minority groups and ultimately in 1956, would lead to the 'border campaign' of the IRA.

•

Ireland was not completely immune from having to deal with some of the ongoing legacies of the Second World War, albeit at a relatively low level, such as compensation for wartime destruction and attempts by former Nazi agents, officials and sympathisers to enter Ireland. Senior officials in the Department of Justice at this time generally favoured a restrictive immigration policy. They were, however, less concerned about the reputational damage arising from the possible presence of suspected war criminals on Irish soil than their counterparts in External Affairs.

Anglo-Irish and Irish-American relations had been the main focus of Aiken's foreign policy during his first term in office, but Ireland's relations with the states of Western Europe were becoming increasingly significant given the emergence of European integration. Despite its refusal to join NATO, Ireland had, as already noted, been a founder member of the Council of Europe in 1948. It also welcomed the establishment of the European Coal and Steel Community (ECSC) in 1950, but, lacking any reserves of coal and steel, it was not invited to participate in this organisation. In any case, the prospect of a dilution

The promotion of Ireland as an international tourist destination became increasingly significant in the post-war era. This Bord Fáilte poster from the 1950s, featuring an express train drawn by a diesel-electric locomotive built in Britain by Metropolitan-Vickers and introduced into service in 1955, depicts the modernisation of Ireland's railway network.

CURRAN
Ireland
WELCOMES
you
CIE
IRELAND'S TRANSPORT COMPANY
TICKETS AND INFORMATION HERE
Printed in the Republic of Ireland by DOLLARD, Dublin

of hard-won sovereignty in any sphere did not appeal to Dublin. The government saw the point of European integration, but until Seán Lemass's appointment as taoiseach in 1959, Ireland displayed a preference for voluntary co-operation between the states of Europe rather than any form of European federation.

Ireland was still reluctant to submit its underdeveloped economy to the supranational control that would emerge through the Common Market established by the 1957 Treaty of Rome. Ireland's trade policy remained protectionist and was reliant on access to British markets. The Irish economy had not yet opened up to free trade, though economic relations with the states of continental Europe on OEEC conventions went a limited way to broadening Ireland's foreign trade outside the traditional confines of the dominant British market. As yet, Irish governments were unwilling to contemplate full free trade in agriculture or manufactured goods.

In the mid-1950s Ireland had bilateral relations with five of the original six European states that had commenced the integration process (Luxembourg was the exception). But by that point, this semi-detached stance ensured that Irish diplomats in European capitals found themselves outside the mainstream of international relations. The paucity of high-level information

Irish coffee is a cocktail consisting of hot coffee, Irish whiskey, cream and sugar. It was invented and first served at the international seaplane terminal at Foynes, Co. Limerick during the Second World War and became an internationally known drink in the post-war years. Here, the secretary of the Irish Tourist Board, Bord Fáilte (himself a former diplomat) T.J. O'Driscoll (L) with Ireland's ambassador to Spain Michael Rynne (C), raise a glass of Irish coffee with a visitor to the Irish embassy in Madrid in the late 1950s.

from the Irish legation in Bonn on West Germany's critical place in Europe and European integration was noticeable; Ireland was not a major concern for the German foreign office. Bilateral relations with France were cordial, with Paris showing passing interest in Ireland's non-membership of NATO and Dublin's concerns about partition. But as was the case with other states to whom Irish governments addressed such concerns, France did not wish to antagonise the British.

That said, the broader concerns of such major powers were of ongoing interest to Irish diplomats. Irish ambassadors in Paris (Con Cremin and, from 1954, William Fay) followed France's changing international position. Fay was concerned about France's global strategy after its retreat from Indochina following its defeat at Dien Bien Phu in 1954 and the later nation- alisation of the Suez Canal by Egypt and the ensuing Suez crisis in 1956. Fay's reports, along with Frederick Boland's dispatches from London, offered an insight into Britain's declining world role. At the same time John Hearne, who had been appointed as Irish ambassador to the United States in 1950, provided insights into the United States' growing designs in the Middle East.

Such reports gave Dublin a multidimensional view of evolv- ing international issues in the years leading up to the Suez crisis. As Ireland had no diplomatic missions in Eastern Europe until embassies were opened in Moscow and Vienna in 1974, External Affairs was unable to provide in-depth reporting and analysis on events in the Communist Bloc or on the Soviet stance in the Cold War. There was a similar lack of an Irish diplomatic pres- ence in another region of growing significance: the Middle East.

Though Ireland had left the British Commonwealth in 1949, the Commonwealth Relations Office remained Ireland's channel to the British government, and there was still a desire in Iveagh House for access to the shared information and partici- pation in the multilateral meetings—if only as an observer—that Commonwealth membership provided. As the Commonwealth expanded to include India and Pakistan, Irish interest in the organisation continued. These states would achieve the status of being republics within the Commonwealth, a status that de Valera would have been content with but had not obtained.

Ireland had mixed relations with the original members of the Commonwealth. In 1950 the Irish and Australian missions in

an ROINN ʒNóṫaí eaċṫraċa
Department of External Affairs

baile áṫa cliaṫ.
Dublin

305/14/212

23 January, 1952.

P.S.
Pl. attach to
file. I should
like to see the file
upon which we
have the pps dealing
with this.
J.S.
27/1.

Dear Fred,

Just a note to confirm that as you
surmised the "British spokesman" who expressed himself
as "longing" for a United Ireland provided that we could
woo **the Six** Counties successfully was Churchill himself.
He made these remarks in an off-the-record discussion to
members of the working press at a lunch in the Mayflower,
Washington. Apparently, the understanding was that
the remarks could be quoted if the source was not
identified.

Yours sincerely,

His Excellency F. H. Boland,
Irish Embassy,
LONDON.

PS. I enclose copy of relevant cable from our Washington
Embassy.

Canberra and Dublin respectively were raised to embassy rank,
but Canberra would not accept the constitutionally defined title
'President of Ireland' and refused also to accept Dublin's credentials for the incoming Irish ambassador to Australia. Deadlock
ensued, with Canberra finally cancelling the appointment of the
Australian ambassador to Dublin in January 1954. From 1956
to 1964 Ireland would be represented in Canberra by a chargé
d'affaires and not by an ambassador. The Australian capital was,
nonetheless, another important listening post from which Ireland
could follow the growing international influence of China, India
and the new states of south-east Asia. Ireland had no other diplomatic missions in the region, and contacts with diplomats from
these states were generally via third-party meetings in Britain,
the United States or Australia. Asian expressions of parallels and
links with Ireland and its independence struggle were noted by
Irish diplomats, but more significant issues concerned the recognition of China and the related safety of the small number of Irish
Catholic missionaries remaining in China and Asia generally.

Ireland at this time declined to establish diplomatic ties with
Communist states. A slight loosening of the official barriers to
trade with the Communist bloc, however, was agreed in early
1954, and this continued following the change of government
in Dublin in June that year. Irish and Eastern Bloc diplomats
met unofficially at social and some official events, but strict
rules for contact were laid down. Irish officials were instructed
to be reserved and cautious in their contacts with officials from
Communist states. The Irish embassy in London was an exception, and Irish diplomats there could expect to at least socialise
formally with their Eastern European counterparts. From April
1952 low-ranking diplomats and several KGB officers at the
Soviet embassy in London began to make low-level contact with
Irish diplomats to find out more about Ireland. These contacts
had limited effect, but they gave the Department of External
Affairs its first serious exchanges with Soviet officials.

Ireland would not have diplomatic representation in Moscow
for another twenty years. Dublin still refused visas to Soviet and
Soviet Bloc diplomats wishing to visit Ireland and discouraged
official and business contacts between Ireland and the Soviet
Union.

•

The arrival of Liam Cosgrave (son of W.T. Cosgrave) in Iveagh House in 1954 as Fine Gael Minister for External Affairs in the second Inter-Party government saw no reorientation of Ireland's international position. Issues which had faced Aiken from 1951 to 1954, such as promoting anti-partition propaganda in the United States, contacts with the nationalist community in Northern Ireland, the welfare of Irish emigrants in Britain and the overseas adoption of Irish children, were also of concern to Cosgrave.

During the 1950s the Department of External Affairs continued to facilitate the provision of passports to infants (usually orphans or children born outside marriage) within the large network of institutions administered by the Catholic Church, to enable their adoption by families in the United States. Overseas adoption was often the subject of negative international publicity, such as that which surrounded the adoption by Hollywood actress Jane Russell of an Irish child in 1951.

Yet while some queries were raised, no official felt that it was necessary to curtail the process, and there was little inclination to look into the manner in which such adoptions were facilitated. Officials let the Catholic Church and Catholic adoption societies decide the family with which infants were to be placed. That said, some officials in External Affairs were becoming increasingly unhappy with the behaviour of some United States Catholic adoption societies and their vetting procedures when seeking prospective families with which to place infants. Adoption was put on a legal basis under the Adoption Act of 1952, but the overseas adoption of children continued to be facilitated by the Department of External Affairs. In this regard, the attitude of the department was in line with the deferential attitude to the Catholic Church exhibited by most branches of the Irish state.

With regard to Northern Ireland, the basic tenets of Aiken's policy remained intact under Cosgrave. External Affairs aimed to promote a policy of limited co-operation with Northern Ireland whilst highlighting concerns over official discrimination against its minority Catholic population. Cross-border visits continued, and External Affairs sought information from missions in Britain and the United States on support for the IRA amongst the Irish diaspora. After the outbreak of the IRA's border campaign ('Operation Harvest') in December 1956, which involved attacks on Royal Ulster Constabulary (RUC, the Northern Ireland police force) barracks along the border, Dublin made it clear to the British that it would not tolerate the unlawful use of force by paramilitary groups and would act against the IRA within its own jurisdiction. To that end, internment was re-introduced for IRA suspects, but Dublin also made it clear that it would not extradite suspects or pass information to security authorities in Northern Ireland. By early 1957 the IRA campaign led External Affairs to try to piece together a feasible blueprint for a new Northern Ireland policy and the ending of partition by peaceful means. It took advice from nationalist community leaders in Northern Ireland, and the scheme devised included raising discrimination in Northern Ireland with the British government and even at the United Nations; trying to restrain Irish citizens from joining the IRA; and promoting constitutional means to gain Irish unity.

The five years following the collapse of the first Inter-Party government in 1951 had seen Irish foreign policy stagnate. Outside the United Nations, the Commonwealth, NATO and the developing European integration process, Ireland was on the side-lines of international decision-making (the Council of Europe was an exception), and the concerns facing Iveagh House were taking on a much narrower focus. Some diplomats pondered privately, in the relative pessimism of the 1950s, if Ireland even had a foreign policy. The attention of the Department of External Affairs was largely devoted to Anglo-Irish relations. This would all change dramatically in December 1955 when Ireland finally joined the United Nations.

IRISH EMBASSY

B.111/3.

17 Grosvenor Place,
LONDON, S.W.1.

22nd August, 1952.

The Secretary,
Department of External Affairs,
Dublin.

Mr Fay.

     I enclose herewith, for your information, a copy
of a letter with enclosures which I have received from the
National Council for the Unmarried Mother and her Child.
The documents speak for themselves. I have simply acknow-
ledged the letter with an assurance that it will receive
our careful consideration.

     I don't suppose that any single question has been
given more anxious and painstaking consideration in the
Department within the last seven or eight years than this
matter of the migration of young and immature Irish girls
to this country. If my recollection is correct, it consti-
tutes one of the largest files in the Department and was
the subject - as recently as 1948 or 1949 - of a report by
an interdepartmental committee on which Mr. Gallagher acted
for our Department. Previously the material means of
stopping the traffic existed because the travel permit system
was still in force; the essential difficulty was that any
official action in the matter involved the substitution of
the State for the parents as the judge of the best interests
of the female minor. Nowadays, however, the travel permit
system has gone and it is not easy to see - even assuming
the essential difficulty referred to did not exist - what
effective action should be taken in the matter other than
measures of publicity.

Ambassador.

DFA/6/433/26/14 (1)

AMBASSADE D'IRLANDE

P. M. B. 2421,
LAGOS.

19 March 1962

Urgent

For Information and
Political Divisions.

Secretary,
Department of External Affairs,
Iveagh House,
DUBLIN.

ST. PATRICK'S DAY IN LAGOS, 1962.

I have the honour to report that we gave a large
Reception on the evening of St. Patrick's Day at our
residence, 3 Ilado Close, Ikoyi. Five hundred guests
attended, including the Governor General, H.E. Dr. Nmandi
Azikiwe; the Minister for Justice, Dr. T. O. Elias; the
Minister of Health, Dr. M. A. Majekodunmi and his wife;
Mr. Mbu, Secretary of the Navy; and the Acting Minister of
Foreign Affairs, Senator N. Bamali, (Mr. Jaja Wachuku is
at Geneva). The Ambassadors of all the countries accredited
in Lagos also came with most of their staffs. A feature of
the Reception was the presence of a large number of Nigerians
who had studied in Ireland, e.g., Chief and Mrs. Akirelli,
Miss O. Wackuku, niece of the Foreign Minister, and manyothers.
About two hundred Irish citizens living in the vicinity of
Lagos attended, including almost all the Irish S.M.A. and
C.S.Sp. missionaries here. Archbishop Taylor was away but he
was represented by Rt. Rev. Dr. Aggey, the Auxiliary Bishop
of Lagos. Finally, the Representatives of the main trading
firms in Lagos also were present.

The Police Band of Nigeria, forty members strong,
were in attendance in the garden and played the Nigerian
and Irish National Anthems at the arrival and departure of
the Governor General, and a selection of Irish airs in
between. The Tricolour was of course flown and shamrock
presented to all the guests on arrival. The Governor General
wore his shamrock throughout the reception. Irish beverages
and Irish cigarettes were served.

Opening page of Ambassador Eamonn Kennedy's report detailing the first ever St Patrick's
Day celebrations hosted by the Irish embassy in Lagos, the Nigerian capital, in 1962. Kennedy
became Ireland's first ambassador to an African state when he was appointed to Nigeria in 1960.

ST PATRICK'S DAY

St Patrick's Day has been celebrated on 17 March since at least the seventeenth century. The date is presumed to mark the death of the fifth-century Christian cleric Patricius—Patrick—the most well-known of the missionaries who brought Christianity to the island of Ireland. He is deemed by the Catholic Church to be Ireland's 'patron saint'. The celebration of St Patrick's Day was exported over the centuries by Irish emigrants (it was marked in Boston as early as 1737). By the twentieth century it had become well-established in Irish communities worldwide. It was designated a national holiday in Ireland in 1909.

The St Patrick's Day period is the busiest time of year for many Irish embassies and consulates, which host, organise and participate in thousands of community, business, cultural and political events worldwide. The highest profile of these is the presentation of a bowl of shamrock by the taoiseach to the sitting US president. Bowls of shamrock were intermittently presented at the White House from 1952, but the meeting between the taoiseach and the president has been an annual fixture since 1993.

The most ambitious programme of St Patrick's Day events to date took place in 2019, as members of the Irish government visited 56 countries. This included visits to all EU member states: a very public indication of Ireland's ongoing commitment to the EU against the backdrop of the UK's planned departure from the union.

1955–
1957

The United Nations

Taoiseach John A. Costello arrives at the UN Secretariat in New York on 24 March 1956 to meet Secretary-General Dag Hammarskjöld. It was the first meeting between the head of an Irish government and a United Nations secretary-general.

The League of Nations had been created to maintain international order in the aftermath of the First World War. It had obviously failed to do so, but the idea of a co-operative global body to maintain international peace was ever more relevant in the aftermath of the Second World War; hence the creation of the United Nations. Just as Ireland had sought to engage meaningfully with the League of Nations, so it would seek to do the same with its successor organisation.

While the Soviets had blocked Ireland's initial attempts to join the UN, the Irish application for membership remained live, but there seemed to be little likelihood of it succeeding. This changed when Canada tabled a resolution at the UN's tenth General Assembly, in 1955, to admit a balanced package of new Western and Soviet-aligned members, including Ireland (by then twenty-two states were waiting to join). The Canadian initiative commanded widespread support within the UN, including that of the US and Soviet Union, and on 8 December it was formally adopted by the General Assembly.

Less than a week later, on 14 December 1955, Ireland became one of 16 states admitted to the UN. The Irish application was approved unanimously when the country's name was called. Jack Conway, Ireland's consul general in New York, became Ireland's first UN delegate when he took his seat in the General Assembly the next day. He informed Dublin that Secretary-General Dag Hammarskjöld 'welcomed me warmly'.

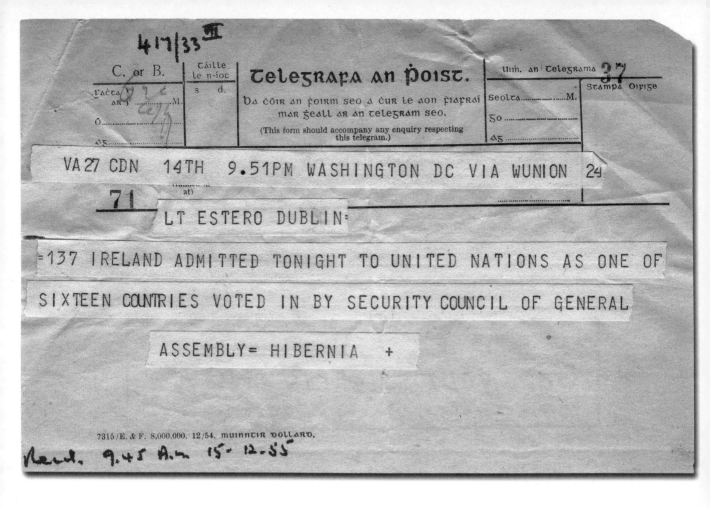

Official confirmation from the Irish embassy in Washington, DC, to Department of External Affairs headquarters at Iveagh House in Dublin that, after a nine-year wait due to a Soviet veto of its 1946 application, Ireland had at last been admitted to the United Nations, 14 December 1955.

So too did delegates from Canada, the United States, the Soviet Union, the United Kingdom, France, India, New Zealand and the Philippines, and the Indian Jesuit Jerome D'Souza (who was actually a member of the Indian delegation) blessed Ireland's General Assembly seat.

Conway noted the expectation, especially on the part of members from Asia, the Middle East and Latin America, that Ireland would play an active role in the United Nations. Ireland's first General Assembly vote was in a secret ballot for Security Council membership. Conway voted for the Philippines, but as the tenth Assembly was drawing to a close, his presence was largely symbolic. Nevertheless, it did provide an opportunity for more substantial preparations for the impending eleventh General Assembly, due to take place in 1956. In the meantime, two keynote speeches prior to the General Assembly that year, on Ireland's engagement with the United Nations, set the tone for the country's involvement in the institution; it would soon be one of the cornerstones of Irish foreign policy.

A startled-looking Jack Conway takes Ireland's seat in the UN General Assembly for the first time, 15 December 1955. Conway, who was Ireland's consul-general in New York from 1955 to 1961, doubled as Ireland's interim representative to the United Nations until October 1956. He was replaced by Frederick Boland, who became Ireland first permanent representative (ambassador) to the United Nations.

In March 1956 John A. Costello (serving as taoiseach in the second Inter-Party government) gave a speech at Yale University Law School in Connecticut, in which he stated how Ireland's United Nations policy would be based on Christian principles; be strongly anti-Communist; and be pro-Western. Three months later, in the Dáil, Costello's Minister for External Affairs, Liam Cosgrave, outlined the key principles underpinning Ireland's United Nations policy: Ireland unequivocally supported the UN Charter; it would 'maintain a position of independence' in the UN; and it would 'support wherever possible those powers principally responsible for the defence of the free world in their resistance to the spread of Communist power and influence'.

Both speeches, with a distinct pro-Western emphasis, were uttered against the backdrop of the Cold War. But they also contained much that remains familiar in Ireland's twenty-first

century UN policy: the idea that Ireland would act as a peace-maker, as a neutral mediator seeking international justice and peace, conscious of the rule of international law and working for the improvement of what Costello termed 'human affairs'. The fundamental point was that Ireland would unequivocally support the United Nations.

•

Ireland's first UN General Assembly delegation was led by Cosgrave (coincidentally, in 1923 W.T. Cosgrave had led the Irish Free State's first delegation to the League of Nations). The delegation to the eleventh General Assembly in 1956 consisted of seasoned diplomats such as Frederick Boland (now Ireland's

A pioneering generation of Irish diplomats: members of the first Irish delegation to the United Nations pictured in the General Assembly, 21 November 1956. L–R: Sheila Murphy, Conor Cruise O'Brien, Paul Keating (a future secretary of the department), Frederick Boland, Eamonn Kennedy, and Minister for External Affairs Liam Cosgrave.

ambassador to the United Nations) and Sheila Murphy, along
with newer members of the External Affairs department such as
Conor Cruise O'Brien, Eamonn Kennedy and Paul Keating (the
latter two would both serve as Irish ambassadors to the UN in the
1970s). Boland was a veteran of the League of Nations and well
versed in multilateral diplomacy. The eleventh General Assembly
was, however, punctuated by two serious international crises and
proved to be a baptism of fire for most of the new delegation.

The first was the Suez Crisis. The Anglo-French invasion of
the Suez Canal Zone in the autumn of 1956, in the wake of hostilities between Egypt and Israel, was a secretly agreed pretext
for taking over the Suez Canal, which had been recently nation-
alised by the Egyptian president, Gamal Abdel Nasser. The
invasion of Egypt was perceived, especially by the United States,

as a neo-colonial act that could not be supported. Hopes for a peaceful solution were pinned on a firm reaction by the UN to these violent events. After much deliberation, the Irish response came down firmly on the side of maintaining the new international obligations stipulated by the UN Charter.

Ireland therefore condemned Israel, Britain and France for violating the Charter and using force, and supported both a United States-sponsored resolution calling for an immediate cease-fire in Egypt and a Canadian motion seeking the establishment of a UN force to oversee the cessation of hostilities; the latter would have major implications for Ireland's subsequent international role.

This page and opposite: Japan's first minister plenipotentiary to Ireland, Akira Ohye, formally presents his credentials to President Seán T. Ó Ceallaigh at Áras an Uachtaráin, 31 October 1957. The presentation was followed by a more informal conversation between the two, apparently on the nature of Japanese Kanji script.

Facing increasing condemnation, especially from close allies such as the US, Britain and France withdrew their forces with the help of this new UN entity: the United Nations Emergency Force (UNEF). With its creation, a new chapter in UN history began, and 'Peacekeeping', as it became known, would soon become a central pillar of Ireland's United Nations involvement. UNEF was deployed to Sinai to facilitate the transition of authority in the Suez Canal Zone following the departure of Anglo-French forces, and to act as a buffer between Israeli and Egyptian forces (it remained operational until 1967).

There was speculation as to whether Ireland could contribute soldiers to UNEF if asked by Hammarskjöld, as domestic

legislation required amendment to allow the Defence Forces to serve outside the state. On 4 December 1956 Ireland signalled its support for the UN's first peacekeeping mission by contributing $26,600 to UNEF for 1957 (just over $232,000 in equivalent terms at time of writing). Symbolically, the day before UNEF came into being, Cosgrave signed a formal declaration that Ireland 'unreservedly' accepted the obligations of the Charter of the United Nations and undertook 'to honour them.'

The second international crisis of 1956 was the Soviet invasion of Hungary in October, and the overthrow of the popular nationalist government of Imre Nagy, which had begun moves to break away from the 'Warsaw Pact', the Soviet-dominated military alliance established in 1955 to rival NATO. Ireland took a hard line on the matter, attaching itself to Western condemnation of the USSR and supporting the US-sponsored resolution condemning the invasion. Speaking in the Assembly on 9 November, Boland highlighted Hungary's right to self-determination, and Ireland's empathy for small states invaded by more powerful neighbours. He also asserted the moral authority of the United Nations and indicated that the Soviet action was a challenge to the values that the UN and the Charter represented. Ireland co-sponsored a resolution in early December,

Dag Hammarskjöld brings the visiting Irish delegation on a personal tour of the General Assembly building and secretariat in New York, 24 March 1956. L–R: Ambassador John Hearne, Alexis FitzGerald, Taoiseach John A. Costello, Charles Brennan, Hammarskjöld, Joseph Brennan and Jack Conway.

calling for the withdrawal of foreign troops from Hungary and the despatch of UN observers to the country. This was followed by a second resolution in January 1957 calling for the establishment of a UN investigation into events in Hungary.

The pro-Western and anti-Communist character of Ireland's stance on Hungary in December 1956 and January 1957 was obvious. Yet, it also indicated that Ireland was beginning to take a more prominent role at the UN as an active, pragmatic and constructive member—promoting international peace and security and seeking consensus to preserve the rights of smaller members of the organisation. This approach had been foreshadowed in Cosgrave's debut speech at the UN on 30 November 1956, in which he focussed on the crises affecting the globe and the role of the UN in facing up to them. Britain, France, Israel and Egypt were criticised for events at Suez, being reminded by Cosgrave that 'the Suez Canal is not just an Egyptian interest and not just a colonialist interest: it is a world interest.' He emphasised that 'ordinary people throughout the world' were 'conscious of the terrible dangers which hang over us'. Cosgrave mixed anti-Communism with a critique of colonialism, asking the 'freedom-loving peoples of Asia and Africa' to recognise 'the true nature of Soviet imperialism'. This speech pointed to the direction that Irish foreign policy at the UN would take over the next few years, and at what would give it a distinctive character.

Irish ambassador to the United States John J. Hearne presents President Eisenhower with a Waterford Glass crystal bowl of shamrock on St Patrick's Day in the mid to late 1950s; a tradition of 'soft' diplomacy initiated by Hearne that continues to this day.

President Seán T. Ó Ceallaigh gives a speech in the Mayflower Hotel in Washington, DC (the venue for Winston Churchill's unguarded comments on Irish unity mentioned earlier), during his 1959 official visit to the United States; President Dwight Eisenhower can be seen to the left of the podium, with Frank Aiken to the right.

Following pages: A telegram from prominent Irish-Americans Anne and Eugene F. Kinkead to President Seán T. Ó Ceallaigh and his wife Phyllis on the occasion of their return to Ireland. They had been on a two-week official visit to the United States of America in March 1959 at the invitation of President Dwight D. Eisenhower. Ó Ceallaigh's was the first official visit by a president of Ireland to the United States.

Bon *V*

WESTER

NZO81   RX BON PD=TDNK SOUTH

=HON AND MRS   SEAN T OKELL

=SS FLANDRES WEST 48 ST

AT THE CLOSE OF YOUR HISTORI

WE SEND YOU OUR LOVE. YOUR

AND RESPECT AMERICANS HAD F

SAFE PLEASANT AND RESTFUL TR

GIVE YOU MANY MORE YEARS OF

AFFECTIONATELY=

    ANNE AND GENE KINKEAD=

oyage

UNION

RANGE NJER 31 925AME=

1959 MAR 31 AM 10 19

L VISIT TO THE UNITED STATES

Y HAS DEEPENED THE REGARD

OUR RACE. WE WISH YOU BOTH A

HOME. MAY GOD PROTECT YOU AND

ALTH AND HAPPINESS

1957–
1968

Multilateralism, peacekeeping and Europe

In 1957 Cosgrave was succeeded as Minister for External Affairs by Frank Aiken, and in the late1950s and early1960s Irish engagement with the UN intensified dramatically. Aiken was personally firmly committed to the UN, knowing it was a vital forum in which small nations like Ireland could voice their views. Aiken emphasised support for the UN Charter over the pro-Western stance of Cosgrave. He made the UN central to Irish foreign policy, and his stance on the 'China Vote' in 1957 and from the late 1950s on his attitude towards the non-proliferation of nuclear weapons both capture his and Ireland's UN policy in this era.

The annual UN 'China Vote' had become a Cold War ritual by 1957. The United States insisted that the People's Republic of China be excluded from the 'China' seat, which was held instead by the Republic of China, based in Taiwan. In 1957 Ireland controversially voted in favour of discussing representation of the People's Republic of China in the General Assembly. To Aiken, a vote in favour of discussion was pragmatic, though it was denounced by the US Catholic hierarchy as 'a vote for Red China'. Aiken remained keen to demonstrate Ireland's independence at the UN, and the vote on China was a testament to this. It was balanced some years later when Ireland co-sponsored several resolutions on Tibet.

Aiken's support for discussing the representation of the People's Republic of China in the United Nations caused anger in Washington and in Irish Catholic circles in the United States. Yet Aiken's action was fully in accord with Ireland's belief that all states should be represented in the United Nations and paralleled de Valera's views on the admission of the Soviet Union to the League of Nations in 1934.

In the late 1950s Aiken also highlighted the dangers facing the world from the spread of nuclear weapons. In a far-sighted initiative at the 1958 Assembly, he advocated the non-proliferation of nuclear weapons. Each year thereafter, Ireland sought support for a so-called Irish resolution on nuclear non-proliferation, a final version of which was successfully passed by the UN General Assembly in December 1961. It was a forerunner to the eventual 'Treaty on the non-proliferation of nuclear weapons' (NPT). The NPT was finally agreed in 1968; Aiken was invited to Moscow to become its first signatory, in recognition of the Irish efforts in campaigning on its behalf. Aiken's initiative remains a keystone UN achievement.

Aiken saw the United Nations as a forum within which to promote decolonisation, a cause that, given its own recent history, Ireland was bound to sympathise with. Aiken felt strongly about this; he had, in his early years, been a senior member of the IRA in its struggle against British rule. Although his support for decolonisation secured the backing of the developing world, his strong views generated tension with Ireland's European neighbours, particularly France and Portugal. Ireland backed the General Assembly's 'Declaration on the Granting of Independence to Colonial Countries and Peoples' in December 1960, and also took a strong anti-apartheid stance against South Africa from the 1960s.

The global crisis of the world wars had placed an intolerable strain on what remained of the European empires, and decolonisation intensified after the Second World War. When Ireland joined the UN there were 76 members; by 1965 there were 117, and the majority of the new members were newly independent African and Asian states. Decolonisation reshaped the UN as the European colonial powers faced these new members at the General Assembly. Having been ruled by Britain to 1922, Ireland's attitude to imperialism became evident in the eleventh UN General Assembly in relation to Algeria, where France was fighting a colonial war, contending that Algeria was part of its metropolitan territory.

Ireland's membership of the UN led to involvement in its peacekeeping operations. Col. Justin McCarthy, pictured here, was the most senior of 50 Defence Forces officers to serve with the United Nations Observer Group in Lebanon (UNOGIL) in 1958. UNOGIL was set up to monitor the traffic of weapons from the United Arab Republic, comprising Egypt and Syria, to rebel forces in Lebanon. Ireland was firmly in the Western fold during the Cold War but was not a member of any post-war military alliance and did not have an imperialist past; in that sense, Ireland was neutral on two fronts and thus became a candidate for active involvement in UN missions. UNOGIL was the first of many, and on the completion of its mission some of the Irish officers involved (including McCarthy, who had been second-in-command of UNOGIL) moved to the United Nations Truce Supervision Organization (UNTSO) in the Middle East on the borders of Israel and its Arab neighbours. Born in England, McCarthy was a highly regarded career soldier; he died in a car crash in Leopoldville in October 1960 while serving with ONUC, the UN mission in the Congo. He remains the most senior of the 87 Irish soldiers killed whilst serving with UN missions between 1958 and 2018.

This was a view that Aiken and Dublin, mindful of Ireland's own past, could not agree with. Boland told the French delegation that Ireland's history meant it was impossible not to sympathise with the Algerian demand for self-determination, but tempered this by saying that a negotiated settlement offered the best outcome. Ireland, perhaps also thinking of Northern Ireland and Anglo-Irish relations, ultimately voted with France that the Algerian problem could not be solved at the UN. It was a prime example of Aiken's, and Boland's, preferred policy on decolonisation at the UN. As the latter put it, 'a moderate, balanced, dispassionate approach', which favoured self-determination and an end to colonial rule. Issues relating to sovereignty and independence naturally attracted Irish sympathies; later, during the Six Day War of 1967 Ireland was unwilling to condemn Israel unreservedly, arguing for its right to defend itself against attack from its Arab neighbours.

Frank Aiken's Aer Lingus travel bag, presented to him by the airline and used by him on his frequent overseas (especially transatlantic) flights. It was initialled by him using the Irish version of his name: 'PMcA' (Proinsias MacAogáin).

•

A detail from a photograph of a United Nations committee in session in November 1956 shows a rare shot of Ireland's most senior female diplomat, Sheila Murphy, conferring with an Israeli colleague. Having served as private secretary to Joseph P. Walshe during the Second World War, Murphy was one of the key officials involved in the conduct of Ireland's wartime neutrality. Post-war she became the department's institutional memory, as her service went back to the 1920s. Her extensive experience was vital to Ireland's General Assembly delegation. She retired in 1964 at the rank of assistant secretary—equivalent to ambassador.

Éamon de Valera served as taoiseach for the last time from 1957 to 1959. He was then elected president of Ireland in succession to his old colleague Seán T. Ó Ceallaigh. Viewed as something of an elder statesman, he is pictured here in Áras an Uachtaráin with Ghanaian prime minister Kwame Nkrumah in June 1960. In the background is a picture of the cultural nationalist and republican leader Patrick Pearse, who was executed by the British for his role in the Easter Rising of 1916.

438/21/92

P.S.M.

    In conversation today with Mr. ÓFlatharth-
aigh, Aras an Uachtaráin, he mentioned that
Dr.Nkrumah expressed a wish to the Minister
to purchase Pearse's works. The Minister at
once said he would procure a set for him
and,when the Prime Minister said he would like
to get them next day, the Minister said it
might not be so soon but it would certainly
not be delayed.

    Mr. Ó Flathartaigh said perhaps I might
check if they had been sent as he was sure the
Minister would like it done before he left.

24/6/60

P.S.S.

Two volumes of Pearse's
works were purchased by
Mr Horan and sent by
bag to London for Dr.
Nkrumah. They were
I understand handed to
Nkrumah in London

RH6.

Cuba's Fidel Castro responds to Ireland's Frederick Boland from the speaker's podium in the UN General Assembly, 26 September 1960. Boland was held in high regard amongst his peers in the UN, and in 1960 was elected president of its fifteenth General Assembly. He called Castro to order after the latter tried to discuss the imminent US presidential election in what was apparently, at nearly four-and-a-half hours, one of the longest speeches ever delivered at the General Assembly.

Opposite: A memo noting that Prime Minister Nkrumah had expressed an interest in obtaining an edition of Pearse's works during his visit to Ireland. The Irish independence struggle was of great interest to many countries in the decolonising post-war world; Ireland was seen as a country that had grappled with the challenges of gaining independence from a more powerful state, but at an earlier stage. Nkrumah had overseen Ghanaian independence from Britain, and was an iconic figure for many African independence movements; his interest in Pearse was therefore understandable. The query was dealt with. The memo is initialled by May Mooney, the private secretary to the department's secretary (P.S.S.) Con Cremin, and by Róisín Ennis, the private secretary to the minister (P.S.M.), Frank Aiken.

By the early 1960s Ireland had become more considerate of its Western neighbours at the UN, while still seeking to maintain an independent position that appealed to the Third World. Thus, the US and the 'Western European Group' supported the election of Ireland's ambassador to the United Nations, Frederick Boland, as president of the 1960 General Assembly (at one point in October 1960 he shattered his gavel while attempting to call Soviet Premier Nikita Khrushchev to order in an exceptionally heated exchange with a Philippines delegate; Khrushchev later sent Boland a case of wine by way of apology). The Western powers also supported Ireland's election to the Security Council for a half-term in 1962. It was the first of three occasions on which Ireland would serve on the Security Council, and it coincided with the Cuban missile crisis, during which Ireland took a pro-western stance.

Taking on the obligations and responsibilities of UN membership, Ireland contributed to United Nations peacekeeping operations from 1958. In 1958 and 1959 small groups of Defence Forces officers deployed with the United Nations Observer Group in Lebanon (UNOGIL), and with United Nations Truce Supervision Organisation (UNTSO) missions both in Lebanon and along the Israeli-Egyptian border. In the summer of 1960 this emerging involvement in UN peacekeeping expanded dramatically when Ireland was asked to contribute to the Opération des Nations Unies au Congo (ONUC), a large-scale mission to maintain law and order in the newly independent Congo.

Ireland was chosen as a contributor due to its neutrality and its non-membership of Cold War military alliances. The mission, which began as a peacekeeping operation and ended in outright war, was a step into the unknown for the Irish Defence Forces. It saw contingents from an army that had not seen active service since the Irish civil war of 1922–23 go into action in late 1961 with Indian and Swedish units under the UN flag, in an attempt to end the secession of the Congolese province of Katanga from Congo (this action was unsuccessful, but the secession was ultimately ended by 1964).

The actions in Katanga—including the deaths of nine Irish soldiers in an ambush at Niemba in Northern Katanga in November 1960 and later the vigorous defence of an almost open location at the mining town of Jadotville by 150 Irish troops—revealed that better training and modern equipment were required for the Defence Forces if Ireland were to remain involved in peacekeeping. Though Commandant Pat Quinlan's troops at Jadotville ultimately were forced to surrender when their ammunition and water ran out, Quinlan got all his men out with only minor injuries. His achievement in doing so, however, was not fully recognised by the Defence Forces until the 1990s. Twenty-six Irish soldiers had lost their lives serving with ONUC by the time that mission concluded in 1964.

Another indication of Ireland's rising 'middle power' role in the United Nations was the secondment of Conor Cruise O'Brien, the head of the United Nations Section in the Department of External Affairs, to serve as the special representative of the UN secretary-general in Katanga in 1961 and the concurrent appointment of Lieutenant General Seán MacEoin, Chief of Staff of the Irish Defence Forces, as the force commander of ONUC. MacEoin was seen as a safe pair of hands to oversee ONUC after the removal of the headstrong Swedish General Carl von Horn. O'Brien's was a much more problematic appointment. He interpreted his mission as being to bring Katanga's secession to an end, forcibly if need be. With Hammarskjöld's authorisation, in September 1961 he initiated 'Operation Morthor', a military plan to do just that.

Opposite: Emily Coll of the UN Department of Public Information Visitor Services (who was originally from Bruree, Co. Limerick) briefs a group of visitors to the UN in New York, 16 October 1958.

Opposite: Conor Cruise
O'Brien, Robert McDonagh and
Joseph Shields during a debate
in the UN General Assembly's
Special Political Committee, 21
October 1960.

Frederick H. Boland and Sir
Patrick Dean, the British
permanent representative to
the UN, in conversation before
a session of the UN Security
Council during the Cuban
missile crisis, 23 October 1962.
Ireland was one of the non-
permanent members of the
Security Council in 1962.

This involved troops under UN command taking an offensive role, rather than simply peacekeeping; it failed, and O'Brien
was publicly (and unfairly) blamed for acting outside his orders
by Hammarskjöld. The latter flew to Congo to try to engineer a
peace settlement and was killed in mysterious circumstances in
a plane crash during this mission. O'Brien ultimately resigned,
writing his account of the period in *To Katanga and back*, a
strongly polemical work that was highly critical of the UN. It
remains an essential source on one of the organisation's murki-
est and most destructive chapters.

Involvement in ONUC built on the smaller UNTSO and
UNOGIL deployments and inaugurated a stronger Irish
commitment to UN peacekeeping. Even before the last Irish
contingents were withdrawn from Congo in 1964, Irish peace-
keepers had been despatched to Cyprus as part of the United
Nations Interim Force in Cyprus (UNIFCYP), an operation
aimed at keeping Greek and Turkish Cypriots from clashing.
This was a policing mission; very different from what had
become a war in Katanga. Peacekeeping thus became, and
would remain, a defining element of Irish foreign policy.

After the termination of ONUC in 1964, Aiken sought to secure consensus on proposals for the future financing of peace-keeping missions but met stern opposition from France and the Soviet Union. While Ireland was broadly in line with the Western powers on many issues (for example, in condemning the Soviet invasion of Czechoslovakia in 1968), such was not the case in relation to condemnation of US actions in Vietnam. From the mid-1960s the expansion of the organisation and the assertiveness of the major powers in effect diluted Ireland's voice in the UN. Furthermore, Ireland's own priorities had changed. Under the influence of Taoiseach Seán Lemass the focus of the state's foreign policy shifted towards gaining membership of the European Economic Community (EEC).

•

Members of the 35th Infantry Battalion prepare to board a US Globemaster transport aircraft at Baldonnell Aerodrome outside Dublin, en-route to service with the ONUC mission, June 1961. The soldiers are wearing Second World War issue 'bull's wool' uniforms but were issued with tropical service uniforms on arrival in the Congo. They are armed with 7.62mm FN FAL battle rifles and Carl Gustav 9mm submachine guns. Defence Forces Chief of Staff Major-General Seán Collins-Powell and Minister for Defence Kevin Boland (in trilby hat) stand to the left.

Irish soldiers on duty with ONUC in Katanga province in the Congo in the summer of 1960 converse with members of local tribes at Lububu station. Providing guards on train services from Albertville west to Kabalo and further south to Kamina was a regular duty undertaken by Irish soldiers in the province.

Irish foreign policy had an economic as well as a political imperative. By the late 1950s it had become obvious that the protectionism of the 1930s had failed. Ireland remained economically on the periphery of Europe, with its industries sheltering behind protective tariff barriers safe from international competition. While Europe enjoyed a post-war economic boom Ireland stagnated. Indeed, the point was occasionally raised as to whether, given this economic crisis, Irish independence was even viable. Calls for economic reforms had been made since the aftermath of the Second World War, and a number of initiatives had been undertaken from the late 1940s on—the 1948 trade agreement with the UK, the creation of bodies such as Córas Tráchtála and the Industrial Development Authority (respectively to promote exports and foreign investment in Ireland, and to create and develop Irish industries) and even tax

Lieutenant-General Seán MacEoin, chief of staff of the Irish Defence Forces, was appointed force commander of the UN's ONUC mission in Congo in January 1961. MacEoin is seen here during his farewell visits to ONUC troops in Stanleyville in March 1962, reviewing an Ethiopian ONUC unit parading alongside the members of the Armée Nationale Congolaise band.

1.

ONUC

SPECIAL COURTESY PASS

M̶r̶. General Sean Mac Eoin
....

a̶ ̶m̶e̶m̶b̶e̶r̶ ̶o̶f̶ ̶t̶h̶e̶ For D-48
....

is hereby accorded the facility of entering the compound of the « Royal » building for the purpose of conducting official business.

Léopoldville
Date : 12/6/61

Chief Admin. Off.

A courtesy pass issued to MacEoin in his capacity as force commander of ONUC.

Minister for External Affairs Frank Aiken and UN Secretary-General U Thant of Burma (Myanmar) leaving Iveagh House on 14 July 1962. It was the first Irish visit by a UN secretary-general and came as Ireland was serving on the Security Council.

exemptions on export profits. Despite such efforts, however, it was apparent that Ireland was becoming worse off compared with other European states that were shifting towards free trade and manufacturing.

The accession of Seán Lemass as taoiseach in 1959 offered the prospect of building on these initiatives in a more meaningful way. Although he had once been a protectionist, Lemass took on board the drastic suggestions of T.K. Whitaker, the secretary of the Department of Finance. In 1957 Whitaker had devised proposals for economic expansion, based not on protectionism, but its polar opposite: opening up the Irish economy to global trade in an increasingly interconnected post-war world. The second Inter-Party government had seen the value of Whitaker's ideas and had taken steps such as joining the International Monetary Fund and the World Bank in 1957. The Lemass era would prove to be a more decisive turning point in Ireland's economic fortunes.

Lemass's term as taoiseach from 1959 to 1966 encompassed a concentrated period of relatively significant growth. Ireland's new economic policy, emphasising both exports and foreign investment, began to produce results, but Lemass and Whitaker realised that for their new departure to achieve its full potential, Ireland would have to come in from the protectionist economic cold in which it had languished since the end of the Second World War. They identified membership of the EEC as an essential strategic goal.

In part, this reflected the realisation that if the Irish economy were to diversify, it would have to break its traditional dependence upon the British market and trade with Europe. Lemass believed that Ireland's economic regeneration could only come about by expanding foreign trade into Europe and joining the

Involvement in UN peacekeeping missions became a regular feature of service in the Defence Forces in the 1960s. Here, Irish soldiers with the United Nations Force in Cyprus (UNFICYP) escort Turkish Cypriots to safety from an area in Famagusta that had previously been fired on by Greek forces; 24 April 1964.

Ireland's first resident diplomatic mission in Africa was to Nigeria, with an Irish embassy opening in Lagos in 1960. Here, Irish ambassador Eamonn Kennedy pays an official call on H.E. Sir Adesoji Aderemi, governor of Nigeria's Western Region, 17 January 1962.

EEC's free trade area. Accordingly, Europe moved to the centre stage of Irish foreign policy from 1960.

•

Through the 1960s Lemass placed greater emphasis on Ireland joining the EEC. Diplomatic relations with the Community were established and the road to Europe opened up. The pace of engagement with Europe hastened when Britain sought EEC membership in the summer of 1961. British–Irish trade was so important that Ireland had sent in its own membership application days before the British one (it was sent directly from Lemass's office, and the chargé d'affaires at Brussels, Eamonn Gallagher, only heard about it after the fact from British colleagues). Vague notions circulated about Irish unity within a

united Europe, but the nightmare scenario facing Dublin was that Britain might gain EEC entry before Ireland. This would have two major consequences: partition would be further strengthened as Northern Ireland would be inside the EEC while Ireland remained outside, and furthermore Ireland would be cut off from its main market, the United Kingdom.

Ireland applied for full EEC membership in July 1961. The country's economic shortcomings were evident, but associate membership of the EEC was ruled out by Lemass on the grounds that it implied Ireland was economically underdeveloped. The likelihood of admission was also drawn into question because Ireland was not a member of NATO, and the state's non-membership of military alliances was considered at that time as a complication to European designs for foreign policy and defence cooperation. That said, in July 1962, Lemass publicly stated that Ireland would be prepared to accept 'a military commitment' as

Minister for Industry and Commerce Seán Lemass arrives in Milan in April 1959 to visit industrial facilities in northern Italy. Later that year he replaced Éamon de Valera as taoiseach and shifted the broad trajectory of Irish economic development towards export-led growth. This was also an essential criterion for membership of the EEC, for which Ireland first applied in 1961 and achieved in 1973.

Frank Aiken and his wife Maud meet German chancellor Konrad Adenauer in Bonn in August 1960. While the focus of Aiken's foreign policy remained firmly centred on the UN, Taoiseach Seán Lemass ensured that Ireland strengthened its relations with the six members of the EEC. Ensuring German support for Ireland's membership of the Common Market was a priority for Lemass. Con Cremin, the then secretary of the Department of External Affairs, is on the far left.

Future chancellor of the Federal Republic of Germany Willy Brandt welcomes Pádraig Ó hAnnracháin, the director of the Irish Government Information Bureau to his Berlin office, 17 September 1960. Brandt was, at the time, 'governing Burgomaster' (regierenden Bürgermeister) of West Berlin; the equivalent position of lord mayor, though with strong executive powers.

a consequence of European integration. When accession negotiations began in October 1962 Lemass visited the capitals of the six EEC states and successfully managed to counter suggestions that Ireland was unprepared for EEC membership.

The Council of Ministers agreed to open entry negotiations with Dublin for full membership. Yet Ireland's strong economic links with Britain posed an obstacle of a different nature. In January 1963 the French president, Charles de Gaulle, raised doubts over Britain's suitability for EEC membership and vetoed London's application. He did not veto Ireland's, but with its main trading partner apparently destined to remain outside the EEC, there was no point in Ireland joining on its own. As a result, Ireland's application went into cold storage.

British–Irish relations, so sensitive since 1921 and difficult during the Second World War, had improved considerably by the 1960s, and Lemass continued to promote Irish economic modernisation in a British–Irish context. Further Anglo-Irish trade barriers were removed, and the Anglo-Irish Free Trade Area Agreement (1965) created the appropriate trading environment in Ireland for eventual EEC membership. Lemass wished to show that Ireland was responding to the economic changes taking place in Western Europe, but hopes of even an interim trade deal with the EEC failed as Anglo-French tension continued to cloud the enlargement process.

Lemass resigned in November 1966 and was succeeded as taoiseach by his minister for finance, Jack Lynch. When Lynch met Prime Minister Harold Wilson in December 1966 he learned that Britain was considering a fresh EEC application. Wilson assured Lynch that Dublin could count on London's support for an effort at simultaneous British and Irish accession. When Britain's second application was submitted on 11 May 1967, Ireland's followed fifteen minutes later. Five days later de Gaulle's 'velvet veto' explained that conditions were not right for Britain to join the EEC. Lynch undertook courtesy visits to the capitals of the six EEC members in the second half of 1967, and even held a successful meeting with de Gaulle in early November, but as 1967 ended the prospects of EEC membership for Ireland remained as far away as ever. Ireland would have to adopt a 'wait and see' attitude towards Europe.

•

Opposite: *Time* magazine's July 1963 cover featuring Taoiseach Seán Lemass and highlighting his programme for Ireland's economic modernisation. The message was driven home by the Leprechaun pulling back a curtain to reveal a shining factory in the background. As the 1960s progressed Irish diplomats became increasingly involved in promoting Ireland's economic development and international trade.

THIRTY CENTS

JULY 12, 1963

TIME

THE WEEKLY NEWSMAGAZINE

IRELAND
New Spirit in the Ould Sod

PRIME MINISTER
SEAN LEMASS

VOL. 82 NO. 2
(REG. U.S. PAT. OFF.)

A poster for the inaugural 'Irish Export Fashion Fair', held in Dublin in 1964. The Lemass government encouraged foreign investment in Ireland as a driver of economic growth, but the promotion of Irish export goods was also a crucial element of this strategy.

An unidentified model wears a striking checkerboard outfit by Rose Slowey at the third Irish Export Fashion Fair, held in Dublin in 1966. This image is taken from the files of Ireland's embassy in Rome, indicating how Ireland's diplomatic missions were by the 1960s promoting a wide range of domestic industries across Europe. By their nature, photos and products such as this also conveyed a more modern image of Ireland.

Following pages: A depiction of diplomatic procedure and protocol: the map for the route taken by US president John F. Kennedy after his arrival on Air Force One at Dublin Airport for his official visit to Ireland in June 1963. The visit was part of a wider tour of Europe, and Kennedy was the first sitting US president to visit Ireland. It had an immense symbolic value for many Irish people, as Kennedy was descended from Irish emigrants and was the first Catholic US president. The perception of youthful modernity that his presidency seemed to encapsulate added to a sense that Ireland had left behind the relative isolation of the post-war era. The map itself was distributed as part of the 'Press Kit' for journalists covering Kennedy's visit.

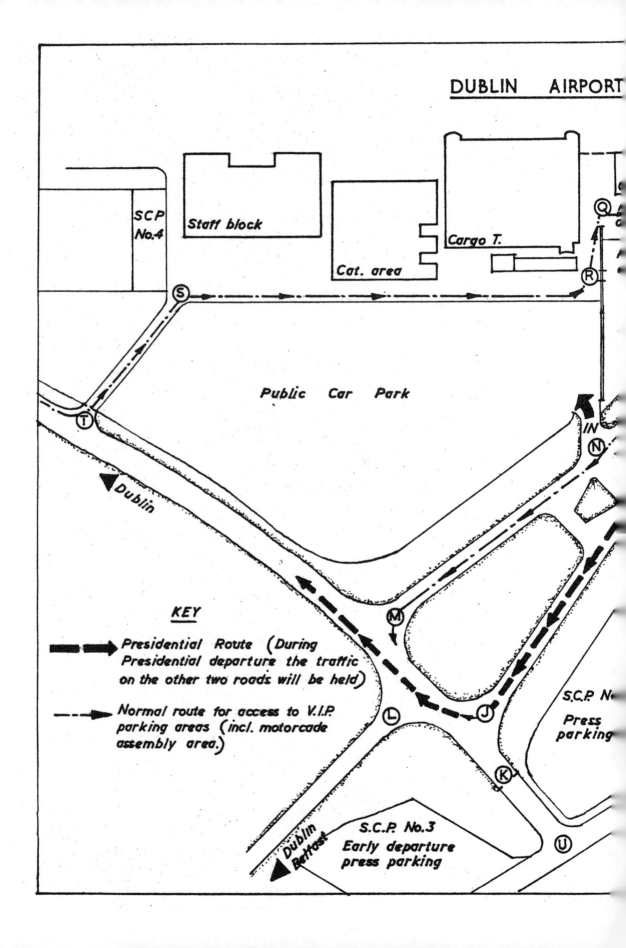

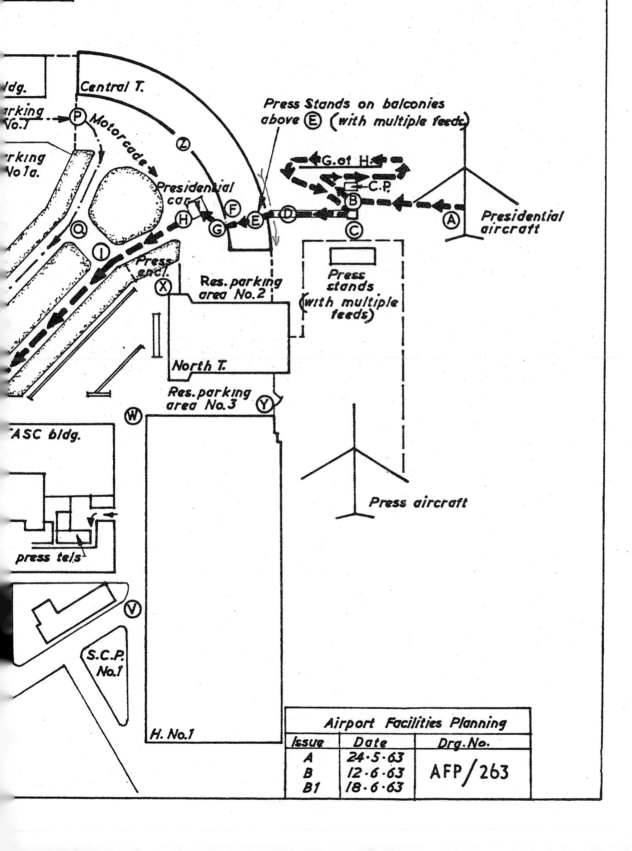

LAYOUT

Central T.

...ldg.

...rking No.1

...rking No.1a.

P Motorcade

Presidential car

Press Stands on balconies above Ⓔ (with multiple feeds)

G. of H.

C.P.

Presidential aircraft

Ⓛ

Ⓗ Ⓖ Ⓕ Ⓔ Ⓓ

Ⓑ

Ⓒ

Ⓐ

Ⓠ

Ⓘ

Press encl.

Ⓧ

Res. parking area No.2

Press stands (with multiple feeds)

North T.

Res. parking area No.3

Ⓨ

Ⓦ

...ASC bldg.

press tels

Ⓥ

S.C.P. No.1

Press aircraft

H. No.1

Airport Facilities Planning		
Issue	Date	Drg. No.
A	24·5·63	
B	12·6·63	AFP/263
B1	18·6·63	

Outside the sphere of international organisations, Irish foreign policy developed during the 1960s through the strengthening or indeed forging of links with other key countries. In particular, US investment was encouraged and facilitated, including through the visit in 1963 of President John F. Kennedy to Ireland. This visit could be seen in purely symbolic terms as the return of the descendant of Irish emigrants to his ancestral homeland. Indeed, some regarded it as a sentimental indulgence.

Kennedy had, however, developed a genuine interest in his Irish ancestry and in fact had visited Ireland twice previously. His 1963 visit was the last stop on a European tour that was intended to highlight US support for Western European allies in the shadow of the Soviet Union (it was on this trip that he famously claimed 'Ich bin ein Berliner'). The ever-pragmatic Lemass had discreetly lobbied for a presidential visit to Ireland, and consequently it became the last stop on Kennedy's tour. The Ireland he saw in 1963 was one undergoing enormous

President Kennedy addresses a crowd at Redmond Place in Wexford, 27 June 1963, having had the honorific 'freedom' of Wexford bestowed on him by Lord Mayor Thomas Byrne, who is seated directly behind him; the scroll and silver chest presented to Kennedy can be seen on the right. Kennedy's paternal great-grandfather had emigrated to the US from Wexford in the mid-nineteenth century; Kennedy himself met a number of his relatives in the county during the visit.

PRESIDENT KENNEDY IN IRELAND
JUNE 26-29, 1963

Previous page: A tape reel of audio recordings of President Kennedy's state visit to Ireland sent to Padraig Ó hAnnracháin by the White House, with a photomontage of the visit on the cover of the box.

Irish Defence Forces cadets at President Kennedy's funeral in Arlington National Cemetery, Washington, November 1963. Kennedy had become increasingly interested in his Irish heritage in the years before his death. During his visit to Ireland he had attended a ceremony at the graves of the executed 1916 Rising leaders in Arbour Hill in Dublin. Kennedy was particularly impressed by the ceremonial 'Queen Anne' drill conducted by Defence Forces cadets on that occasion. After his death, his widow Jacqueline requested that they conduct the same drill by his graveside. It remains the only occasion on which members of another state's armed forces have officiated at the funeral of a US president.

Padraig Ó hAnnracháin adjusts Éamon de Valera's hair during an official trip in the early 1960s. Ó hAnnracháin's role as director of the Government Information Bureau was the equivalent of the modern role of government press secretary.

President Éamon de Valera lays
a wreath of white carnations
and chrysanthemums at
the Canadian National War
Memorial, Ottawa, 2 June
1964. During the visit de Valera
and Canada's External Affairs
minister Paul Martin found an
unexpected link via the Holy
Ghost Fathers. The religious
order had educated Martin in
Québec and employed de Valera
as a teacher in Dublin.

changes as it emerged from the stagnancy and demoralisation
of the 1950s downturn.

Kennedy received rapturous welcomes across the country,
most especially in New Ross, from where his Wexford ancestors
had emigrated. From a US perspective, with an election looming,
images of delighted crowds could do no harm, Ireland's strategic insignificance notwithstanding. But that lack of significance
ensured that one glaring issue could be strenuously avoided:
partition. According to Thomas J. Kiernan, the Irish ambassador
to the US, Kennedy was 'more British than Irish' and would act
accordingly. He did spend more time in Ireland than in the UK
during this European visit, but ultimately Britain was America's
most important ally. That said, Kennedy's visit to Ireland was
a sign that, despite having remained neutral during the Second

ÉIRE
IRELAND

IRIS sheachtainiúil na Roinne
Gnóthaí eachtracha

WEEKLY BULLETIN OF THE
DEPARTMENT OF EXTERNAL AFFAIRS

Uimhir (No.) 664: 15-VI-1964.

President Lyndon B. Johnson welcomes President Eamon
de Valera in Washington.

Frank Aiken signs the Treaty on the Non-Proliferation of Nuclear Weapons (NPT) in Moscow, 1 July 1968. As early as 1958 Aiken began to argue strongly for the control of nuclear weapons. By 1961 he secured US and Soviet support for an Irish UN resolution calling on member states to agree on the control of nuclear weapons, and to restrict their proliferation. The resolution was adopted unanimously on 4 December 1961 and the eventual outcome was the NPT. In recognition of his efforts, Aiken was invited to be its first signatory. The NPT remains the principle global framework for the control of nuclear weapons and one of the major achievements of post-war Irish foreign policy.

Opposite: De Valera's visit to Canada was immediately followed by an official visit to the US; he is pictured here on the cover of the official Department of External Affairs bulletin with US president Lyndon Johnson.

World War and having remained outside NATO, by the 1960s Ireland was still part of the Western fold. The economic implications of this were of particular importance, as the visit showcased a modern, outward-looking Ireland ready for EEC membership.

Irish foreign policy in the 1960s also began to take a direct interest in Asia. This focus on the East was a result of policies of export-led economic growth on the one hand, and, on the other, a desire to fill the long-standing void of Irish representation in Asia. External Affairs had hoped to establish an Irish embassy in post-independence India, especially to liaise with the Irish missionary presence there and elsewhere in Asia, but it had proven financially unviable throughout the 1950s. It should be said that India had not appointed a dedicated ambassador to Ireland until 1951, despite the good relations between the two countries. Prior to that the Indian ambassador to the UK was also accredited to Ireland.

With regard to Irish relations with countries in the Far East, Japan was to the forefront. Japan had appointed an honorary consul in Dublin in September 1926. It had maintained a temporary resident mission in Ireland during the Second World War, though its eventual status as the consulate of a belligerent power and its contacts with both IRA activists and Indian separatists were of concern to the de Valera government. The late 1950s saw the beginning of a new era in Irish–Japanese relations as, in March 1957, both governments agreed to establish formal diplomatic ties. On 27 August that year, the Irish government agreed to the appointment of 53-year-old veteran diplomat Akira Ohye as Japan's first minister plenipotentiary to Ireland, though Dublin was, initially, reluctant to establish an embassy or mission in Tokyo. The prohibitive cost was the principal reason; some within the Department of External Affairs pressed for the allocation of departmental resources to other regions.

Whereas the Irish government was beginning to look to Asia for trade opportunities, limited resources meant that hard choices needed to be made regarding the setting up of embassies in competing jurisdictions. An embassy in New Delhi remained the principal alternative to Tokyo, and a mission was finally opened in the Indian capital in 1964. The trajectory of Irish–Japanese economic and trade contacts did, however, continue upwards during the 1960s and by the end of the decade Japanese brands and goods were increasingly well known in Ireland; Honda, for instance, held a 60% share of the Irish motorcycle market.

In August 1968 Taoiseach Jack Lynch and his wife Máirín arrived in Japan for a formal three-day visit (the first by an Irish taoiseach) and subsequently, the Japanese embassy increased its visibility in Dublin. There was a growing belief in the Department of External Affairs that Ireland now 'owed' Japan an embassy and, it was argued, an embassy would in fact foster improved trade relations. Ireland's first ambassador to Japan, Robin Fogarty, arrived in Tokyo on 1 September 1973, with a brief to further improve trade relations. By the end of that year, Córas Tráchtála had opened offices in Japan. Irish state and semi-state bodies were now well represented in Tokyo. Yet this reaching out to the wider world was taking place at a time when Ireland's closest international relationship came to the fore once again.

Jack and Máirín Lynch in Yokohama, 15 August 1968, during the first official visit to Japan by an Irish leader. The visit was prompted by an invitation for Máirín Lynch to launch the supertanker pictured in the background, the *Universe Ireland*, which was intended to serve the oil refinery at Whiddy Island in Bantry Bay, Co. Cork. Diplomatic and economic links between Ireland and Japan had expanded throughout the 1960s; Japan had appointed its first resident ambassador to Ireland in February 1968 and Ireland reciprocated in Tokyo in 1973.

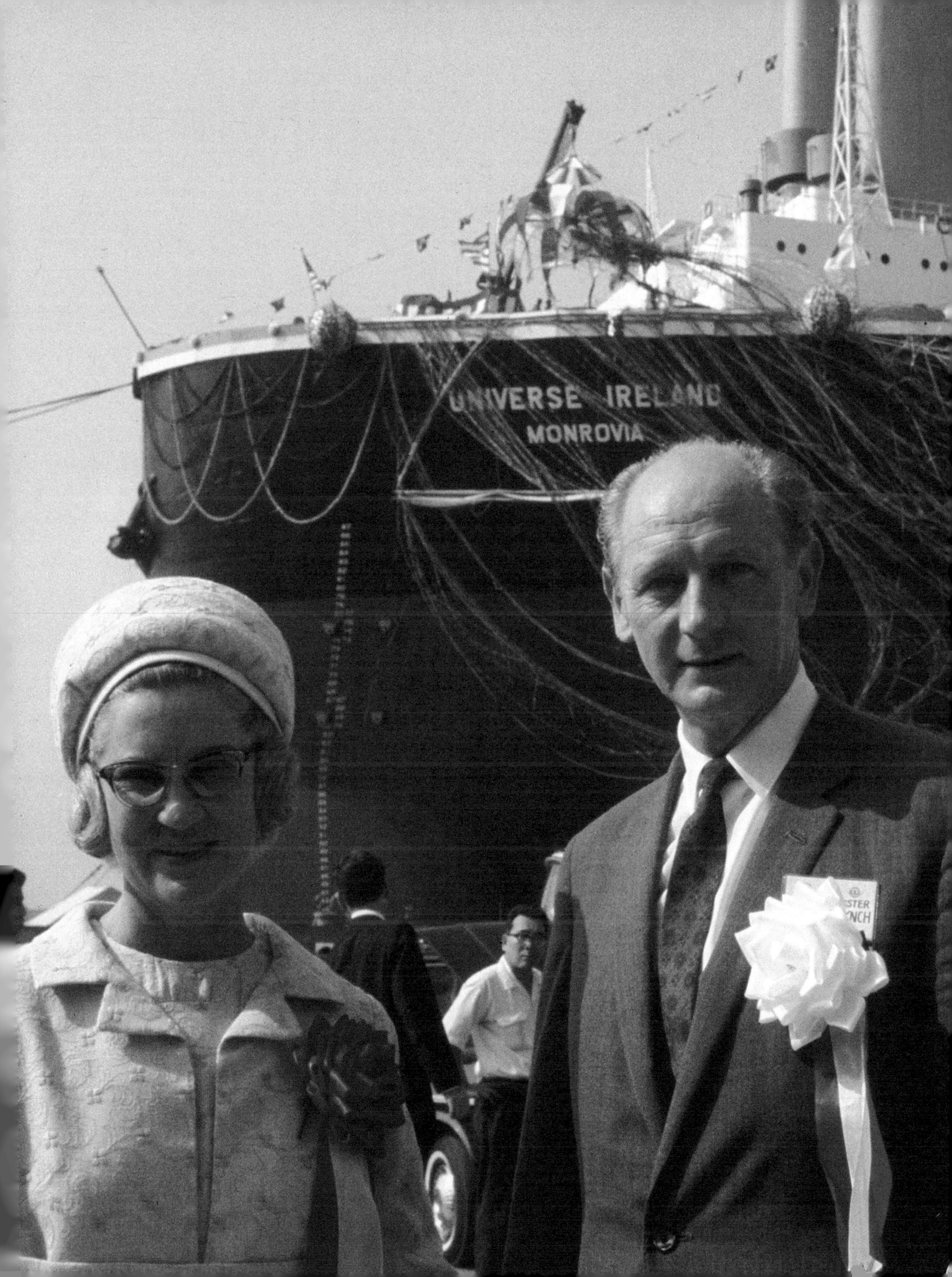
UNIVERSE IRELAND
MONROVIA

LOCAL STAFF

In 1927 the Department of External Affairs had approximately 50 staff members at home and overseas. As of 2019 the Department of Foreign Affairs and Trade has over 1,800 staff members. Irish diplomatic missions worldwide benefit from the expertise and knowledge of local staff recruited in host countries, who bring a range of country-specific skills, linguistic skills and experience that Irish diplomats can draw upon, especially in terms of delivering front-line services to Irish citizens overseas.

A case in point is the embassy of Ireland in India, which opened in New Delhi in 1964 as the first Irish embassy in the Asia/Far East region. As of 2019, in addition to India, this embassy is accredited to four other countries—Bangladesh, The Maldives, Nepal and Sri Lanka. The embassy's staffing reflects its broader working environment: while the working language is English, local staff members speak numerous additional languages, such as Hindi, Punjabi, Tamil, Bengali and Nepalese.

The contributions made by local staff can often be overlooked, but they play a vitally important, if not essential, role in supporting members of the Irish diplomatic service worldwide.

1968–
1973

The late 1960s and early 1970s saw three new developments redefine the scope of Irish foreign relations: the outbreak of conflict in Northern Ireland, Irish membership of the European Economic Community, and the formal establishment of the provision of overseas aid as a meaningful aspect of foreign policy. This chapter considers these three vital themes in turn.

The 'Troubles'

Seán Lemass meets Northern Ireland Prime Minister Terence O'Neill at the Northern Ireland parliament at Stormont outside Belfast, 14 January 1965. While civil servants and ministers from Dublin and Belfast had liaised on numerous occasions since the 1920s, this was the first meeting at leadership level since the Boundary Commission of 1925. It was followed by a second meeting in Dublin the following month. The thaw in relations was not welcomed by all shades of unionist opinion.

Dublin had not engaged in substantive dialogue with Belfast since the unsatisfactory outcome of the Boundary Commission in 1925. Few attempts were made to recognise mutual north-south interests, but discreet contacts had occurred between north and south. These were largely at a civil service level and covered technical cross-border matters such as the operation of railways and electricity generation.

After 1959, however, Lemass proposed freeing north-south trade, and he unilaterally reduced tariffs on some goods from Northern Ireland. With the arrival of the more liberal Terence O'Neill, who became prime minister of Northern Ireland in 1963, Lemass's cross-border co-operation was reciprocated, and a carefully managed rapprochement in non-contentious areas commenced. This led to the first north-south summit meeting since 1925 when, in January 1965, Lemass visited O'Neill at Stormont, the parliament building outside Belfast that housed the unionist-dominated government. O'Neill made the return visit to Dublin in February 1965.

Such efforts to normalise relationships were short-lived. O'Neill's attempts to introduce reforms to address nationalist grievances provoked opposition within his own Unionist party and the wider unionist community, with the evangelical preacher (and future founder of the Democratic Unionist Party) Ian Paisley coming to particular prominence. When Lemass's successor Jack Lynch met O'Neill for talks in December 1967 and January 1968, the situation in Northern Ireland was deteriorating. In April 1969 O'Neill resigned. Dublin, Stormont and Westminster were unprepared for the widespread rioting in Derry's Bogside and in Catholic areas of Belfast that erupted during August 1969 as loyalist attacks on the burgeoning and largely Catholic-led civil-rights movement, demanding an end to discrimination in the allocation of jobs and housing and in electoral practices, spiralled out of control.

Hugh Foot, Lord Caradon, British permanent representative to the UN, listens impassively to his Irish counterpart, Con Cremin, prior to the UN Security Council meeting of 20 August 1969 at which Ireland unsuccessfully tried to have the outbreak of conflict in Northern Ireland considered on the agenda. In the early years of the 'Troubles', the British position was that the conflict was an internal matter for the UK alone; the meeting in question adjourned without the Irish item being adopted.

Dublin unsuccessfully warned London of the prospect of violence in Northern Ireland in the summer of 1969; the improvement of British-Irish relations in the 1960s did not, however, stretch to Northern Ireland affairs. London saw Northern Ireland as an internal United Kingdom matter, but British claims that all was under control there were belied by rioting and the burning of Catholic homes in autumn 1969. This led to hundreds of refugees from Derry and Belfast fleeing south for safety. Stormont was incapable of managing the escalating crisis, one that by its nature seemed to have an international dimension.

On 13 August 1969 Lynch announced that Dublin could 'no longer stand by and see innocent people injured and perhaps worse'. The growing violence in Northern Ireland was brought to the attention of the United Nations Security Council by Lynch's foreign minister, Patrick Hillery, and Ireland's ambassador to the UN, Con Cremin, and Lynch advised against the deployment of the British army to restore order in Northern Ireland. Nevertheless, British troops were deployed shortly afterwards, and Dublin realised that Western Europe and the United States were not prepared to intervene in what they saw as a British domestic matter.

Hardliners within Fianna Fáil viewed the Northern Ireland crisis as an opportunity to remove Lynch, whom they regarded as being without sufficient 'republican' credentials. In addition, they hoped to use the crisis to achieve national unification. Demands grew for Irish military intervention and for the government to arm Northern nationalists for their own self-defence. Lynch maintained a moderate line and rejected the use of force to solve intercommunal differences in Northern Ireland; he went so far as to dismiss two members of his cabinet, Neil Blaney and Charles Haughey, on suspicion that both ministers were involved in gun-running to nationalists in Belfast (they were later charged with attempting to import arms illegally; the charges against Blaney were dropped and Haughey was acquitted).

Lynch remained consistent in his efforts to seek a peaceful solution to the accelerating 'Troubles' (as the conflict came to be known), though he also maintained the traditional Fianna Fáil commitment to Irish unity. He found himself trying to juggle a range of issues arising from the spiralling crisis. He had to try to alleviate the sufferings of northern Catholics, minimise the radicalisation of the nationalist community, denounce IRA and loyalist violence, and prevent the Troubles from spilling over the border.

To some degree, engagement with Northern Ireland and the issues it presented was new territory for the Department of External Affairs itself, and it was now obliged to inform itself comprehensively. A key figure in doing so was Eamonn Gallagher, a first secretary from Letterkenny, Co. Donegal, who from August 1969 had begun to use family contacts to reach out to John Hume and other members of the newly founded Northern Ireland Social Democratic and Labour Party (SDLP) and to report his findings back to Dublin. Gallagher was soon appointed to lead a new section of the department dealing solely with Northern Ireland matters, and in 1972 this was followed by the establishment of the dedicated Anglo-Irish Division, led by Bob McDonagh. The Department of Foreign Affairs (the name was changed in 1971 because the original name was seen to reflect its origins in the Commonwealth, and in line with similar changes in other countries), and the Irish government more generally, were learning about Northern Ireland anew. Their approaches to its problems were worked out laboriously in the drafting and redrafting of speeches and articles setting forth the Irish position. The precision needed in public statements of this kind rested on a great deal of private analysis, debate and consultation with ministers and a range of civil servants, drawing on whatever information they had at their disposal; this was the cut and thrust of policy making.

The Irish government's opposition to paramilitary violence in Northern Ireland had to be juggled with its criticisms both of the Stormont government's handling of the situation and wider British policy. At the same time, the government hoped to persuade the British of the necessity for reforms in Northern Ireland. All of this had to be communicated to the world at large, and especially to British and international media outlets that had now turned their attention to the upheavals taking place in Northern Ireland. The Irish government as a whole retained a private agency to deal with the media on its behalf. Patrick Hillery was unenthusiastic about this approach and requested that Noel Dorr, who had been based at the Irish embassy in Washington, DC, until 1970, overhaul the department's own internal Press and Information section.

ICE PARTY   MR L COSGRAVE   MR E HEATH   MR ABD FAULKNER

The signing of the Sunningdale Agreement, 9 December 1973, which created the short-lived power-sharing executive in Northern Ireland that collapsed in the summer of 1974 under loyalist pressure. L–R: Oliver Napier (Alliance Party) Taoiseach Liam Cosgrave, Brian Faulkner (Ulster Unionist Party), Prime Minister Edward Heath and Gerry Fitt (Social Democratic and Labour Party).

This was one form of diplomatic activity, but it was not the most important; that remained the direct contact between the British and Irish governments, and their respective officials. Lynch was influenced by the views of John Hume, which were relayed to him by Eamonn Gallagher. He sought to persuade the British Labour government of Harold Wilson that the Irish government should have a political role in finding a solution to the emerging crisis in Northern Ireland, and that the system of devolved government at Stormont, based as it was on the Westminster model, was wholly unsuited to ruling the divided community in Northern Ireland. His arguments were rejected, even though the British government recognised Lynch's role as a moderating force. Dublin now worked closely with other members of the SDLP, led by Gerry Fitt and later by John Hume himself, but its input on unfolding events in Northern Ireland was limited.

Violence increased in Northern Ireland in 1971 as the newly formed and more overtly militant Provisional IRA (originally a splinter group of the main grouping of the IRA) intensified its own armed campaign. The loyalist response targeted Catholic areas of Belfast, leading to thousands of Catholic refugees fleeing south of the border in 1971–72. National and international outrage followed 'Bloody Sunday' on 30 January 1972, when British paratroopers opened fire on unarmed anti-internment protestors in Derry, killing thirteen people. Lynch temporarily recalled the Irish ambassador to the United Kingdom from London and, in a furious popular reaction to Bloody Sunday, the British embassy in Dublin was burned down by protestors.

Edward Heath's Conservative government suspended Stormont and introduced direct rule from London on 20 March 1972. It was obvious that any replacement government in Northern Ireland would have to follow a different model. The British subsequently outlined ideas involving devolution based on power-sharing between nationalist and unionist

The aftermath of a bomb attack on Dublin's Talbot St, May 1974. The conflict in Northern Ireland increasingly made itself felt south of the Irish border. On 17 May 1974 a sequence of no-warning car bombings in Dublin and Monaghan killed 33 people. The bombings were the work of loyalist paramilitaries, though collusion with elements of the British security forces has long been alleged. This was the bloodiest single day of the 'Troubles'.

representatives in Northern Ireland, and recognition of what they now termed the 'Irish dimension' to the issue. Elections to a new assembly in Northern Ireland took place in June 1973, with negotiations on government formation subsequently taking place with those parties—the SDLP, the Ulster Unionist Party and the Alliance Party—who were willing to accept this new approach.

The Sunningdale conference of December 1973 came after lengthy negotiations and was attended by representatives of the two governments and the three political parties. The outcome was the establishment of a new power-sharing executive that was set up in January 1974; it was intended that a north-south 'Council of Ireland' would be established at a later stage. Support for the settlement was weak within the broader unionist community, however, and the Council of Ireland never came into being. The executive agreed on at Sunningdale itself worked reasonably well for a few months, but it was brought down in May 1974 by loyalist protests and a general strike that paralysed Northern Ireland. The new Fine Gael-led government of Liam Cosgrave had hoped to uphold the executive, but it was dismayed by the fact that the British government, led once more by Harold Wilson from February 1974, did not defend the Sunningdale agreement more assertively. Attempts to secure a settlement in Northern Ireland fell by the wayside for the remainder of the decade.

Joining the EEC

Francis Biggar (on the right),
Ireland's first ambassador to the
EEC, presents his credentials
to Walter Hallstein, the first
president of the European
Commission, in Brussels, 24
February 1961. Biggar's posting
was of critical importance as
Ireland began to negotiate its first
application for EEC membership
in the summer of 1961.

In the early 1960s Seán Lemass identified membership of the
European Communities (EC) as an essential foreign policy
objective, and this remained the case in the early 1970s. The
three separate 'Communities' (the European Coal and Steel
Community, European Atomic Energy Community and the
European Economic Community) had been brought together
in 1967 as the European Communities, although in everyday
parlance they were known as the EEC or the Common Market.
Following de Gaulle's resignation as French president on 28
April 1969, EC enlargement again became possible, but there
would be no overnight Irish accession.

Patrick Hillery had become Minister for External Affairs after
the June 1969 general election, replacing the United Nations-
focussed Frank Aiken, and his appointment signalled Dublin's
determination to achieve EC membership. Ministerial visits
to the European Commission and to the capitals of the six EC
founder states took place through summer 1969, with the aim
of promoting a positive image of Ireland across the European
Communities. Hillery had to overcome a proposal that Britain's
membership application be dealt with before Ireland's, potentially separating Ireland from its main export market.

Ireland's accession negotiations eventually began on 30 June
1970, with the first face-to-face talks between Ireland and the
European Commission commencing in September that year. As

a result of the decision to fully develop the Common Market, and commence steps towards a European Monetary System and greater foreign policy co-ordination, the Europe that Ireland was negotiating to join was a more advanced entity than the original Common Market of 1957. Protecting Irish interests during the entry negotiations and the transitional period following entry, particularly in trade, agriculture, industry and fisheries were Ireland's main concerns. Despite the fraught state of Anglo-Irish relations, and what turned out to be the worst phase of the Northern Ireland Troubles coinciding with the entry negotiations, Hillery and his officials worked closely with their British counterparts to ensure that Britain and Ireland understood matters of joint concern during the negotiations.

Five-year transitional measures were agreed for Ireland's industry and agriculture. More complex was the application of the Common Fisheries Policy (CFP) to Irish waters. Ireland relied on inshore fishing and, with no deep-sea fishing fleet, wanted to protect its territorial waters from external fishing fleets. Ireland eventually obtained a ten-year extension of its fisheries to a twelve-mile limit from Lough Foyle to Cork and in the Irish Sea, which essentially allayed Irish concerns. Membership of the EC would involve participation in a nine-member European

Éamon de Valera and Charles de Gaulle at Áras an Uachtaráin, 17 June 1969. De Gaulle had resigned as president of France for the last time only weeks prior to this meeting. Freed from the responsibilities of office, he chose to embark upon a holiday in Ireland with his wife. De Gaulle specifically requested to meet de Valera, for whom he had previously expressed his admiration. Arguably both men, now considered elder statesmen, held a similar view of Europe's destiny as an association of distinct states as opposed to a more federal arrangement.

A 1971 pamphlet on 'Irish cultural influences in Europe' from the sixth to the seventeenth century, with emphasis on the activities of Irish Christian clerics and missionaries. The author was Fr Tomás Ó Fiaich of St Patrick's College, Maynooth, Co. Kildare, a leading medieval historian who, in 1977, became Roman Catholic archbishop of Armagh. The pamphlet was published by the Cultural Relations Committee of the Department of External Affairs, and it can be seen as an example of cultural ('soft') diplomacy at a time when Irish entry to the EEC was being actively pursued. The dissemination of information and publicity material was an ongoing, and surprisingly extensive, aspect of the department's activities.

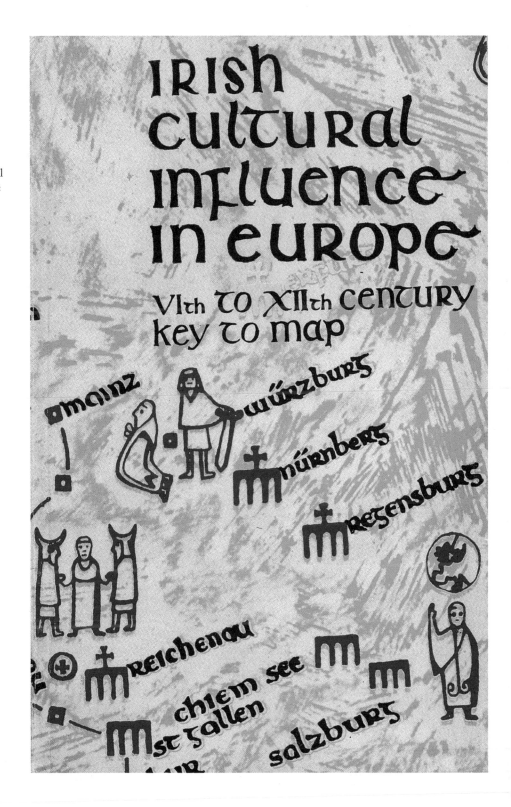

customs area with free trade between members and a common external tariff, but Ireland was able to maintain aids and incentives to industries such as motor assembly and steel production and could thus participate in a progressive manner with the EC's customs union.

Yet while the reforms of the 1960s had made Ireland's economy fit for EC membership, it was not strong enough to deal with the strains of membership at national level. Ireland's increased prosperity was not shared equally. It varied significantly from region to region. European Regional Policy aimed to ensure comparable levels of prosperity across the Community, and the most immediate benefits of membership to less-developed areas of Ireland were expected to be from the Common Agricultural Policy (CAP). During the negotiations Patrick Hillery argued that the EC would need to supplement ongoing Irish national measures for regional development, such as industrial incentives, grants and fiscal measures as well as various infrastructural development projects. Without a well-structured EC regional policy Ireland would suffer greatly under full-scale economic and monetary union, which was initially envisaged by 1980. It was also hoped that regional development could assist

Taoiseach Jack Lynch and the Irish EEC entry negotiations team outside the Berlaymont Building in Brussels, 1972. On the far-right of the photograph is Minister for Foreign Affairs Patrick Hillery, who would soon be appointed Ireland's first European commissioner, holding the Social Affairs portfolio from 1973 to 1976; he also served as a vice-president of the European Commission.

Opposite: A Fianna Fáil poster advocating a 'Yes' vote in the 1972 referendum on Ireland's admission to the EEC. Ireland voted on 10 May 1972 to join the EEC by 83% in favour and 17% against. Ireland then entered the EEC on 1 January 1973.

UNITE WITH
EUROPE

VOTE YES

Published by Fianna Fáil

INTO

EUROPE

Ireland
and the
EEC

the development of Irish border areas and thus assist in bringing peace to the island.

The final entry negotiations session took place on 18 January 1972. The chairman, Luxembourg's permanent representative to the European Communities, Jean Dondelinger, declared all outstanding problems solved and the proceedings closed with appropriate toasts. On 22 January 1972, at the Palais d'Egmont in Brussels, Lynch and Hillery officially signed Ireland's accession to the EC.

•

Ireland's accession to the European Communities required a change in the Irish constitution and so the matter was put to a popular vote via a referendum on 10 May 1972. The 'Yes' campaign had the support of the government and main opposition party, Fine Gael, as well as interest groups and the media. The 'No' campaign was a much smaller grouping made up of the Labour Party, Sinn Féin, the main trade unions and a broad grouping of the Irish Left.

Arguments relating to protecting Ireland's sovereignty and neutrality were widely deployed by the 'No' campaign. Arguments that membership would bring economic growth were met by counter-arguments that the loss of economic resources and economic sovereignty would have the opposite effect. The Department of Foreign Affairs, working closely with the Irish Council of the European Movement, developed a 'Yes to Europe' campaign deliberately designed to counter the 'No' campaign. Prior to 1995, the Irish state did not have to provide matching information on the pros and cons of any referendum issue and could freely use state funding in this way.

Very little government time was spent highlighting the possible drawbacks of EC membership. The key points in government campaigning were selling the immediate benefits of membership, in the form of increased prices via the CAP, to the agricultural community, and the longer-term benefits to industry and employment that access to European markets could bring. The 'Yes' publicity campaign operated via regular speeches, accessible pamphlets, specialised leaflets and newspaper articles. It also used popular prime time television programmes to get pro-EC entry arguments across.

One of the greatest assets for the 'Yes' campaign was Taoiseach Jack Lynch; his image as a modest and honest everyman helped to convince people of the benefits of EC membership. Lynch argued that those who wished to vote 'No' were voting to increase Ireland's dependence on Britain. To Patrick Hillery, as Minister for Foreign Affairs, the difference between EC membership and staying out was as straight forward as a full order book if Ireland became a community member, or an empty one if Ireland stayed out.

The 'Yes' campaign was successful, and Ireland joined the EC on 1 January 1973 without fanfare in either Dublin or Brussels (the UK and Denmark joined at the same time, in the first enlargement of the EC since its foundation). RTÉ, the national broadcaster, presented no coverage of what was the greatest change in Ireland's sovereignty and international relations since independence. A small number of low-key events did take place. The new Minister for Foreign Affairs Brian Lenihan spoke at a celebratory lunch; tree-planting ceremonies were held in every county; and children born on New Year's Day 1973 were presented with a special medal. Patrick Hillery became Ireland's

Minister for Labour Patrick Hillery and his wife Maeve are shown around the German owned Liebherr crane factory in Killarney, Co. Kerry on the tenth anniversary of its opening, 19 May 1969. The company's founder, Hans Liebherr, was the inventor of the tower crane. His company opened a factory in Ireland as it sought to extend into overseas markets, a decision that coincided with Lemass's policy of encouraging foreign direct investment into Ireland on a large scale and which also hinted at the possible economic benefits of Ireland joining the single market. In July 1969 Hillery replaced the long-serving Frank Aiken as Minister for External Affairs.

Taoiseach Jack Lynch escorts President de Valera at Áras an Uachtaráin prior to the latter's signing of the Act of the Oireachtas bringing Ireland into the EEC, 13 December 1972. De Valera was reputedly distressed by the implications of joining the EEC, on the grounds that it diluted Ireland's hard-won sovereignty. The accession of Ireland to the EEC marked a fundamental refocussing of Irish foreign policy towards Europe; it marked the biggest single re-orientation of Ireland's international affairs since 1922.

first European Commissioner, and within weeks he and other Irish ministers, along with Irish officials, began serving in the various European Community institutions.

Ireland was now a member of the largest trading bloc in the world and part of an economy second-richest only to that of the United States. This was a milestone that, for many, marked the culmination of the process of full independence from Britain. As *The Irish Times* put it, in somewhat purple prose, in its editorial on New Year's Day 1973, Ireland was embarking on 'an adventure which, like all adventures, will have perils and problems it will also have rich opportunities, not the least being the help of friends and neighbours. For we are amongst friends'.

Development aid and human rights

The *Columcille*, owned by the charity Africa Concern (now Concern), leaves Dublin en route to Biafra with a shipment of relief supplies, 6 September 1968. Africa Concern had been set up to facilitate public appeals for aid to relieve the humanitarian crisis caused by conflict in the Nigerian province of Biafra.

The early 1970s saw the development of a strand of Irish foreign policy under the auspices of the Department of Foreign Affairs: development aid. The notion of providing overseas aid or charity was by no means unknown in Ireland due to the strength of Catholic (and, to a lesser extent, Protestant) missionary traditions; in 1971 there were 6,000 Irish people involved in private voluntary work overseas, but only 400 of these were lay people. The state itself had developed aid programmes to war-torn Europe in the immediate aftermath of the Second World War, and in the 1960s there had been some technical aid programmes for civil servants from African nations such as Zambia.

Agricultural development in Africa was supported via the organisation Gorta (the Irish word for 'hunger'). This had been established in 1965 as 'Gorta: The Freedom from Hunger Council of Ireland' following a request from the UN's Food and Agricultural Organization that the Irish government create an agency that would raise general awareness and public support for long-term agricultural development on the continent. Gorta's first project was an agricultural training school in Tanzania. Such official initiatives were limited in scope, but the Biafran famine of 1967–70 in Nigeria was a seminal moment in raising Irish public awareness of the horrors of underdevelopment. That crisis prompted the establishment of Concern, one of the first Irish non-governmental organisations established to provide development aid.

The creation of such bodies as Concern was part of a broader European phenomenon, and as early as 1969 Patrick Hillery, as Minister for External Affairs, had accepted that there would have to be an official policy on the matter. Membership of the EC spurred more concrete actions by Irish governments. The departments of Foreign Affairs and Finance discussed the best means of providing development aid. One was to administer any official programme that emerged, while the other was to pay for it. The state's resources were limited, and so the question was how best to maximise these. It was decided that any aid programme would place an emphasis on food aid and technical assistance, and that the focus of the programme would be on a limited number of countries. The eventual outcome was the establishment in 1974 of Irish Aid by Minister for Foreign Affairs Garret FitzGerald, as an official section of the Department of Foreign Affairs.

Membership of the UN and its agencies had made it easier for the Irish state to contemplate such a step. The UN classed the 1970s as a 'development decade' after the global changes of the 1960s. The maintenance of the international order was linked to the moral imperative of development aid, but the contours of the Cold War had a major impact on the destination of aid flows. Ireland aligned itself with Scandinavian countries in this regard (though the oil crisis of the 1970s put pressure on the flow of aid to the developing world).

For Ireland, the African states of Lesotho, Sudan, Tanzania and Zambia were to be the main focus of its aid efforts (initial plans to provide aid in India were dropped due to the logistical challenges posed). The missionary tradition had placed Africa prominently within Irish public awareness, and there were natural links with former British colonies that shared a working language with and had similar governing structures to Ireland.

There was a humanitarian dimension to Irish aid from the outset. The promotion of human rights was linked to economic self-sufficiency, and local participation was essential. Over time, aid efforts would extend to Albania, Cambodia, Bangladesh and Vietnam. Rural development, health and education were key planks of the Irish aid programmes, which suited the self-image of the Irish state as a bridge between the West and the developing world. From the outset, the provision of Irish development aid was intended to widen the scope of Irish foreign policy, and to facilitate international peace and justice. After 1974 a great deal of aid was funnelled through the EC as well as directly from Irish Aid; the overall sums involved in Ireland's development aid programme increased from €1.5m in 1974 to €200m in 2000.

Alongside this commitment to development aid naturally came a greater awareness of the issues of human rights. Development aid, by its nature, sought to redress an economic and social imbalance, which implied that economic and social equality was its ultimate objective. The achievement of political equality followed on from this. The notion of individual rights and international solidarity had been, to some extent, foreshadowed in Irish foreign policy since its inception. The rhetoric of the 1919 declaration of independence sought to reach out to other small nations, while individual rights were touched upon in clauses of both Irish constitutions. Universalist principles were articulated by the League of Nations (such as in the 1926 convention to suppress the slave trade, which Ireland had signed in

1930) and de Valera's May 1945 speech at the end of the Second World War had effectively set out a case for the rights of small nations in a multilateral world.

Furthermore, Sean MacBride, as Minister for External Affairs, had been involved in drafting the 1949 European Convention on Human Rights, which was ratified in 1953. Ironically, the first case brought in the European Court of Human Rights (ECHR) was taken against the Irish government by Gerard Lawless, who unsuccessfully argued that his internment in 1957 for republican activities breached the convention; none other than MacBride represented the plaintiff. Yet the Irish state also broke new ground in the 1970s, when it took a case against the United Kingdom for allegations of torture against a number of men whom the British had interned without trial in Northern Ireland as suspected IRA members. The ECHR ultimately adjudicated that the men in question had been subjected to 'inhumane and degrading treatment', though it stopped short of defining this as torture.

Throughout the 1970s and into the 1980s Irish governments ratified a range of international human-rights instruments, but were sometimes criticised for not ratifying others. A number of cases were taken against the state on human-rights grounds,

Irish links to the advocacy of international human rights, and especially ongoing condemnation of apartheid South Africa, were highlighted in May 1974. The UN Special Committee on Apartheid embarked on a two-week special session in Europe to publicise the UN stance on apartheid; the session included a visit to Dublin. This coincided with the tenth anniversary of the foundation of the Irish Anti-apartheid Movement, members of which are pictured here with some of the UN committee, including Nigerian diplomat Edwin Ogebe Ogbu, chairman of the special committee, who is making a statement.

Barry and Aisling Denham, children of Ireland's ambassador to Zambia Donal Denham, playing with two unidentified security guards at the newly opened Irish embassy in Lusaka, late 1980s. The image touches on two elements of Ireland's foreign relations that can often be overlooked: the fact that Irish missions abroad, like so many others, depended, and continue to depend, upon the services provided by local, non-Irish staff; and that the families of diplomats play a vital, if indirect, role in supporting those same diplomats.

Irish Aid director general, Ruairí de Búrca (back row, fifth from left), at St Joseph's Compound, a school for hearing impaired children supported by Irish Aid, in Sierra Leone, 2019.

notably that by Trinity College Dublin academic David Norris, who successfully brought a case to the ECHR in 1988 arguing that the criminalisation of sexual activity between males in Irish law was a breach of the ECHR's rulings (it was decriminalised in Ireland in 1993). At the same time, Irish diplomats were often actively involved in the development and furtherance of human-rights concerns at the UN (in the early 1980s Declan O'Donovan chaired the UN's third committee, which largely dealt with human rights, and as such was involved in brokering the 1981 'Declaration on the Elimination of All Forms of Intolerance or Discrimination based on Religion or Belief').

Development aid and human-rights issues were not always interlinked during the Cold War, but its end in 1989 ensured that there was a broader trend internationally during the 1990s to link the provision of aid to the establishment of human rights and democracy in those countries to which aid was provided. Yet there was an inevitable tension between promoting core values (such as human rights) and upholding the interests of the Irish state in other areas, most obviously economic well-being. Irish politicians and diplomats viewed their primary responsibility as ensuring the well-being of the state and its citizens. In practice, this could mean trying to maintain as friendly a relationship as possible with states with whom Ireland might otherwise disagree profoundly on the question of human rights. Ireland was no exception in having to negotiate such a delicate path.

1973–
1985

Ireland's foreign policy during the period from 1973 to 1985 was dominated by two major issues. The first was multilateralism, most especially in terms of Ireland's exploration of the possibilities and opportunities offered by membership of the EC. The second key issue was the ongoing attempt to deal with the continuing conflict in Northern Ireland, in terms of both how it impacted upon Ireland and how the basis for a political settlement that could bring an end to violence might be created. These two broad themes will be examined in turn.

European integration

Minister for Foreign Affairs Garret FitzGerald in Brussels, 10 July 1975, with the iconic Berlaymont Building visible in the background. FitzGerald was an ardent Europhile and Francophile; his fluency in French and his energy and grasp of his portfolio greatly helped the development of Ireland's place in the European Communities in the early years of the state's membership. To the immediate left of the car is Brendan Dillon, Ireland's permanent representative to the EEC.

Irish entry to the EC in 1973 meant joining a sphere of international relations that would have a profound bearing on life in Ireland, as the EC evolved into the European Union. The initial Irish approach to the European Communities was shaped to some degree by a change of government, as Jack Lynch's Fianna Fáil was replaced by a Fine Gael–Labour coalition led by Liam Cosgrave. Whereas Labour had originally opposed joining the EC, the overwhelming support for membership as registered in the referendum on entry ensured that the party accepted the matter as settled; moreover, the new Minister for Foreign Affairs, Fine Gael's Garret FitzGerald was himself an enthusiastic Europhile and he rapidly began to make a mark. In April 1973 he recalled all Irish heads of overseas missions for a conference on the implications of Irish membership of the EC and soon

outlined his own approach in a speech to the Dáil in which he set out five basic principles of the foreign policy that he intended to follow. As he put it, these were:

> To help maintain world peace and reduce tensions between the super-powers, between blocs, and between states; to resolve, even on a provisional but open-ended basis, the Northern Ireland problem and to pursue relations with the United Kingdom Government to achieve this purpose; to contribute to the development of the European Communities along lines compatible with Irish aspirations and to the creation within the Community

A 1973 debate in the UN's Special Political Committee on Israeli activity in the occupied territories of the West Bank and Gaza Strip. Ireland's delegate, Marie Keating (later Cross), is seated in the back row, beside the Israeli delegate who is speaking.

of a stable democratic and healthy society; to secure Ireland's economic interests abroad, thus facilitating economic and social progress at home, and particularly to secure our interests in the economic, social and regional policies of the EEC; to contribute to the Third World in a manner and to an extent that will meet our obligations, satisfy the desire of Irish people to play a constructive role in this sphere, and add to our moral authority in seeking to influence constructively the policies of other developed countries towards the Third World.

These were, essentially, the core principles of foreign policy that the Irish state would follow.

This new emphasis soon found concrete expression, in the form of an expansion of the Department of Foreign Affairs at Iveagh House in Dublin, the opening of new embassies in Luxembourg and Japan in May 1973, and the establishment of new provisions for overseas aid. Ireland also, for the first time, established relations with a Communist country, in this case the USSR: an embassy opened in Moscow in 1974 (a Soviet embassy also opened in Dublin, though Irish military intelligence—G2—kept the staff there under surveillance). Ireland subscribed to instruments such as the International Convention on Economic, Social and Cultural Rights, and the International Convention on Civil and Political Rights.

The nature of the EC posed particular challenges for the Irish state, most obviously regarding the necessity to seek multilateral consensus between states with very different systems of law and government. On the other hand, membership of the EC offered Ireland an opportunity to come out from Britain's shadow as a member of a broader political and economic project. Despite having been associated with the UK for so long, the Irish approach to the EC was different from Britain's from the outset. Ireland adopted a more positive approach to Europe that contrasted with the wariness displayed by the British towards the EC, though this may have been shaped by the reality that British influence was far more substantial than that of Ireland.

Nevertheless, Ireland was seen by its new peers as being broadly in favour of the European project.

The positive approach adopted by Ireland in the early years of EC membership was largely shaped by FitzGerald. A willingness to seek consensus on issues was in part dictated by a concern that the larger EC states might seek to exert an influence at the expense of smaller members in what was intended to be a partnership of equals. The benefits for Ireland, still a largely agricultural economy, of membership of the CAP and the common market would be manifold (farmers quickly benefitted from the CAP), yet the full realisation of such benefits lay in the future. In the early 1970s some Irish industries did suffer as the market was opened up; an economic blow exacerbated by the reverberations of the 1973 global oil crisis. Alongside economic convergence, Ireland also committed itself to 'European Political Co-operation', a much less developed attempt to ensure that the various EC states would align their foreign policies in relation to states outside the bloc. The structures that would facilitate this were less well-defined. Instead of being able to rely on a central institution such as the European Commission, political co-operation was to be managed via the country that held the EC's rotating presidency at any given time.

Garret FitzGerald, as 'President in office of the Council of the EC'—the formal leader of the EC on the occasion in question—speaks to Mauritian prime minister Seewoosagur Ramgoolam at the signing of the Lomé Convention in Togo, 28 February 1975. The convention marked an important stage in the development of trade and aid relations between the EEC and the states of Africa, the Caribbean, and the Pacific—the ACP—countries.

PRESIDENT

Taoiseach Liam Cosgrave, with Minister for Foreign Affairs Garret FitzGerald to his right, chairs a meeting of the European Council at Dublin Castle, 10 March 1975, during the first Irish presidency of the EEC. Coincidentally, both men held governmental positions in the 1970s occupied by their respective fathers in the 1920s. W.T. Cosgrave had been president of the Executive Council of the Irish Free State (the equivalent of the position of taoiseach) from 1922 to 1932, while Desmond FitzGerald had been minister for External Affairs from 1922 to 1927.

EC membership touched on so many issues that all the key government departments involved in the accession negotiations were forced to expand through the second half of the 1970s, and especially after Ireland began to assume the rotating EC presidency (in addition, the Department of Foreign Affairs would triple its number of overseas missions between 1973 and 2011). Ireland first held the presidency in 1975. The major meetings were held in Dublin Castle. Ireland oversaw the first meeting of the European Council, the signature of the Lomé Convention (establishing trading relations with 71 African, Caribbean and Pacific countries), and the re-establishment of relations with the oil-producing states of the Middle East after the oil crisis. When holding the 1979 EC presidency, Ireland had to co-ordinate the EC's common UN policy (though as the community was not a state, its members, some of which were also permanent

THE IRISH SOLDIER IN UNIFIL

IRELAND

UNITED NATIONS

A sketchbook of paintings by Sgt. M Clarke.

M. Clarke.

members of the Security Council, retained their individual presence in the UN).

From an Irish point of view, the multilateralism of the EC differed in one important respect from that of the UN. As early as 1961, the Department of Foreign Affairs had been concerned over the possible implications that EC membership might have for Irish neutrality. The fact that Ireland might be used as a transatlantic transit point by belligerent powers in a Third World War was simply a geopolitical reality, and had been considered by the Irish Defence Forces as a possibility since the mid 1950s. In February 1979, for instance, the United States considered using Shannon Airport as a transit point for troops on NATO duty, which posed a difficulty that was only avoided by the US changing its mind. Major Defence Forces exercises held in the early 1980s centred around the possibility of a belligerent power attempting to take Shannon airport to use it as a staging post for an East–West conflict in mainland Europe. In 1981 a Department of Defence memo suggested that if Britain were attacked, Ireland would be as well, and the memo privately assessed what logistical and military support could be provided to the UK in the event of another European, or global, war.

The first page of a sketchbook complied by Sergeant M. Clarke of the Defence Forces, illustrating a tour of duty with the United Nations Interim Force in Lebanon (UNIFIL). This UN peacekeeping mission had been established in 1978, after Israel invaded south Lebanon, to monitor the Israeli withdrawal from the area. Given the continuing tensions in the region, UNIFIL remains an ongoing mission and is the longest and most substantial peacekeeping mission to which the Irish Defence Forces have contributed. Service in the Lebanon came to occupy a prominent place not only in Defence Forces' overseas service, but also in Irish popular culture in the 1980s. Forty-seven members of the Defence Forces were killed serving with UNIFIL between 1978 and 2001.

Minister for Foreign Affairs Garret FitzGerald lays a wreath at the tomb of the unknown soldier in Moscow, December 1976. Ireland's diplomatic and trading relationship with Moscow had developed considerably in the 1970s as a result of Ireland's EEC membership; reciprocal embassies were opened in Moscow and Dublin. Ireland's first ambassador to the Soviet Union, Dr Edward Brennan, had been appointed in 1973.

Ambassador of Ireland to India Denis Holmes (third from left) at the Loreto Convent in Darjeeling, April 1977. The presence of Irish Christian missionaries in India can be traced back to the nineteenth century; it reflected Irish involvement in the East India Company, and especially the British Raj after 1857. Many of the Indian nationalist elite had been educated by Irish missionaries.

Such considerations were part and parcel of the reality of the Cold War and ensured that small states such as Ireland remained invested in the multilateralism of the United Nations. This stance was shaped by pragmatism as well as principle. States such as Ireland had a natural vested interest in a rules-based international order that sought to give them some degree of parity with their larger and more powerful counterparts.

Following the first Israeli invasion of Lebanon in 1978, the United Nations Interim Force in Lebanon (UNIFIL) was established, to supervise the withdrawal of Israeli forces and restore peace and security. With UNIFIL, Ireland's role in UN peace-keeping took its most concrete form since the 1964 deployment to Cyprus; there has been an almost continuous contribution of a battalion to UNIFIL since 1978. This commitment may have aided Ireland's election to non-permanent membership of the UN Security Council in 1981–2, in a tenure that coincided with a second Israeli invasion of Lebanon. The Middle East would become a particular focal point for Irish defence, foreign and trade policies throughout the 1980s and beyond.

Liam Cosgrave and Harold Wilson at the entrance to 10 Downing Street, London, 5 April 1974. Wilson had returned to power in March 1974, replacing Edward Heath as British prime minister. Wilson's arrival marked a critical change in British policy towards Northern Ireland, as the Sunningdale Agreement came under increasing pressure due to ongoing opposition by loyalists.

Managing the 'Troubles'

While the broad thrust of Irish foreign policy since the 1950s had emphasised the forging of links and a broader engagement with the wider world, by the early 1970s the ongoing conflict in Northern Ireland ensured that the Department of Foreign Affairs was increasingly preoccupied by the Anglo-Irish relationship; its new Anglo-Irish section, formed, as already noted, as a response to the outbreak of the Troubles, would increase in size throughout the 1970s. At the same time as Ireland formally joined the EEC, it was also obliged to deal with the failure of the Sunningdale Agreement and its aftermath in Northern Ireland.

The Department of Foreign Affairs played a role on the ground in Northern Ireland throughout the Troubles. This was a legacy of Eamonn Gallagher's attempts to forge contacts in the late 1960s, and the value of such personal engagement was not lost on Irish governments. While Northern Ireland was outside their jurisdiction, Irish officials—nicknamed 'travellers' within the Department of Foreign Affairs itself—maintained quiet contacts across the nationalist and unionist communities and with their representatives. They travelled discreetly, usually for a couple of days at a time, sometimes following a geographic route, or alternatively meeting people from one segment of society, whether religious, political or from civic society (they never had direct meetings with paramilitaries). Their discussions took place in neutral venues and were discreet rather than surreptitious. Those they met knew that they were meeting Irish diplomats. 'Travelling' continued from the 1970s up to the

FATAL CASUALTIES IN NORTHERN IRELAND

1969 - 31st December 1976

	1969	1970	1971	1972	1973	1974	1975	1976	TOTAL
Total Number of Civilians Killed	12	23	114	323	170	167	211	245	1,265
*of which Sectarian Assassinations									
Roman Catholic victims	-	-	-	90	51	78	92	98	4C9
Protestant victims	-	-	-	39	32	40	57	91	259
Total Number of assassination victims	-	-	-	129	83	118	149	189	668
Security Forces casualties:									
Prison Officers								1**	1
Army	-	-	43	103	58	29	14	13	26C
UDR	-	-	5	24	9	5	7	16	66
RUC	1	2	11	17	13	16	11	24	95
Total Number of Security Forces casualties	1	2	59	144	80	50	32	54	422
TOTAL CASUALTIES	13	25	173	467	250	217	243	299	1,687

* No records for 1969-1971.

* Figure from October 1976.

1990s and was intended to gather information: to keep Dublin informed of political realities and better equipped to formulate a policy to address these. Many northern nationalists after all, most especially in the SDLP, looked to the Irish government to advocate on their behalf.

    While the Official IRA became increasingly inactive in the 1970s, from 1975 onwards the Provisional IRA began to reorganise in a manner that was intended to sustain a war of attrition that aimed to slowly grind down British resolve and lead to a British withdrawal. Such a withdrawal was, in the mid-1970s, considered a real possibility, one that troubled both the Irish government and the Department of Foreign Affairs, which harboured doubts over the British Labour Party's commitment to Northern Ireland. In May 1974 Seán Donlon of the Department's Anglo-Irish division reported that the SDLP leader John Hume was deeply pessimistic that the Irish government might align itself with a British argument for withdrawal, given that this

The human cost of the Troubles: an extract from a list of fatalities in Northern Ireland, as compiled by the Department of Foreign Affairs in 1976.

Senator Edward Kennedy, Taoiseach Garret FitzGerald and SDLP leader John Hume in Washington, DC, in the early 1980s. Hume was the decisive intellectual influence on the Irish government's approach to a settlement in Northern Ireland. Both the SDLP and successive Irish governments recognised that Irish-American political leaders such as Kennedy (the youngest brother of President John F. Kennedy) could potentially exert a great deal of influence on Irish issues within the US political system. Irish-American political and business leaders played a crucial role in the development of the eventual 'peace process' in the 1990s.

might expose the nationalist community to loyalist attack. This bleak prospect was compounded in June 1974, when the Department of Foreign Affairs produced an assessment of the likely impact of a British withdrawal, at a time when it was privately perceived as a genuine possibility.

The assessment considered a range of scenarios, none of which was positive: repartition, a renewed refugee crisis, and the intensification of sectarian conflict were all very real possibilities. Massive force—beyond what was available to the Irish government—would be needed to control Northern Ireland in the event of the latter, with no prospect of outside intervention. The possibility of a declaration of independence was also considered. The assessment noted that any Irish military build-up would be likely to alarm and provoke unionists, and a decision was made to explore other possible avenues, and to make contact with unionists and indeed any interested parties that could help to improve relations.

The Irish government's preferred option was for the British to remain, with an eye to a solution further down the road. Harold Wilson's Labour government, however, had little appetite for new political initiatives in Northern Ireland following the collapse of Sunningdale and the subsequent constitutional convention. Dublin, on the other hand, was concerned that a political vacuum would create a space for paramilitarism, especially given the hints of a possible British withdrawal during a period that witnessed increased sectarian killings. Ulster unionism was fragmenting and the ascendancy of Ian Paisley's Democratic Unionist Party (DUP) undermined prospects for a power-sharing settlement at this juncture.

This did not mean, however, that the Irish government could ignore the security implications of what was happening in Northern Ireland. Taoiseach Liam Cosgrave was inclined, just like his father, to take a harsh line against republicans whom he and his government felt were intent on undermining the republic itself. The prospect of the northern conflict spilling across the border was widely feared; the single bloodiest day of the Troubles was caused by no-warning car bombings in Dublin

The aftermath of the assassination of British ambassador to Ireland Christopher Ewart-Biggs on 21 July 1976, in which Judith Cooke, an official in the Northern Ireland Office, was also killed. A large bomb had been placed in a road culvert near Ewart-Biggs's residence in the south Dublin village of Sandyford. The Provisional IRA later claimed responsibility. An experienced career diplomat, Ewart-Biggs had only taken up his post twelve days earlier. Such an attack on a diplomat in Ireland was unprecedented and caused widespread outrage; it also prompted the Cosgrave government to introduce further emergency legislation to deal with paramilitaries.

and Monaghan on 17 May 1974 that killed 33 people. The IRA assassination of the British ambassador to Ireland, Christopher Ewart-Biggs, outside Dublin on 21 July 1976 was seen to foreshadow what might yet happen if the conflict did escalate across the border (Cosgrave specifically mentioned the killing of Ewart-Biggs in a subsequent Dáil debate on an Emergency Powers Bill).

Equally, the Irish government was not oblivious to British security requirements. In June 1976 Cosgrave permitted limited British incursions in Irish airspace. But his stance on such issues posed difficulties in some important overseas constituencies. In March 1976 Cosgrave travelled to America to address Congress during the bicentenary of the founding of the US. The trip was also intended to encourage inward investment into Ireland while discouraging Irish-American support for the IRA. Threats to his life were notified to the Irish consulates in New York and Boston, and there were fears that his visit might be met by protests.

Throughout the 1970s the Department of Foreign Affairs sought to marginalise more militant Irish-American figures and focussed their energies on cultivating relationships with key Irish-American congressional leaders such as Edward Kennedy, Daniel Moynihan and Tip O'Neill, along with Hugh Carey, the governor of New York. It was thanks to their lobbying that the Democratic president Jimmy Carter made an unprecedented public statement on Northern Ireland in August 1977. Carter asserted US support for a peaceful settlement that commanded the backing of both communities and urged Irish-America not to offer any support, direct or indirect, to paramilitary groups. Given the stance of previous US administrations that considered the Troubles an internal matter for the UK, this intervention was a significant symbolic shift in attitude.

Britain remained wary of official Irish involvement in Northern Ireland, and there were enduring tensions between the British emphasis on security and the Irish desire for a political settlement. These tensions survived changes in administrations. In 1976 Harold Wilson had resigned as British prime minister, being replaced by his Labour colleague James Callaghan. Fianna Fáil returned to power under Jack Lynch in 1977. The assumption in Dublin was that, insofar as Northern Ireland was

a priority for the British, Callaghan would lean to a more unionist position to secure the support of unionist MPs for his own government. From an Irish perspective then, the landslide election of the Conservatives led by Margaret Thatcher in 1979 was thought to herald a more significant change.

The IRA murder of Lord Louis Mountbatten, the last viceroy of India, whilst he was on holiday in Sligo in August 1979, was a major incident; it prompted Pope John Paul II not to visit Northern Ireland as part of his official visit to Ireland that year. Mountbatten's murder and the Warrenpoint attack on the same day, in which 17 British troops were killed on the border, resulted in Thatcher warning Lynch about a possible backlash against Irish citizens in the UK. In November Lynch was replaced as Fianna Fáil leader and taoiseach by Charles J. Haughey who wanted a more dynamic northern policy. At their first official summit meeting, in London in May 1980, Haughey sought to impress Thatcher by presenting her with a silver Georgian tea set (by her own admission, she was initially impressed). Yet tensions soon

Patrick Hillery became president of Ireland in 1976. He is pictured here with Pope John Paul II (Poland's Karol Wojtyła) at Dublin Airport during the latter's visit to Ireland from 29 September to 1 October 1979 (with the Aer Lingus Boeing 747 on which the pope travelled in the background). John Paul did not visit Northern Ireland due to security concerns. The major public events he attended in Ireland, culminating in a vast open-air mass in Dublin's Phoenix Park, remain the largest confirmed public gatherings in Irish history. The visit can be taken as the high-point of official Catholicism in independent Ireland.

L–R: Minister for Foreign Affairs Brian Lenihan and Andrew O'Rourke, Permanent Representative of Ireland to the EC and former secretary general of the Department of Foreign Affairs, attending a European Council meeting in Luxembourg, 29 June 1981. Also visible is French president François Mitterrand.

Prime Minister Margaret Thatcher and Taoiseach Charles Haughey at the Anglo-Irish summit held in Dublin Castle, 8 December 1980. To the left of Thatcher are Sir Geoffrey Howe, Chancellor of the Exchequer, and Lord Carrington, Secretary of State for Foreign and Commonwealth Affairs. Key Irish figures include Minister for Finance Michael O'Kennedy (behind Thatcher on her left). Behind him on his right is Eamonn Kennedy, then ambassador to the UK, and on his left is Sean O hUiginn, who later played a key role in the peace process as head of the Anglo-Irish division of the department and also served as Irish ambassador to the US.

crept into the relationship between the two leaders. A dispute between Dublin and London came in December 1980 over the meaning of the phrase 'totality of relationships', as used in the joint communique issued by Haughey and Thatcher after the Anglo-Irish summit held on 8 December. Their very different public interpretations of the implications of these words led to an acrimonious rift between Dublin and London.

Since the late 1970s the question of the status of republican prisoners in Northern Ireland's jails had been emerging, and this soon came to constitute a crisis in its own right. Hunger strikes by republican prisoners in Irish prisons had been condemned by the Vatican on humanitarian grounds in 1977, which prompted a stern rebuke to the Holy See from the Cosgrave government. By late 1978, however, Lynch's government was raising allegations of the mistreatment of prisoners in Northern Ireland with the British, though any communications on the matter fell short of recommending that the prisoners be accorded any special, or political, status. In 1981 ten republican prisoners starved themselves to death in Northern Ireland in a protest against their official categorisation as criminals. The hunger strikes in the 'H-Blocks' of the Maze Prison (so-called after their physical layout) prompted an enormous wave of public sympathy that made itself felt at the ballot box. Provisional IRA hunger striker Bobby Sands was elected to the British parliament in 1981, before he died following 66 days without food (two other hunger strikers were elected to the Dáil). The votes for the hunger-strike candidates suggested that there was a constituency that would offer political support to militant republicanism.

What appeared to be a cordial, if not yet constructive, rapport between Thatcher and Haughey was seriously damaged by the unwillingness of the Irish government to support the renewal of EC sanctions against Argentina (which it had previously supported) after the British sinking of the Argentine naval cruiser *General Belgrano* in May 1982 during the Falklands War with the loss of over 300 lives. Later that year Haughey's government fell, however, and after a sustained period of instability, it was replaced in 1983 by a new Fine Gael and Labour Party coalition, led by Garret FitzGerald as taoiseach.

The official advice FitzGerald had received from the Department of Foreign Affairs on taking office for the second

Noel Dorr, as president of the
UN Security Council, calls a
meeting of the council to order,
1 August 1982. Ireland has been
elected as a rotating member on
the Security Council on three
occasions (the most recent term
served was in 2000–01), and as
of 2019 is seeking a fourth term.
Directly behind Dorr are Irish
officials Jeremy Craig (seated)
and Declan Kelleher (standing).

time was that Thatcher did not see Northern Ireland as an
automatic priority. But the hunger strikes of 1981 cast a long
shadow. Given the degree of public sympathy that was registered electorally for the hunger strikers, there were very real
fears that republicanism in the form of Sinn Féin could dislodge
the constitutional nationalism of the SDLP. The 'New Ireland
Forum' of 1984 was the result of this prospect; a consultative
body established by the Irish government to map out possible
paths to a settlement.

The Irish government remained wary of the conflict spilling
over the border, but was by now firmly convinced that addressing nationalist alienation in Northern Ireland was essential to
any resolution of the conflict. It also believed that this had to be
pressed home to a British government preoccupied with finding
a military and security solution to what the Irish side interpreted
more broadly as a political problem.

FitzGerald took the view that Thatcher could be persuaded
that the improved security cooperation that was her particular concern could best be secured by according the Irish

government a more substantial political role, and even perhaps a security presence on the ground in Northern Ireland, in return for a more explicit acceptance by Dublin of the existing status of Northern Ireland. He instructed Michael Lillis of the department's Anglo-Irish division, to privately convey an informal proposal along these lines to David Goodall, deputy secretary of the Cabinet Office, on the occasion of a meeting in Dublin in the autumn of 1983.

Thatcher was initially unenthusiastic but following a summit meeting with FitzGerald at Chequers in November 1983 she agreed to further exploratory contacts with Dublin at official level. This developed into intensive confidential negotiations, extending over nearly two years, between teams comprising four or five officials from each side, led by the respective Cabinet secretaries, Dermot Nally and Sir Robert Armstrong. In addition to the senior officials from home departments— Foreign Affairs, Justice and the Attorney General's office on the Irish side and from the Foreign Office, and later the Northern

Noel Dorr in conversation with Zehdi Labib Terzi of the Palestinian Liberation Organisation (PLO) in the Security Council chamber, 6 August 1982. The Israeli invasion of Lebanon was intended to be an attack on the PLO, then based in Lebanon. This meeting of the UN saw the adoption of another resolution calling on Israeli forces to be withdrawn from the vicinity of Beirut, though the US abstained from the vote.

Ireland Office, on the British side—the respective ambassadors were also involved. In the Irish embassy in London, a middle-level diplomat, Richard Ryan, was assigned the particular role of cultivating contacts with backbench British MPs (particularly on the Conservative side) to gain support for the Irish government's case on the necessity of a political settlement in Northern Ireland—a task that FitzGerald later described in his memoirs as 'dining for Ireland'. At each stage the negotiators reported to their respective ministers and ultimately to the heads of their government. FitzGerald and Thatcher followed the negotiations closely, gave direction to the negotiators at all stages and also discussed progress both at bilateral summits and on the margins of numerous EC meetings.

While these negotiations were under way, the deliberations of the New Ireland Forum commenced in Dublin. In the end, four nationalist political parties took part—Fianna Fáil, Fine Gael, Labour, and from Northern Ireland the SDLP. Unionist parties did not attend. The proceedings extended from May 1983 to May 1984 and in its final report, the forum set out a series of broad principles that emphasised the need for respect for both the nationalist and unionist identities in Ireland and the need for 'the political arrangements for a new and sovereign Ireland...to be freely negotiated and agreed to by the people of the North and by the people of the South'. While it expressed its preference for 'a unitary state, achieved by agreement and consent, embracing the whole island of Ireland with guarantees for both identities', the report also outlined two other possibilities: a 'federal/confederal state', and a system of 'joint authority' to be exercised by both governments.

Thatcher strongly and publicly rejected the three main recommendations of the forum report, but FitzGerald remained conciliatory, and the confidential negotiations between the two governments continued. The Irish government took the view that the statement in the forum report that the parties remained 'open to discuss other views which might contribute to political development', provided a good basis for its decision to maintain negotiations.

The eventual outcome was the Anglo-Irish Agreement, signed by the two prime ministers at Hillsborough Castle in Northern Ireland on 15 November 1985. In it the two governments agreed

Ambassador Denis Holmes with his son Michael on the roof of the Irish embassy in New Delhi. The mobile nature of diplomatic life could bring pressure to bear on the families of diplomats, though equally, families provided invaluable and often overlooked support to diplomats in their various postings.

Opposite: The official menu for a state banquet in Tokyo in honour of President of Ireland Patrick Hillery in September 1983. Hillery was the first Irish head of state to visit Japan. In March 1985 Crown Prince Akihito and Princess Michiko paid a reciprocal state visit to Ireland. Through the 1970s and the 1980s Japan and Ireland developed important bilateral investment and trade links, though these links also grew within the wider context of Japan–EEC relations.

WELCOME DINNER

in honour of

His Excellency Dr. Patrick J. Hillery

The President of Ireland

and

Dr. Maeve Hillery

Thursday, September 15th 1983

at Restaurant Tsuruya, Kyoto

that 'any change in the status of Northern Ireland would only come about with the consent of a majority of the people of Northern Ireland'; and they also agreed, that, if in the future a majority consented to a united Ireland, they would give effect to that wish.

The agreement (which was subsequently registered at the United Nations) gave the Irish government an unprecedented role in relation to Northern Ireland. It would be entitled to put forward views and proposals to the British government and 'determined efforts' would be made to reach agreement. An incentive to the Northern Ireland parties to agree to a sharing of power at local level was that any Irish role in relation to the internal affairs of Northern Ireland would apply only insofar as the matters in question were not the responsibility of a devolved administration. An Intergovernmental Conference was also established to deal with judicial, political, security and legal matters, as well as with the promotion of cross-border cooperation. Finally, a joint Anglo-Irish Secretariat, headed by Michael Lillis on the Irish side, was set up in Belfast to service the conference and to provide an established channel for sustained input from the Irish government.

The Irish delegation to the United Nations at the thirty-ninth regular session of the General Assembly, 25 September 1984. (L–R): Ted Barrington (Department of Foreign Affairs), Assistant Secretary Pádraig MacKernan, Michael Sanfey (at back left, hand to mouth), Ambassador Bob McDonagh, Pat O'Connor (at back, hand to mouth), and Minister for Foreign Affairs Peter Barry. In general, foreign ministers attend the General Assembly in person during the early weeks of its annual session, which in this case had commenced on 18 September.

US president Ronald Reagan speaks to the press on the steps of the White House during the St Patrick's Day Shamrock Ceremony, March 1986. During Reagan's presidency Irish attempts to solicit US influence in favour of a political settlement continued. This may have led to Reagan's encouragement of Margaret Thatcher to accept the Anglo-Irish Agreement of 1985. Reagan is flanked by (L–R) Pádraig MacKernan (ambassador of Ireland to the US), Dermot Nally (secretary general, Department of the Taoiseach), Seán Donlon (secretary general, Department of Foreign Affairs), George Schultz (US secretary of state), George Bush Sr (US vice-president) and Taoiseach Garret FitzGerald.

The agreement was met with outrage by unionist parties in Northern Ireland, and by mass street protests over several years. The Irish officials who were seconded to the secretariat were based at Maryfield outside Belfast, where they lived for a number of years under the most stringent security arrangements; even their families had to be placed under 24-hour police protection for fear of loyalist paramilitary attack. The two governments continued to work the agreement over the following years, however, and, as its structure was wholly intergovernmental, it could not be brought down as the Sunningdale Agreement had been brought down by the loyalist strike of May 1974.

The conflict continued on the ground in Northern Ireland, but there was now, for the first time, a structured channel within which to address problems and difficulties, as well as improving security cooperation, between the two governments. Although it was vehemently opposed by republicans and loyalists at the time, the Anglo-Irish Agreement had an important effect on both, in different ways; it helped to pave the way for the 1998 Good Friday ('Belfast') Agreement that ultimately superseded it.

The British and Irish teams negotiating the Anglo-Irish Agreement pictured together at Chevening, the country residence of the British foreign secretary, May 1985. The Anglo-Irish Agreement of November 1985 was the outcome of two years of intensive exchanges between the British and the Irish governments, during which the two teams of officials met for some thirty-six confidential sessions on one or other side of the Irish Sea. There were also frequent meetings and exchanges at ministerial level and between Taoiseach Garret FitzGerald and Prime Minister Margaret Thatcher. Back row (L–R): David Goodall (Foreign and Commonwealth Office and also for a time deputy Cabinet secretary); Tony Brennan (deputy secretary, Northern Ireland Office); Seán Donlon (secretary, Department of Foreign Affairs); Andy Ward (secretary, Department of Justice); Michael Lillis (assistant secretary and head of Anglo-Irish Division, Department of Foreign Affairs); Henry Darwin (legal adviser, Foreign and Commonwealth Office); Tony Stephens (Northern Ireland Office), Declan Quigley (senior legal assistant, Office of the Attorney General); Christopher Mallaby (Foreign and Commonwealth Office, who succeeded David Goodall as deputy Cabinet secretary). Front row (L–R): Sir Alan Goodison (UK ambassador to Ireland), Dermot Nally (secretary to the Irish government) Sir Robert Armstrong (British Cabinet secretary); Noel Dorr (Irish ambassador to the UK).

Taoiseach Garret FitzGerald
and Prime Minister Margaret
Thatcher at the centre of a
media throng during the press
conference at Hillsborough Castle
outside Belfast to announce
the signing of the Anglo-Irish
Agreement, 15 November 1985.

Unionist protestors at a rally in Belfast opposing the Anglo-Irish Agreement on 25 November 1985. The agreement gave the Irish government an unprecedented consultative role in Northern Ireland affairs. This was a tangible recognition that any settlement in Northern Ireland would have to incorporate an 'Irish' dimension, and that the Irish government had a stake in a settlement. For this reason, the agreement was met with widespread opposition from within the unionist and loyalist community.

Below: The Anglo-Irish Agreement established a secretariat staffed on the Irish side by members of the Departments of Foreign Affairs and Justice at Maryfield, just outside Belfast. Some of the Anglo-Irish Secretariat staff and British officials are pictured here outside the secretariat building. Back row (L–R): Noel Ryan (assistant secretary general, Department of Justice), Barry Noonan, Steve Hewitt (assistant secretary, Northern Ireland Office). Middle row (L–R): Mary Quealy (Department of Foreign Affairs), unidentified, Valerie Steele (principal officer, Northern Ireland Office), Dáithí O'Ceallaigh (Department of Foreign Affairs), Daire Ó Críodáin (Department of Foreign Affairs), Front row (L–R): Michael Lillis (Department of Foreign Affairs, Irish joint-secretary), Roger Miller (Northern Ireland Office), Caroline Bolger (Department of Foreign Affairs), unidentified, Mark Elliott (Foreign and Commonwealth Office). The secretariat staff conducted their business under conditions of strict security, due to the real prospect of attack by loyalist paramilitaries; their families were also placed under police protection.

President Patrick Hillery with President of China Yang Shangkun outside the Great Hall of the People in Beijing on the first state visit by a president of Ireland to the People's Republic of China, May 1988 (though former president of Ireland Cearbhaill Ó Dálaigh had visited China in 1977 after he left office). Ireland and China had established diplomatic relations in June 1979, and Ireland's first ambassador to China, John Campbell, presented his credentials in May 1980. President Hillery visited many historical and cultural locations in China, but developing trade between both countries was the important wider context to the visit; Minister for Industry and Commerce Albert Reynolds headed a trade mission to China the previous month.

CONSULAR SERVICES

In 1942 the Irish writer (and future Nobel laureate) Samuel Beckett found his freedom of movement restricted when he was residing near Avignon under the Vichy regime. Consequently, he contacted Con Cremin at the Irish legation in Paris for assistance. Offering support to Irish citizens travelling and living abroad is an everyday reality of the work of Irish diplomats, and helping citizens in distress or during . crises is generally the most commonly reported consular activity. Providing protection, assistance and services to the Irish abroad has been a mainstay of consular work since the foundation of the Irish diplomatic service.

The Irish consular network can trace its origins to the Dáil Éireann foreign service, and it expanded from the 1920s onward. Some of the first consular records relate to the issuing of Irish visas in New York to Americans planning to disembark from transatlantic liners in Cobh, Co. Cork. During this era, a network of Irish consulates grew rapidly. The vast majority were headed by honorary consuls: men and women holding essentially voluntary appointments across the globe. As of 2019, Ireland has 15 consulates and 99 honorary consuls across the world.

Consular work continues to be a core function of almost every diplomatic mission. More Irish people are travelling than ever before, and to more destinations, therefore consular services have to keep up with the demand. Every embassy has an officer on 24-hour call, and in the twenty-first century consular assistance is also delivered online. The provision of such services remains a vital part of Irish diplomatic officers' responsibilities overseas.

1985–
1998

The end of the Cold War, European integration, and paths to a settlement in Northern Ireland

Soviet leader Mikhail Gorbachev meets Taoiseach Charles Haughey at Shannon Airport, Co. Clare on 2 April 1989. Since 1980 Shannon had been used as a stop-over point by the Soviet state airline, Aeroflot, for refuelling and repairs. Gorbachev's visit took place as part of a wider tour of Western European states undertaken as part of his 'Glasnost' (openness) policy, which ultimately led to the ending of the Cold War. To Gorbachev's right is Soviet Foreign Minister (and future president of Georgia) Eduard Shevardnadze. On Haughey's right is Minister for Foreign Affairs Brian Lenihan, while Minister for Finance (and future taoiseach) Albert Reynolds can be seen second from the end of the table, with Dermot Nally, secretary to the government, on his left at the end of the table.

Irish government policies, whether foreign or domestic, in the 1980s were shaped by an economic reality: recession, the existence of a huge (and increasing) national debt, and the recurrence of emigration on a huge scale—more than 61,000 (out of a population of over 3.5 million) people left Ireland in 1988, two-thirds of whom went to the UK. In 1984 there had been fears that an intervention by the International Monetary Fund (IMF) would be required to place the Irish state back on a secure financial footing (precisely what would happen in 2010). In these circumstances, the Department of Foreign Affairs was not immune to cutbacks. In the mid 1980s there were attempts to rein in expenditure on entertaining visiting dignitaries; there were always exceptions, however, and entertainment could be laid on in style for dignitaries such as US president Ronald Reagan (in the case of the latter, however, at the state dinner accompanying his visit in 1984, the best wine was reserved for the top table rather than being served across the board).

For a small state such as Ireland, foreign policy often reflected economic policy and the expansion of one could potentially be held back by the requirements of the other. In 1980, for example, Taoiseach Charles Haughey had been invited to visit Iraq. Foreign Affairs, wary of how the visit might look to outside

observers, suggested that because the potential economic links were of great importance, any such visit ought to coincide with a trade fair. The visit was postponed due to the outbreak of the Iran–Iraq War, but the debate around it illustrates the balance that foreign policy had to establish.

The Middle East and the Muslim world became an important export market for Irish beef throughout the 1980s, though US outrage at state-sponsored terrorism by Libya, including support for the IRA, posed problems for Irish beef exports to that country. Ireland managed to remain broadly independent of the UK and US throughout the 1980s on issues ranging from the Falklands conflict to Libya. Both states were trading partners, but Irish economic growth in the later twentieth century was rooted in another development: the acceleration of the process of European integration.

●

Ireland held the EC presidency in 1984, when reform of the CAP and enlargement negotiations with Spain and Portugal

Irish links to the Middle East extended beyond Lebanon. Here, Niall Holohan, chargé d'affaires at the Irish embassy in Tehran, moves to shake hands with Iranian foreign minister Ali Akbar Velayati in Tehran, 1985. The man in the black turban to his left is Iranian president (and current supreme leader of the Islamic Republic) Ayatollah Ali Khamenei.

Ireland

VON NATUR AUS GUT

Halle 2.1   Stand F2/G4   Halle 13.2   Stand M9

ANUGA • KÖLN 10.– 15.10.1987

The cover of the Irish brochure issued at the Anuga trade fair in Cologne, October 1987. The promotion of Irish manufacturing overseas was made all the more important in the challenging economic climate of the 1980s. Anuga remains one of the world's largest agrifood trade fairs.

loomed large. In terms of foreign policy, 1985 proved to be a crucial year. Alongside the negotiation of the Anglo-Irish Agreement, it witnessed the beginnings of the historic rapprochement between the US and Soviet Union, which led to the ending of the Cold War. It also saw the most significant potential change in the EC since its establishment in 1957. The negotiation of the Single European Act prepared the way for the single market and opened the door to further European integration by formalising and expanding the powers of bodies such as the European Commission and European Parliament. It also expanded the range of treaty commitments by member states into neglected areas such as the environment. Furthermore, it challenged Ireland's traditional neutral stance, which generally commanded popular assent. Questions about whether the EC might pose a threat to Irish neutrality and, indeed, Irish sovereignty, would become a recurring theme of public debate about Europe. Indeed, neutrality was raised as a general election issue in 1987 by both Fianna Fáil and the left-wing Workers Party.

In 1987, following a case taken by economist Raymond Crotty, the Irish Supreme Court adjudicated that the Single European Act could not be ratified, except by referendum. A referendum had, after all, been required for Ireland to join the EEC in the first place. From then on Irish governments could not avoid public debates about Europe. This prompted Charles Haughey (who had become taoiseach once again in 1987) to reassure Helmut Kohl of Germany and François Mitterrand of France that Irish commitment to the EC was not in any doubt. Subsequently, Irish governments sought to raise public awareness of the EC—which would change its name to the European Union (EU) after the ratification of the 1992 Maastricht Treaty—as it seemed inevitable that the various stages of meaningful European integration would have to be put to the Irish electorate. (This shift towards raising awareness of the benefits of EU membership was also evident in other EU member states).

The implementation of European Monetary Union and the development of the single market were the core issues for the EC in the late 1980s. Both proved beneficial to the Irish economy as Haughey's government embarked upon a recovery strategy with the tacit assistance of its Fine Gael opponents. Foreign direct investment, so crucial to economic policy since the 1960s, was encouraged across a range of sectors, such as chemicals, electronics and pharmaceuticals. The European single market made Ireland a far more attractive prospect to US firms willing to base themselves in an Anglophone country that was committed to a European single currency (later called the 'euro'), and which was to benefit in the 1990s from major injections of EU structural funding aimed at overhauling Ireland's infrastructure. By then, the success of this economic strategy would be evident.

The fourth Irish EC presidency, in 1990, coincided with the collapse of the Soviet Union and the ending of the Cold War.

Diplomatic relations between the Czech Republic and Ireland were officially established on 1 January 1993, and the embassy of Ireland to the Czech Republic opened in Prague in 1995. Here Marie Cross, Ireland's first ambassador to the Czech Republic, is pictured with Czech president Vaclav Havel, in July 1999, on her farewell visit. Ireland had hoped to open its first diplomatic mission in Central Europe in Prague in 1947, but this plan was abandoned after the Communist coup of February 1948. While trade links were established in the 1970s, diplomatic relations prior to 1995 were conducted through Czech and Irish ambassadors resident in, respectively, the United Kingdom and Austria.

Haughey was widely praised for overseeing the brokering of broad European support for German reunification, despite the reservations of France and the UK. Another key outcome was the opening of the discussions that led to the 1992 Maastricht Treaty, which formally established the European Union. Irish neutrality again became an issue, as Maastricht proposed deeper arrangements for European security co-operation. Specific provisions ensuring that such a common agreement would not supersede individual member states' security policies were incorporated into the final version of the treaty. Ireland's 1990 presidency also introduced innovations such as bilateral European meetings with the US president. As European integration continued to progress, Ireland located itself firmly within the project. The original Irish focus on the EEC had emphasised how membership of the communities could be in Ireland's national self-interest; but over time, this almost transactional approach had evolved into an awareness that Irish interests were also served by the broader success of the EU.

Ireland's increasing commitment to the emerging EU did not dilute the significance of the UN for the Irish state, which still devoted a good deal of attention to peacekeeping in the Middle East. Tensions with Israel were compounded in 1987 by the death of Corporal Dermot McLaughlin, killed in what was believed to have been the deliberate targeting of a UN post in Lebanon. The incident prompted a debate on whether or not to withdraw from UNIFIL completely. At the same time, tentative commercial links with Iran were not pursued when the backdrop of the Iranian Revolution ensured that one major power in the Middle East was firmly defined as an enemy of Britain and the US; Ireland was in no position to alienate either, and so prospective Iranian links were set aside.

One international cause that came to public prominence in Ireland was opposition to the apartheid regime in South Africa. This issue had gathered increasing public support, as demonstrated by the lengthy strike undertaken by staff of the supermarket chain Dunnes Stores in protest at being obliged to handle South African produce. The government was of the view that unilateral sanctions against South Africa would be ineffective (though there were running tensions with the Irish Rugby Football Union over its willingness to continue engaging with its South African counterpart in defiance of international sporting boycotts). Instead, Ireland co-sponsored a UN resolution in 1985 advocating rolling sanctions on South Africa.

•

The most significant development in Irish foreign policy in the late 1980s and early 1990s was the pursuit of a peace process in Northern Ireland and the negotiations that led to the Good Friday Agreement of 1998. The elements for a successful settlement in Northern Ireland had essentially been mapped out in the 1970s as part of the Sunningdale Agreement. Equally, Irish governments and diplomats had slowly and patiently sought to convince their British counterparts that any settlement would have to contain elements that extended beyond the six counties of Northern Ireland: its relationships with Ireland, and with the rest of the UK, would have to be incorporated into any successful package. The broad contours of what was required had been established. The question now was how to ensure that the various parties could negotiate an acceptable settlement within those parameters. This was not an easy process: unionist parties found the prospect of negotiating with Sinn Féin, which commanded a significant electoral mandate but was, in their view, inextricably linked to the paramilitary Provisional IRA, unacceptable at this early stage. Moreover, any settlement that did not ensure peace was bound to be undermined. Nor, at this stage, was Margaret Thatcher's government prepared to place engagement on a process that was not guaranteed to lead to a settlement in Northern Ireland above its own security needs. The British emphasis on security, especially in regard to what it viewed as a porous border with Ireland from which IRA attacks could be planned, did not automatically tally with Irish concerns for the status of nationalists in Northern Ireland.

Fianna Fáil returned to power in 1987 and, despite having roundly condemned the Anglo-Irish Agreement, the party was content to continue to implement it. Tensions over security matters emerged in relation to the question of the extradition of suspects such as Patrick Ryan (a Catholic priest accused of involvement in the IRA) to the UK. Given that Ireland had signed the European Convention on the Prevention of Terrorism in 1986, this was interpreted by the British as Irish unwillingness to tackle problems of concern to them. Haughey's government, for its part, was unimpressed by British actions such as the abandonment of an inquiry into alleged shoot-to-kill policies by British security forces, the upholding of the convictions of the Birmingham Six (wrongly accused of carrying out lethal no-warning pub bombings in Birmingham in 1974), and a number of contentious killings by British security forces. It was becoming clear, however, that the Anglo-Irish Agreement had not reached its full potential; as early as February 1988 Haughey spoke privately of the possibility of direct dialogue with parties in Northern Ireland. Such an eventuality was some way off. John Hume had met the Sinn Féin leader, Gerry Adams, in 1988 to discuss a possible IRA ceasefire, but nothing came of this. Nevertheless, the assumption was that paramilitaries were not wedded to war for its own sake, and that a shift to achieving objectives by solely political means was possible.

In 1992 a series of talks took place in Belfast involving the British and Irish governments and the main democratic parties in Northern Ireland, including the DUP. These were the first

discussions of this kind since partition. They were inconclusive, but might be seen in hindsight as a watershed, the major figures had, at least, been prepared to speak to each other in this way. Some of the most significant actors, however, were absent: the paramilitary organisations that were responsible for the vast majority of killings.

More meaningful progress came in the early 1990s with the advent of a new Conservative prime minister, John Major, and a new Fianna Fáil taoiseach, Albert Reynolds, who decided to take a more pro-active approach to seeking a settlement in Northern Ireland. The secretary of state for Northern Ireland, Peter Brooke, had declared in 1992 that Britain had no 'selfish strategic or economic interest' in remaining in Northern Ireland. There emerged from the British government a sense of willingness to facilitate a political settlement, a stance confirmed by the 1993 Downing Street Declaration. It set out the broad parameters of a settlement and committed both governments to negotiations with all relevant parties should they be committed to 'exclusively peaceful methods'. It also committed the British government to recognising a right of self-determination

Taoiseach Albert Reynolds and Prime Minister John Major attend the Five Nations rugby match between England and Ireland at Twickenham in London, 19 February 1994 (Ireland won the match 13–12). Major succeeded Margaret Thatcher as prime minister in 1990. Reynolds succeeded Charles Haughey as taoiseach in 1992, and immediately made the securing of an embryonic peace process in Northern Ireland a priority. Both men had established a rapport whilst serving as minister for Finance and chancellor of the Exchequer respectively, and the Joint Declaration (Downing St Declaration) signed by the British and Irish governments on 15 December 1993 became one of the cornerstones of the emerging peace process.

Tánaiste and Minister for Foreign Affairs (and Labour Party leader) Dick Spring leaving Castle Buildings at Stormont during all-party talks in June 1996. The IRA ceasefire of August 1994 had ended with the bombing of London's Canary Wharf in February 1996. Sinn Féin was excluded from these talks until the reinstatement of the IRA ceasefire in July 1997.

for the island of Ireland as a whole, to be exercised on either side of the border, and to recognise any settlement that might be agreed, up to and including a united Ireland. This document was drafted between the two governments with the hands-on assistance of Irish officials such as Sean O hUiginn, the head of the Anglo-Irish Division, and advisers such as Fergus Finlay and Martin Mansergh. The agreement committed the two governments to discussing the future of Northern Ireland with all parties in the event of paramilitary ceasefires. Figures such as the Catholic priest Alec Reid, who had facilitated the 1988 meetings between Hume and Adams, and the Presbyterian minister Roy Magee acted as discreet but essential conduits to republican and loyalist paramilitaries respectively.

Highly secret negotiations between the British and Irish governments and both republican and loyalist paramilitaries resulted in ceasefires being called in 1994. The path to substantive negotiations was, however, impeded by the fall of Reynolds's government and the shifting political arithmetic of Westminster. British demands for the decommissioning of paramilitary weapons (interpreted as a necessity for Major's government to retain the support of unionist MPs at Westminster) were seen by the IRA as an unacceptable attempt to humiliate it with a symbolic surrender. IRA bombings in London and Manchester in 1996 ended their first ceasefire. Multi-party talks, chaired by US senator George Mitchell, began in June 1996, with Sinn Féin excluded. Then, the election of new governments in Dublin and London in 1997 (led by Bertie Ahern and Tony Blair respectively) led to intensified negotiations with Sinn Féin present, after the IRA restored its ceasefire (though the DUP absented itself). The outcome of these laborious negotiations was the Good Friday Agreement. The key objective from the Irish side was to maintain the peace that had existed, for the most part, since the 1994 ceasefires, and from that to build a political consensus.

The agreement itself established an elected assembly and power-sharing executive; this internal arrangement within Northern Ireland was the first 'strand' of the agreement, which was firmly located alongside two additional 'strands' dealing with north-south and east-west relations (the latter referring to relations between Ireland and the wider UK). The north-south strand involved the establishment of a North-South Ministerial Council, with a joint secretariat based in Armagh and staffed by civil servants from both Ireland and Northern Ireland. The political structures established under the agreement were to be accompanied by commitments on human rights and equality, policing reform, and rolling programmes of demilitarisation and prisoner releases.

The agreement also addressed fundamental matters of both ideology and identity: part of the agreement involved the modification of articles 2 and 3 of the Irish constitution, to replace the territorial claim on Northern Ireland, which had long been a contentious issue for unionists, with a peaceful aspiration to unity; it also permitted those living in Northern Ireland to define themselves legally as Irish, or British, or indeed both. The agreement was endorsed overwhelmingly in referenda north and south of the Irish border; this served to address another issue. Since partition, republicans had argued that the exercise of Ireland's right to self-determination could only take place if Ireland was an all-island unit; partition, they claimed, undercut this right, and this was used as an argument to dismiss the legitimacy of the jurisdictions on either side of the border. Given that it was voted on simultaneously north and south, the ratification of the agreement could be deemed an act of self-determination in its own right. The Good Friday Agreement was complemented by a separate British–Irish agreement registered with the UN.

The implementation of the agreement was contentious. The fragility of the process was shown by the fact that a republican splinter group carried out the deadliest single attack of the Troubles on a Saturday afternoon in August 1998: after the agreement was signed. They planted a car bomb in the market town of Omagh, Co. Tyrone, causing the deaths of 29 civilians.

The Good Friday Agreement can be seen as the eventual outcome of what had been a key focal point of Irish foreign policy for successive Irish governments since the early 1970s. Undoubtedly the SDLP leader John Hume was enormously influential in shaping the analysis of the Northern Ireland conflict adopted by Irish diplomats in developing a Northern Ireland policy; it was left to his deputy Seamus Mallon, however, to sum up the continuity between the efforts made to end the Troubles in the 1970s and those of the 1990s that eventually succeeded: the Good Friday Agreement was, according to Mallon, simply Sunningdale for slow learners. Mallon's willingness to invoke the failed settlement of 1973 took place in the very different circumstances of 1998, but it contained a considerable grain of truth: the core planks of the Good Friday Agreement—power-sharing and the need to recognise an all-island dimension to the issue— had been foreshadowed a quarter of a century previously.

Opposite: The official Irish copy of the Good Friday Agreement, signed on 10 April 1998. The republican and loyalist paramilitary ceasefires had provided a basis for a political settlement in Northern Ireland, though formal negotiations towards a settlement did not begin until 1997. Negotiated under the overall chairmanship of the former Democratic leader of the United States Senate, George Mitchell, this was the first political settlement in Northern Ireland to be subscribed to by mainstream nationalist and unionist parties as well as republican and loyalist parties assumed to have links to paramilitary groups. The three 'strands' of the agreement established, respectively, a power-sharing government within Northern Ireland, a set of north-south structures on the island of Ireland, and a set of east-west structures dealing with the wider relationship between Ireland and Britain. The signatories were Taoiseach Bertie Ahern, Minister for Foreign Affairs David Andrews, British Prime Minister Tony Blair and Northern Ireland Secretary Marjorie 'Mo' Mowlam.

In witness thereof the undersigned, being duly authorised thereto by the respective Governments, have signed this Agreement.

Done in two originals at Belfast on the 10th day of April 1998.

For the Government of Ireland

For the Government of the United Kingdom of Great Britain and Northern Ireland

1998–
2019

Irish foreign policy in the twenty-first century

In 1996 the Department of Foreign Affairs set out, for the first time, a comprehensive and public statement of intent. The White Paper *Challenges and opportunities abroad* was a substantial volume drafted with considerable public input; it set out a programme that sought to combine Irish national self-interest with broader commitments to more general ethical principles. It presented an official statement of Ireland's place within the wider world for the first time in almost 80 years, and addressed Ireland's international roles in the UN and the EU, as well as its stance on issues such as peacekeeping, human rights, environmental concerns and development aid, the role of the Irish abroad and the diaspora, and even the democratic accountability of Irish foreign policy. As the twentieth century drew to a close, the White Paper spelled out the signature policies and key areas of international importance to the Irish state. The development of the White Paper, and the appointment of ministers of state (junior ministerial positions) to the Department of Foreign Affairs, indicated how the Irish state now assigned a greater degree of importance to its international profile.

●

As ever, such commitments as the policy document contained did not develop in isolation. Throughout the 1990s Ireland's economy grew at an unprecedented rate, and trade promotion and increasing foreign direct investment remained integral to Irish foreign policy. The 1990s saw a new emphasis on developing Irish links with Asia, but the most crucial markets for Irish business remained closer to home: on 1 January 1999 Ireland joined the euro area (the currency itself came into circulation later) and soon became the fastest-growing economy in the Eurozone.

Beyond the EU, the United Nations remained at the core of Irish foreign policy. Mary Robinson, who had been elected as Ireland's first woman president in November 1990, was appointed UN High Commissioner for Human Rights in 1997 for a five-year term, and Ireland, led by Ambassador to the UN Richard Ryan, held the chair of the United Nations Human Rights Council in 1999. In 2001 Ireland sat on the UN Security Council

A lawyer by profession, Mary Robinson served as president of Ireland from 1990 to 1997 and was noted for supporting a wide range of humanitarian causes throughout her career. She served as UN High Commissioner for Human Rights from 1997 to 2002. She is pictured here in July 2016 in her capacity as special envoy of the secretary-general on El Niño and Climate.

The UN Security Council observes a moment's silence on 12 September 2001 to mark the '9/11' attacks in the US. Ireland was, at the time, serving a third term as a non-permanent member of the Security Council. The Irish delegation, including Ambassador Richard Ryan, are at the top-left of the image.

for a third term. During this term, the 11 September attacks on the United States occurred, and were unanimously condemned by the Security Council. Ireland played a constructive role in peace-making efforts in Timor Leste (including through the provision of a peace-keeping presence there) and in Angola, which was emerging from civil war. Security Council membership also saw Ireland active in the Middle Eastern peace process, seeking a settlement that respected the rights of all parties to the Israel-Palestine conflict and advocating a two-state solution to an issue that was of long-term interest to Irish diplomacy.

Ireland also supported the first Security Council resolution on Iraqi weapons of mass destruction. After its Security Council term ended, Ireland's relatively high profile within the UN system continued, through membership of the Human Rights Commission from 2003 to 2005. Ireland's UN policy promoted enhancing human rights globally, supporting a rules-based international order, and achieving sustainable development goals;

this policy corresponded with greater public interest in such issues as debt relief as a concrete form of aid to the developing world. Ireland also continued to maintain its long-term policy of promoting both conventional and nuclear disarmament.

The role of Ireland's Defence Forces in peacekeeping continued in the early years of the twenty-first century. In 1998 Ireland had signed a memorandum of understanding with the United Nations, committing the Defence Forces to participation in the UN Standby Arrangements System (UNSAS) and offering to provide up to 850 Defence Forces personnel for UN peacekeeping operations at any given time. By the first decade of the twenty-first century, contingents from the Defence Forces could be found serving with the UN in missions in Africa, Asia, the Middle East and Europe. In 1999 Ireland joined the NATO-led Partnership for Peace (PfP). This was not a military alliance, and membership of PfP took into account Ireland's long-standing policy of military neutrality.

Ireland subsequently participated in the NATO-led, UN-mandated SFOR mission to Bosnia and Herzegovina, and in KFOR, the NATO-led peace-support operation in Kosovo. A further development in 1999 was Ireland's obtaining observer status in the Western European Union, and its involvement in the creation of an EU Rapid Reaction Force. These moves were also concerned with improving the capacity of the Defence Forces to participate in international peace-support missions, and with demonstrating that Ireland was fulfilling its European security commitments, while still respecting its traditional neutrality. Defence Forces participation in the United Nations Mission in Liberia (UNMIL), and from 2003 in the European Union EUFOR mission in Chad and later in EU 'Battlegroups', brought more firmly into public discourse the operation of the 'triple lock' mechanism whereby government and Dáil approval and a UN Security Council mandate is required for Irish participation in any form of peace-support or peacekeeping mission.

Public sentiment remained strongly supportive of Irish neutrality. In the aftermath of the 11 September attacks a long-term debate re-emerged as to Ireland's actual attitude to its traditional neutrality, in relation to the United States-led 'war on terror'. The Irish government had, after the US-led invasion of Iraq in March 2003, permitted United States military aircraft bound

A member of the Irish Defence Forces distributes humanitarian aid in Kosovo, under the auspices of the NATO-led Kosovo Force (KFOR). Following the break-up of the former Yugoslavia, Kosovo was governed by Serbia, but resistance to Serb rule and the resulting policy of repression by Serbia, which saw vast numbers of Kosovars being displaced, prompted the UN to recognise an imminent humanitarian crisis. Following NATO airstrikes in 1999 and a Serbian withdrawal, the 50,000 strong KFOR was mandated by the UN to enter Kosovo to stabilise the province. The Irish deployment with KFOR was originally intended to provide logistical and humanitarian support; it later involved active patrolling. Kosovo became independent in 2008.

for the Middle East to transit through Shannon airport. A subsequent UN resolution obliged member states to support the US-led coalition in Iraq, but a critical view on the 'war on terror' remained dominant in public debate in Ireland throughout this period, especially in relation to what cargo—whether detainees allegedly being moved via 'extraordinary rendition flights' or straightforward shipments of troops and possibly weapons—might be passing through Co. Clare.

In parallel, there was a growing public disconnect from the intentions of the European integration project, as was seen by the defeat, by referendum in June 2001, of the Nice Treaty on EU expansion. It had been presumed that the Irish electorate would pass the treaty, which was intended to facilitate the accession of new members from Eastern Europe. This had been the case with all past European referenda. A low turnout and concerns about aspects of the treaty, including that the European Union was marginalising smaller states, ensured its defeat. Yet support in Ireland for European integration remained high. Ireland enthusiastically introduced the euro in January 2002, and a re-run of the Nice Treaty referendum in October 2002 saw a 60% vote in favour with a close to 60% turnout.

Irish economic growth in the late 1990s and early 2000s—the era of the so-called Celtic Tiger—had implications for the continued flow of structural funds from the European Union as Ireland moved to becoming a net contributor of European monies from being a net recipient (the EU also contributed significant resources to projects relating to the Northern Ireland peace process, especially in the border region). In 2004 Ireland held the EU presidency once more. While the most high-profile public event was a ceremony in Dublin's Phoenix Park on 1 May to welcome ten new member states to the EU, the work of the Irish presidency was dominated by its chairing of negotiations on a proposed European constitutional treaty, which successfully concluded with an agreement in June of that year. The treaty was rejected in French and Dutch referendums in 2005, but most of it was later incorporated in the Lisbon Treaty of

Opposite: A portrait by Thomas Ryan of Dermot Gallagher in the secretary general's office in Iveagh House. Born in Leitrim, Gallagher joined the Department of External Affairs in 1969 under Frank Aiken, serving in a wide range of posts at home and overseas before retiring, as secretary general, in January 2009; the portrait was given to him to mark the occasion. Gallagher was twice head of the Anglo-Irish Division at crucial junctures (1987–91 and 1997–2000), and served as ambassador to the US in 1991–97, during the very significant (from an Irish perspective) presidency of Bill Clinton. He was, apparently, the only Irish official involved in the negotiation of both the Sunningdale and Good Friday agreements. He died in 2017.

The ceremony held in Áras an Uachtaráin to mark the accession of ten new member states to the European Union on 1 May 2004, during Ireland's presidency of the EU.

Minister for Foreign Affairs Micheál Martin at a working lunch with his Israeli counterpart Tzipi Livni in Tel Aviv, 10 July 2008, during Martin's first overseas trip as Minister for Foreign Affairs. His itinerary included visits to Cairo, Jerusalem and Ramallah, during a period of rising tension in the region.

Previous pages: Taoiseach Bertie Ahern and Minister for Foreign Affairs Dermot Ahern sign the Lisbon Treaty, 13 December 2007. This was intended to streamline the future expansion of the EU. Ireland was the only member state obliged to ratify it by a referendum. This was held on 12 June 2008 and was defeated. A second referendum passed sixteen months later, after declarations addressing Irish concerns were provided by the EU.

2007. The treaty was, however, rejected in the Irish referendum on ratification that took place in June 2008 (largely arising, it seems, from a poor understanding of its contents). After wide public consultation, which led to guarantees on various points of concern, including a commitment that Ireland's traditional policy of military neutrality would not be compromised (a solution that was much easier than embarking on an immensely complex renegotiation), the treaty was ratified after a second referendum in October 2009.

•

In the years following the Good Friday Agreement the delicate nature of power-sharing in Northern Ireland and the difficulties in building cross-community trust were seen in the matter of the decommissioning of paramilitary weapons and in how issues arising from the devolution of policing and justice powers to the Belfast executive prevented the full implementation of the agreement for 20 months after signature. On the Irish side, discussions on these matters were led by Dermot Gallagher for the Department of Foreign Affairs, with Paddy Teahon and Tim Dalton leading for the departments of the Taoiseach and Justice, respectively.

The power-sharing executive in Northern Ireland created by the agreement collapsed on a number of occasions in the

Northern Ireland's First Minister, Rev. Ian Paisley, and Taoiseach Bertie Ahern greet each other at the opening of the Boyne Visitor Centre at Oldbridge, Co. Meath on 6 May 2007. The Battle of the Boyne was fought in July 1690 between armies led by the Catholic James II and the Protestant William III (William of Orange). The 'Williamite' victory over James's forces is of great historical significance to Ireland's Protestant communities, and retains a powerful symbolism for many Protestants in Northern Ireland; the site of the battle is, however, located south of the border in Ireland. Ahern had played a major role in the development of the peace process in Northern Ireland, and this cross-border meeting at a heritage site exploring Ireland's often divisive history was Ahern's last official function before he stepped down as taoiseach.

early 2000s, most significantly in autumn 2002. Considerable energy was expended by the Irish and British governments and the Northern Ireland political parties to get the executive back up and running. Talks at St Andrews in Scotland in late 2006 produced an agreement that provided the context to bring the executive back into operation in 2007, under the leadership of the diametrically opposed politicians of the DUP and Sinn Féin, who nonetheless struck up a working relationship and kept the executive operating until it collapsed again in early 2017.

The achievements of Irish foreign policy in the first half of the 2000s—at the UN, through the 2004 EU presidency, and specifically through the Northern Ireland peace process (which led to improvement in both north-south relations on the island of Ireland and wider British-Irish relations)—meant that by the second half of that decade Ireland was in a position to take on a more proactive international role as a mediator between the developed and developing worlds. A 2006 White Paper on international aid significantly increased the amount of overseas aid as well as increasing its scope; in 2007 the Defence Forces' base at the Curragh Camp in Co. Kildare was designated an emergency depot for supplies

In May 2008 the Department of Foreign Affairs hosted the Dublin Diplomatic Conference on cluster munitions, attended by over 100 countries and chaired by Dáithí O'Ceallaigh, a former permanent representative to the UN. The conference produced the Convention on Cluster Munitions, which banned the production and use of such weapons; as of 2018, it had been signed by 108 countries.

Micheál Martin at the memorial to Cuban nationalist activist José Martí in Havana, February 2009. This visit took place ten years after diplomatic relations between Ireland and Cuba were established and was the first by an Irish foreign minister to Cuba. In the background is a rendering of Irish artist Jim Fitzpatrick's iconic 1967 two-tone painting of Che Guevara.

under the World Food Programme. The following year Ireland chaired a conference of 107 states and campaigners that resulted in the 2008 Convention on Cluster Munitions—an international treaty that prohibits the use, transfer and stockpiling of cluster bombs. Although the convention does not ban cluster munitions, the convenors of the Dublin conference hoped to stigmatise the use of such weapons, and with growing international support the Convention on Cluster Munitions entered into force in 2010.

•

As an open, globalised trading economy, Ireland was disproportionately affected by the global financial crisis of the late 2000s. Strong domestic economic growth of the 'Celtic Tiger' years was reversed as recessions in trading partner countries in the euro area as well as in the United States and the United Kingdom impacted strongly on the Irish economy. The banking and construction sectors were particularly affected. The government of the day implemented a policy of budget cuts and capital expenditure controls in an attempt to mitigate

Ireland's largest diplomatic mission is the Permanent Representation to the EU in Brussels. Amongst those pictured here, in May 2019, are Ambassador Declan Kelleher (8th from left) and staff from the departments of Foreign Affairs and Trade; Agriculture, Food and the Marine; Business, Enterprise and Innovation; Communications, Climate Action and Environment; Defence; Education and Skills; Finance; Transport, Tourism and Sport; Justice and Equality; Public Expenditure and Reform; and Social Protection.

Opposite: One important benefit of Ireland's membership of the EU was the provision of development or 'structural' funding to improve Ireland's infrastructure. This image, from 2002, depicts an EU-funded project underway in Co. Galway, on the Atlantic coast, connecting offshore island communities (in this case the Aran Islands) to the national electricity grid; prior to this, islanders used independent generators to provide electricity.

the worst impacts of the crisis. Ireland's international reputation was, however, undoubtedly tarnished by the financial crisis of 2008–10.

Ireland was one of a small number of euro-area countries to enter into an economic support programme, backed by the European Central Bank, the European Commission and the International Monetary Fund (IMF). This 'Troika' and its representatives would become familiar figures in Dublin in the following years. A series of economic reforms by Irish governments, some as part of the Troika programme, led to a gradual improvement over time. Nevertheless, the economic crisis saw job losses and a contraction in public expenditure as well as in the overall economy, and the effects were felt across the country. Mitigating the impact of the financial crisis and returning to growth was the priority of successive governments, and it involved a range of departments and government agencies over several years.

Irish Aid had previously moved from Dublin to Limerick in the course of wider government decentralisation policies. In 2011, in the context of the financial crisis, responsibility for EU coordination across the Irish government had been transferred to the Department of the Taoiseach. During the recession, the division of the Department of Foreign Affairs dealing with EU matters was also moved to the Department of the Taoiseach, who from 2011 was Fine Gael's Enda Kenny. (In 2016, it returned, prior to the decision of the UK to leave the EU.) Ireland entered a stringent austerity programme, and the department itself saw cutbacks: the international aid programme was cut and proposals were drafted to close embassies. These resulted in the closure of the embassies to Iran, Timor Leste and the Holy See in 2011.

To restore its credibility Ireland had to rebuild itself internationally as a vibrant state in recovery. The emphasis was on driving traditional motors of economic growth. New markets were sought by exporters, and trade returned to the forefront of foreign policy; a concrete sign of this new agenda came in 2011, when the Department of Foreign Affairs officially became the Department of Foreign Affairs and Trade. The financial crisis did not derail Irish foreign policy: Irish embassies had always been tasked with enhancing Ireland's international reputation. Post-crisis, they now had the task of helping to restore that reputation, while a greater emphasis was placed on economic work. The fact that Ireland was unique among EU member states in maintaining an embassy in every EU capital was of enormous

German chancellor Angela Merkel speaks to Taoiseach Brian Cowen, with US president Barack Obama in the foreground, during the EU–US Summit hosted in Prague during the Czech presidency of the EU, 5 April 2009.

February 2012: Then Chinese vice-president Xi Jinping kicks a ball at Croke Park, Dublin, the headquarters of the Gaelic Athletic Association, the amateur sporting and cultural organisation founded in 1884 to organise and promote Irish sports such as Gaelic football and hurling. The strengthening of Sino-Irish economic links became a feature of Irish foreign policy and diplomacy in the early twenty-first century.

benefit in this regard and offered concrete proof of Ireland's commitment to engaging with the EU.

Conscious efforts were also made by the state to harness the Irish diaspora as part of the recovery. The Global Irish Economic Forum, which met four times between 2009 and 2015, was established to explore how engagement with the diaspora could contribute to Ireland's economic recovery. Another major initiative, in the field of tourism, was 'The Gathering'—a call to those with Irish roots worldwide to visit Ireland in 2013. Its announcement met with sharp criticism in some quarters initially, but The Gathering became an enormously successful grassroots drive by communities across the state, fostering a renewed emphasis on tourism as a driver of economic growth.

The importance of improving the international reputation of the Irish economy was also crucial. This involved concerted efforts to communicate externally on the economic realities in Ireland, and on the steps being taken to return to growth. This work was carried out through the Permanent Representation to

Tánaiste and Minister for Foreign Affairs and Trade Eamon Gilmore, Bono of U2, former US president Bill Clinton and Taoiseach Enda Kenny at the third Global Irish Economic Forum held in Dublin Castle, 4–5 October 2013. The inaugural forum was held in Dublin in September 2009, to explore how business and political leaders could contribute to Ireland's economic recovery through strategic links with the diaspora.

Opposite: Ambassador Emma Madigan presents Pope Francis with a facsimile copy of the Book of Kells, 11 November 2014; the original, a seventh-century illuminated manuscript of the Christian gospels, is retained in Trinity College Dublin. The occasion was the presentation of her credentials as ambassador to the Holy See, which marked the re-opening of the Irish embassy to the Vatican. It had been closed in 2011 due to cutbacks arising from the post-2008 financial crisis, though this was also a period when Irish relations with the Holy See were strained due to the Catholic Church's handling of a range of clerical sexual abuse scandals in Ireland.

the EU in Brussels, led at the time by Rory Montgomery and involving staff drawn from across all government departments, and by embassies in EU countries and other key capitals. State agencies played a crucial role in promoting Irish exports and attracting investment into Ireland.

Membership of the EU had been central to the transformation of the Irish economy and Irish society since 1973. Public faith in Ireland in the European integration project remained high despite the bailout and austerity. May 2012 saw Irish voters approve the European Union's Fiscal Stability Treaty by 60% in a referendum which saw a 50% turnout. In March 2013 Ireland's presidency of the EU helped broker a final agreement on new rules to control government finances to stabilise Eurozone economies. A sign of renewed economic and financial stability was Ireland's 2013 return to the international bond market, raising €5 billion through the issuing of a ten-year bond. Ireland successfully exited the Troika's three-year programme in December 2013. Economic growth accelerated in subsequent years.

The easing of austerity freed up resources: in 2014 new Irish embassies and consulates were announced for Austin, Texas; Croatia; Hong Kong; Indonesia; Kenya; Sao Paulo; and Thailand, while it was also announced that the embassy to the

The financial crisis of 2008 and its aftermath had a profound impact on Ireland, which in 2010 entered a three-year bailout programme orchestrated by the European Central Bank (ECB), the EU, and the International Monetary Fund (IMF). Pictured here at a meeting of the EU's Economic and Financial Affairs Council (ECOFIN) during Ireland's 2013 presidency of the EU are, (L–R), German federal finance minister Wolfgang Schäuble, Ireland's permanent representative to the EU Rory Montgomery, and Minister for Finance Michael Noonan.

A street performer in action at the launch of 'The Gathering' in Dublin, 31 December 2012. 'The Gathering' was a major community-driven tourism initiative developed by Fáilte Ireland (the Irish tourist board) that took place throughout 2013, focusing on links with the Irish diaspora. It reflected a renewed emphasis on tourism as a driver of economic recovery in the aftermath of the ECB/EU/IMF bailout.

Holy See would be re-opened. This expansion was in line with the *Review of the government trade, tourism and investment strategy*, published in 2015 to provide a more strategic and nuanced direction for Ireland's international trade, tourism, investment and education promotion efforts. January 2015 also saw the adoption by the government of a new statement of Irish foreign policy: *The global island: Ireland's foreign policy for a changing world*. An embassy in New Zealand opened in 2018; this was one of six new missions announced in 2017, including embassies in Chile, Colombia and Jordan and consulates-general in Vancouver, Canada and Mumbai, India. All formed part of a plan to double Ireland's global footprint by 2025.

•

Ireland's foreign policy objectives did not deviate from their signature goals during, or as a result of, the global downturn and the financial crisis. Policy emphasised the need to ensure Irish economic growth, but also highlighted the state's ongoing commitments to international peace and security, to human rights, and to the tackling of poverty and hunger globally. Ireland held the chair of the Organisation for Security and Co-operation in Europe (OSCE) for the first time in 2012, and the OSCE Ministerial Council held in Dublin in December 2012 was one of the largest and most significant international meetings of its kind ever held in Ireland, with attendees including the US secretary of state, the Russian foreign minister, the British foreign secretary and the EU's high representative for foreign affairs and security policy.

In 2013 Ireland began a three-year term on the United Nations Human Rights Council, focussing on human-rights conditions in individual countries as well as on a number of thematic priorities, such as ensuring the rights of LGBTI (lesbian, gay, bisexual, transgender and intersex) people, the rights of the child, protection of human-rights defenders, freedom of religion or belief, and internet freedom. Despite the impact of the financial crisis, from 2013 to 2015 Ireland stabilised its development aid budget; in addition, improving national finances meant that in subsequent years a small annual growth in the development aid budget was possible. From €601 million in 2015, development aid grew to €641 million and €651 million over the following two years. The goals of development policy were summarised as reducing hunger and promoting sustainable development, inclusive economic growth and better governance, human rights and democratic accountability. Aid was distributed to nine key partner countries in Africa and South East Asia. The increases in the aid budget pointed towards the Irish development aspiration of providing 0.7% of GNP for Official Development Assistance when economic circumstances permit.

Instability in other regions of the world was increasingly felt on the borders of the EU. Increasing numbers of migrants and refugees—often escaping conflict in Syria, Afghanistan and Africa—arriving on Europe's Mediterranean shores in 2015 saw the EU launch Operation Triton, a maritime operation to tackle increased migration and attempt to save those trying to cross from Libya to Italy and Greece using unseaworthy vessels. Operation Triton saw the first overseas missions as part of an EU force by vessels of the Irish naval service. Through six-month rotations, the Irish vessels provided a search and rescue capability to the European force and undertook humanitarian rescue operations.

In response to ongoing humanitarian crises across the globe, Ireland provided over €150 million in aid, including €25 million to alleviate the impact of the civil war in Syria. In 2015 Ireland played a critical role in securing agreement on a set of UN targets known as the 'Sustainable Development Goals' (SDG). These set an agenda intended to transform the world for the better over the coming generations. The choice of Ireland to lead the SDG negotiations arose from its reputation at the UN as well as its commitment to the organisation and its capacity to build strong relationships with other countries.

Nuclear disarmament, as originally advocated by Frank Aiken in the 1960s, remained one of Ireland's most important priorities at the UN. July 2017 saw the completion of the Treaty on the Prohibition of Nuclear Weapons (TPNN), the first legally binding international agreement to comprehensively prohibit nuclear weapons, with the goal of leading towards their total elimination on primarily humanitarian grounds, although none of the existing nuclear powers has signed the treaty. Ireland was one of the leading proponents of the treaty at the UN, working

President of Ireland Mary McAleese and Queen Elizabeth II of the United Kingdom, followed by Prince Philip and Martin McAleese, walk past busts of former presidents of Ireland (with that of Éamon de Valera first on the left) in Áras an Uachtaráin during the British state visit of May 2011. While Elizabeth II had visited Northern Ireland on many occasions, this was her first visit to Ireland; this was a milestone in the normalisation of Anglo-Irish relations arising from the Northern Ireland peace process.

with Austria, Brazil, Indonesia, Mexico, Nigeria, South Africa and Thailand towards its conclusion, and Ireland signed it on 20 September 2017.

•

The visit of Britain's Queen Elizabeth II to Ireland in summer 2011 and President Michael D. Higgins's reciprocal 2014 visit to Britain highlighted the improvement in British-Irish relations since the signing of the Good Friday Agreement. In 2012 the Irish state embarked on a Decade of Centenaries, in which key milestones in the Irish revolution of a century previously were to be marked. Amongst these was the outbreak of the First World War, the commemoration of which has often been a contentious issue in Ireland. Given the British commitment to marking the centenary of the war, the Decade of Centenaries was regarded as a further opportunity for promoting mutual

Tánaiste and Minister for Foreign Affairs and Trade Eamon Gilmore is pictured here at the Cenotaph in Belfast alongside Northern Ireland First Minister Peter Robinson on Armistice Sunday, 10 November 2013. Commemorating the First World War has a particular resonance for unionists in Northern Ireland, though it has been politically sensitive in Ireland despite the mass enlistment from across the island of Ireland during the war. The poppy is traditionally sold in Ireland and the UK by the Royal British Legion to support its welfare work with current and former members of the UK armed services and their families. Other than in exceptional and limited circumstances, Irish diplomats and politicians, in their official capacity, do not wear a poppy.

Previous pages: Queen Elizabeth II lays a memorial wreath at the Garden of Remembrance in Dublin city centre. The garden commemorates men and women who died in successive campaigns for Irish independence from Britain from 1798 to 1921. The wreath-laying by the British monarch at this venue was seen as a striking gesture of reconciliation.

respect and understanding between nationalists and unionists in Ireland and Northern Ireland, and for improving wider British-Irish relations. This was especially true in relation to the experiences of Irishmen who had enlisted in the British armed services during the First World War (though the programme encompassed far more, on the Irish side, than just the First World War). In 2015 Britain and Ireland took the unprecedented step of signing a memorandum of understanding on deepening future defence and peacekeeping collaboration between their respective militaries.

This remarkable improvement in British-Irish relations was tested by 'Brexit': the 2016 decision of the UK to leave the European Union. The importance of Brexit to Ireland became evident when the question of the future status of the Irish border, in the context of its potential impact on the peace process, trade relations within the island of Ireland, and the long-standing 'Common Travel Area' between Ireland and Britain all came to the fore in the UK's exit negotiations with the EU: the only possible land frontier between the EU and a post-Brexit UK would be between Ireland and Northern Ireland. The reality of geography thus ensures that, as ever, Ireland's foreign policy will need to devote considerable attention to Ireland's closest geographical neighbour. While the British–Irish relationship will, as ever, remain important, Ireland continues to be firmly committed to EU membership. The manner in which Ireland can pursue its objectives in an EU without the UK and manage relations with a UK outside the EU, is, at the time of writing, a matter that can only be resolved in the future.

●

One hundred years ago foreign policy became a key part of Ireland's independence struggle. The past one hundred years have seen the growth of Ireland's international responsibilities. Irish foreign policy and the work of the Irish diplomatic service, which has grown from one mission in Paris in 1919 to a network of over 90 diplomatic missions across the world in 2019, have reflected this.

The issues explored in this book illustrate how many of the signature concerns of Ireland's foreign policies in the twenty-first century remain broadly similar to those set forth a century ago. Issues as diverse as reconciliation, cooperation and economic growth in Ireland; engagement with the Irish diaspora; a commitment to international peace and stability and strong global institutions, as well as to human rights, equality and the rule of law; and solidarity with those suffering from poverty, hunger and disadvantage, have resonated through one hundred years of Irish foreign policy.

IN MEMORIAM
This plaque is dedicated to all the guests who lost their lives in the terrorist attack at the Imperial Marhaba Hotel on June 26th, 2015.

UN Secretary-General Ban Ki Moon and Minister for Foreign Affairs and Trade Charles Flanagan in Dublin Castle at a May 2015 event marking the sixtieth anniversary of Ireland's joining the UN in December 1955.

Below right: President of Ireland Michael D. Higgins at the first World Humanitarian Summit, organised in Istanbul by the UN in May 2016 to discuss future responses to humanitarian crises. Before his election to the presidency in 2011, Higgins had been a Labour Party parliamentarian and minister, with a long-standing record as an advocate of human rights in Ireland and overseas.

Opposite: Ireland's ambassador to Tunisia, and former secretary general of the department, David Cooney, visits a memorial to the attack at the Imperial Marhaba Hotel, Tunis, in which 3 Irish citizens were amongst the 38 killed by a terrorist gunman in June 2015. Cooney (who was also ambassador to Spain and operating from the embassy of Ireland in Madrid), along with the head of the embassy's consular services Caoimhe Ní Chonchúir and their staff, provided consular assistance to Irish tourists and their families in the aftermath of the attack, in conjunction with staff in the department's headquarters at Iveagh House in Dublin. The provision of such assistance to Irish citizens abroad remains a fundamental element of Irish diplomatic activity.

Message from Ambassador Anderson
Teachtaireacht ón Ambasadóir Anderson

The 1916 centenary, celebrated across the world, will have special resonance in the United States. It will of course be particularly meaningful to the 35 million US residents who claim Irish ancestry. But the narrative of the Rising will resonate with all Americans who cherish the principles of freedom and self-determination which shaped their own history.

As we honour and interrogate the 1916 legacy, we will also present the dynamic and multi-faceted Ireland of today. The defining characteristic of our centenary programme will be to present modern twenty-first century Ireland - with 1916 as the point of departure, we will chart the journey and the point of arrival, and seek to position ourselves for the next steps on that great continuing journey.

The Embassy and our six Consulates are extremely grateful for the enthusiastic collaboration of our partner organisations in preparing this centenary programme. Together, we extend a warm invitation to all those of Irish ancestry and to all of Ireland's friends right across the United States – 2016 will be a year of pride and inspiration; please join us and be part of it.

Anne Anderson,
Ambassador of Ireland to the United States

Cé go bhfuil comóradh céid Éirí Amach 1916 á cheiliúradh ar fud an domhain, beidh suntasacht ar leith aige i Stáit Aontaithe Mheiriceá. Rachaidh sé i gcion go mór, ar ndóigh, ar na daoine siúd atá ina gcónaí sna Stáit Aontaithe a mheasann gur de bhunadh na hÉireann iad, 35 milliún duine ar fad. Ach rachaidh scéal an Éirí Amach i bhfeidhm ar mhuintir Mheiriceá go léir ar mór acu an tsaoirse agus an ceart ar a rialú féin, prionsabail is bonn le stair na tíre sin. Bainfidh tábhacht le ceiliúradh an chéid i dtaobh treo a leagan amach dúinn maidir leis an am atá le teacht.

Agus muid ag tabhairt urraime d'oidhreacht 1916 agus á ceistiú, déanfaimid Éire ina lae inniu, Éire atá dinimiciúil agus ilghnéitheach, a chur i láthair freisin. Beidh sé ina shaintréith den chlár comórtha céid Éire nua-aoiseach na linne seo, Éire an aonú haois is fiche, a chur i láthair – ag tosú thiar i 1916, rianóimid an turas agus an ceann scríbe, agus déanfaimid iarracht muid féin a shuíomh i gcomhair na gcéad chéimeanna eile sa turas mór sin atá fós ar bun.

Tá an Ambasáid agus na sé Chonsalacht dár gcuid thar a bheith buíoch as comhoibriú díograiseach ár n-eagraíochtaí comhpháirtíochta agus clár seo an chéid á ullmhú. Táimid ag tabhairt cuiridh ó chroí do gach duine de bhunadh na hÉireann agus do gach duine de shaoránaigh agus cairde na hÉireann ar fud na Stát Aontaithe – bliain bhróid agus inspioráide atá romhainn in 2016; bí linn, le bhur dtoil, agus glac páirt sa cheiliúradh.

Anne Anderson,
Ambasadóir na hÉireann chuig Stáit Aontaithe Mheiriceá

Previous pages: Michel Barnier (third from left), the EU's chief Brexit negotiator, visits the Irish border region in May 2017. The possible economic impact of the British decision to leave the European Union is of particular concern to the agrifood sector on both sides of the Irish border. Also pictured are (L–R): Heather Humphreys, Minister for Arts, Heritage, Regional, Rural and Gaeltacht Affairs; Máiread McGuinness MEP, Vice-President of the European Parliament; and (second from right) Charles Flanagan, Minister for Foreign Affairs and Trade.

The 2016 centenary of the Easter Rising was the subject of major commemorations in Ireland and overseas; here, Ireland's ambassador to the United States of America Anne Anderson introduces the 2016 programme for events in the US. Anderson had joined the Department of Foreign Affairs in 1972. The ban on married women serving in the Irish public sector was lifted in 1973, thus removing a major impediment to the careers of female diplomats. Anderson was the first woman appointed as an Irish ambassador to a number of posts, including France, the EU, UN and US. She was also the first female permanent representative from any EU country.

Members of the Irish Naval
Service from the L.É. *William
Butler Yeats* (visible in the
background) attend to a
boat with migrants in the
Mediterranean Sea, 10 August
2017. Between 2015 and 2018 the
Naval Service was involved in
search and rescue missions for
migrants attempting to cross the
Mediterranean.

Tánaiste and Minister for
Foreign Affairs and Trade
Simon Coveney and German
Federal Foreign Minister Heiko
Maas hold replica copies of the
'Saarbrucken Cecelianschule
Dankebuch' in St Stephen's
Green, Dublin, with the white
façade of Iveagh House just
visible in the background, April
2018. The original book was
a compilation of letters from
German schoolchildren near
Saarbrucken thanking Irish
people for aid donations made
after the Second World War.
The group is pictured beside
'The Three Fates', a statue
gifted to Ireland in 1956 by the
Federal Republic of Germany in
recognition of the post-war Irish
aid effort.

Following pages: In 2009
Tourism Ireland (the cross-
border body promoting tourism
for the island of Ireland as a
whole) launched its 'Global
Greening' initiative, which sees
a range of iconic structures
and locations around the world
illuminated green to mark St
Patrick's Day, 17 March. In 2017
the Scott Base in Antarctica
became the most southerly
location to be included in the
initiative.

Taoiseach Leo Varadkar speaks at the launch of Global Ireland in Dublin, 11 June 2018.
Seated (L–R): Minister of State for European Affairs Helen McEntee, Minister for Foreign
Affairs and Trade Simon Coveney, Minister for Business, Enterprise and Innovation Heather
Humphreys, and Minister for Culture Heritage and the Gaeltacht Josepha Madigan.

GLOBAL IRELAND

On 11 June 2018 the Irish government launched its Global Ireland 2025 strategy. This aimed to double Ireland's global footprint—its diplomatic, cultural, economic and development aid impact abroad—by 2025 by increasing Ireland's engagement with the wider world, through emphasising an increased commitment to the EU; pursuing the objective (originally announced in 2005) of election to the UN Security Council for a fourth term; seeking new markets for exports and sources of investment; and engaging more strongly with the Irish diaspora.

The strategy was launched at a time when the international environment in which Ireland must operate became more challenging, on a number of fronts. For the Department of Foreign Affairs and Trade, the Global Ireland strategy envisioned a significant expansion of Ireland's diplomatic infrastructure at home and abroad, with the establishment of new embassies and consulates in Europe, Asia, Africa and the Americas, and the expansion of key existing missions.

Ireland prospered economically and politically in the past half-century by embracing the liberal and multilateral international economic and political order. The values and institutions that underpin this order have come under threat in the first decades of the twenty-first century as geopolitical power shifts across the globe, political norms mutate, and economic turbulence increases worldwide. The Global Ireland strategy was devised to act as a response to these challenges.

Bon Voyage

by WESTERN UNION

B170CC 3K PD BOSTON MASS 530PME MAR 30 1959

THE HON SEAN T KELLY, PRESIDENT OF IRELAND

    SAILING MAR 31 SS FLANDRE PIER 88 NR NYK

WARMEST GOOD WISHES TO PHYLLIS AND YOU FOR A PLEASANT AND RESTFUL

JOURNEY HOME AFTER YOUR HIGHLY SUCCESSFUL VISIT HERE. BOSTON STILL

TAKING ABOUT YOUR BRIEF VISIT HERE, AND THE WONDERFUL IMPRESSION

YOU MADE. I HOPE YOU AND PHYLLIS WILL COME BACK AGAIN SOON.

        JOE GANNON
        140 FEDERAL ST
        BOSTON

        558PM

Glossary

Opposite: A telegram sent by prominent Irish-American Joe Gannon to President Seán T. Ó Ceallaigh on his departure back to Ireland following his state visit to the US in 1959.

Ambassador
The highest-ranking diplomatic representative. Prior to the appointment of Ireland's first ambassador in 1946, to the Holy See, Irish diplomats were appointed at the lower rank of envoy extraordinary and minister plenipotentiary.

Chargé d'affaires
A diplomat who will deputise for a serving ambassador in his or her absence, or who will be placed in temporary charge of an embassy while awaiting the formal appointment of an ambassador. The post has no relation to diplomatic rank, but is normally held by mid-level or higher-level diplomats.

Consulate/Consulate General
The official representation of a state, assisting and protecting the interests of that state's citizens in another state, perhaps through offices in several locations, each of which is headed by a Consul/Consul General. A Consul General is at higher ranking than a Consul.

Counsellor
A high-level diplomatic rank, below the highest-level position of ambassador. Appointments at this level first began in the Irish diplomatic service in the late 1940s.

Credentials
The documentation confirming the appointment of an ambassador, which is presented to the head of state of the country to which the ambassador is posted.

Dáil Éireann
Literally, 'Assembly of Ireland': the name of the Irish parliament, originally established in 1919 prior to independence.

Diplomatic bag

The term for packages sent between states and their diplomatic missions, which may not be interfered with or opened while in transit.

Embassy

A diplomatic mission comprising the chancery, residence and diplomatic and official staff, and headed by an ambassador.

Envoy extraordinary and minister plenipotentiary

An older term for the head of a diplomatic mission, below the rank of ambassador; often abbreviated in the context of diplomacy to 'minister'; this should not be confused with the religious term or the term for members of a government.

First secretary

A mid-level diplomatic ranking, below the rank of counsellor and above third secretary.

High Commissioner

During Ireland's 1922 to 1949 membership of the Commonwealth, the most senior Irish diplomatic agents in charge of the Irish mission (High Commission) in London and, from 1939, Ottawa, held the senior diplomatic rank of High Commissioner. After the declaration of the Republic of Ireland in 1949, Ireland's High Commissioners to London and Ottawa, and since 1946 Canberra, were redesignated ambassadors.

Legation

A diplomatic mission headed by a diplomat below ambassadorial rank.

Second secretary

A mid-level diplomatic rank, in use from the inter-war years and again in recent years.

Secretary general

The term for the highest official in an Irish government department, though the term 'secretary' was used more commonly for much of the twentieth century.

Taoiseach

Literally, 'chief' or 'leader'. The term for the head of the Irish government under the Irish constitution of 1937; the equivalent of 'Prime Minister'.

Third secretary

The most junior Irish diplomatic rank.

Ministers for External Affairs/ Foreign Affairs/Foreign Affairs and Trade

Count George Noble Plunkett
22 January 2019–26 August 1921

Arthur Griffith
27 August 1921–9 January 1922

George Gavan Duffy
10 January 1922–25 July 1922

Arthur Griffith
26 July 1922–12 August 1922

Michael Hayes
21 August 1922–09 September 1922

Desmond FitzGerald
30 August 1922–23 June 1927

Kevin O'Higgins
23 June 1927–10 July 1927

William T. Cosgrave
14 July 1927–12 October 1927

Patrick McGilligan
13 October 1927–3 April 1930

Éamon de Valera
9 March 1932–18 February 1948

Seán MacBride
19 February 1948–13 June 1951

Frank Aiken
14 June 1951–2 June 1954

Liam Cosgrave
3 June 1954–20 March 1957

Frank Aiken
21 March 1957–2 July 1969

Patrick J. Hillery
3 July 1969–3 January 1973

Brian Lenihan
4 January 1973–14 March 1973

Garret FitzGerald
15 March 1973–5 July 1977

Michael O'Kennedy
6 July 1977–11 December 1979

Brian Lenihan
12 December 1979–30 June 1981

John Kelly
01 July 1981–21 October 1981

James Dooge
22 October 1981–9 March 1982

Gerard Collins
10 March 1982–14 December 1982

Peter Barry
15 December 1982–20 January 1987

Brian Lenihan
10 March 1987–12 July 1989

Gerard Collins
13 July 1989–11 February 1992

David Andrews
12 February 1992–12 January 1993

Dick Spring
13 January 1993–17 November 1994

Albert Reynolds
18 November 1994–15 December 1994

Dick Spring
16 December 1994–26 June 1997

Ray Burke
27 July 1997-7 October 1997

David Andrews
08 October 1997–27 January 2000

Brian Cowen
28 January 2000–29 September 2004

Dermot Ahern
30 September 2004–7 May 2008

Micheál Martin
08 May 2008–19 January 2011

Brian Cowen
20 January 2011–9 March 2011

Eamon Gilmore
10 March 2011–11 July 2014

Charles Flanagan
12 July 2014–14 June 2017

Simon Coveney
15 June 2017–Present

Secretaries and Secretaries general of the Department of External Affairs/Foreign Affairs/Foreign Affairs and Trade

Joseph P. Walshe (acting)
1 September 1922–7 August 1927

Joseph P. Walshe
8 August 1927–6 May 1946

Frederick H. Boland
7 May 1946–25 September 1950

Sean Nunan
26 September 1950–22 May 1955

Seán Murphy
23 May 1955–30 November 1957

Con Cremin
1 December 1957–6 January 1963

Hugh McCann
7 January 1963–9 April 1974

Paul Keating
10 April 1974–24 February 1977

Robert McDonagh
25 February 1977–31 August 1978

Andrew O'Rourke
1 September 1978–26 October 1981

Seán Donlon
27 October 1981–1 March 1987

Noel Dorr
2 March 1987–30 June 1995

Pádraig MacKernan
1 July 1995–6 July 2001

Dermot Gallagher
7 July 2001–24 January 2009

David Cooney
25 January 2009–29 April 2014

Niall Burgess
30 April 2014–Present

Timeline of the opening of Irish resident diplomatic missions

The dates given in this table are when a resident Irish diplomat was first based in the locations concerned. In most cases, diplomatic relations had been established and non-resident ministers and ambassadors had been appointed many years before resident missions were opened.

Prior to 1946 Irish diplomatic missions tended to be either legations or high commissions. Ireland's first 'Embassy' was opened in 1946, when the first ambassador to the Holy See was appointed. Particularly from 1946 onwards, ambassadors in the list of missions below were also accredited to other countries and institutions. After Ireland left the Commonwealth in 1949, what had been high commissions subsequently became embassies. From the 1950s on, legations were regularly upgraded to full embassies. The 'Total' column is cumulative and takes into account the openings, closures and re-openings listed.

Year	Diplomatic mission(s)	Total number of resident missions
1923	United Kingdom League of Nations—Geneva (closed 1940)	2
1924	United States of America	3
1929	Holy See (closed 2011–14) France Germany (closed 1945–50) Boston (Consulate)	7
1930	New York (Consulate)	8
1933	Chicago (Consulate) San Francisco (Consulate)	10
1935	Spain	11
1938	Italy	12
1939	Canada	13
1940	Switzerland	13
1942	Portugal	14
1946	Australia Sweden	15
1947	Argentina (First mission in Latin America)	16
1950	The Netherlands Belgium	19

Year	Diplomatic mission(s)	Total number of resident missions
1956	Permanent Mission to the United Nations—New York	20
1960	Nigeria (First mission in Africa)	21
1962	Hamburg (Consulate) (closed 1982) Denmark	23
1964	India (First mission in Asia)	24
1965	Permanent Mission to the United Nations and other International Organisations—Geneva	25
1966	Permanent Representation to the EEC—Brussels	26
1973	Japan Luxembourg	28
1974	Lebanon (closed from 1976 to 1979 and permanently in 1986) USSR (now Russia) Austria	31
1976	Egypt (First mission in the Middle East) Saudi Arabia Iran (closed 2011)	33
1977	Greece	34
1978	Lesotho—Development Co-operation Office (closed 2014)	35
1979	Kenya (closed 1988) People's Republic of China Tanzania—Development Co-operation Office	39
1980	Zambia—Development Co-operation Office	40

Year	Diplomatic mission(s)	Total number of resident missions
1985	Anglo-Irish Secretariat—Belfast (closed 1998)	41
1986	Iraq (closed 1990)	41
1989	Republic of Korea (South Korea)	41
1990	Poland	41
1993	Finland Organisation for Security and Co-operation in Europe—Vienna	43
1994	Ethiopia South Africa Uganda	46
1995	Czechoslovakia (now Czech Republic) Hungary Malaysia	49
1996	Israel Mozambique	51
1998	Cardiff (Consulate) (closed 2009–19) Edinburgh (Consulate) Turkey	54
1999	Council of Europe Mexico Partnership for Peace liaison office—Brussels North-South Ministerial Council Joint Secretariat—Armagh Sudan—Development Co-operation Office (closed 2003)	58

Year	Diplomatic mission(s)	Total number of resident missions
2000	Sydney (Consulate) Shanghai (Consulate) Palestinian National Authority—Ramallah Singapore	62
2001	Brazil Cyprus Estonia Norway Slovakia Slovenia	68
2003	Organisation for Economic Co-operation and Development—Paris United Nations Educational, Scientific and Cultural Organisation (UNESCO)—Paris	69
2004	Timor Leste—Development Co-operation Office (closed 2011)	70
2005	Sierra Leone—Irish Aid Office Bulgaria Latvia Lithuania Malta Romania Vietnam	77
2007	Malawi	78
2009	United Arab Emirates	78
2010	Atlanta (Consulate) Liberia—Irish Aid Office	80

Year	Diplomatic mission(s)	Total number of resident missions
2014	Austin (Consulate) Thailand Hong Kong (Consulate) Indonesia Kenya Sao Paolo (Consulate) Croatia	84
2018	Vancouver (Consulate) New Zealand	86
2019	Jordan Colombia Mumbai (Consulate) Chile Los Angeles (Consulate) Frankfurt (Consulate)	93

Select bibliography

The principal source for the study of Ireland's foreign policy is Michael Kennedy, Catriona Crowe, Ronan Fanning, Dermot Keogh, Eunan O'Halpin, Kate O'Malley and Bernadette Whelan (eds), *Documents on Irish Foreign Policy* (11 vols, Dublin, 1998–), the early volumes of which are available at http://www.difp. ie/. The release of the Department of Foreign Affairs and Trade's archives is governed by the so-called 30-year rule for the release of state papers, but the annual releases of more recent papers are widely covered in the national media. The summaries of the state paper releases by John Bowman (in *The Irish Times*) and the late Ronan Fanning (in the *Sunday Independent*) are particularly useful. A great deal of audio-visual material of relevance can be accessed through the online archives of RTÉ, the Irish state broadcaster: http://www.rte.ie/archives/

For the specific study of Irish foreign policy, Michael Kennedy and Joseph Morrison Skelly have provided both a historiographical review and extensive bibliography of works published prior to 2000 in their book *Irish foreign policy, 1919–1966: From independence to internationalism* (Dublin, 2000). The principal scholarly journal in the field is *Irish Studies in International Affairs* (1979–), published by the Royal Irish Academy and available on the JSTOR database. Alongside an extremely wide range of studies and personal perspectives on the formulation and conduct of Irish foreign policy since 1919, the annual reviews of Ireland's foreign relations and foreign aid (authored most recently by Donnacha

Ó Beacháin and Helen O'Neill, respectively) published in this journal have been extremely useful in the development of the present work.

Biographical studies of many diplomats and political figures can be found in the *Dictionary of Irish Biography* (9 vols, Cambridge, 2009) and its online supplements: http://dib. cambridge.org/. The historiography of Irish foreign policy is intertwined with the wider historiography on Irish history since 1919; many standard studies, and especially biographies of key figures, contain material of relevance. The list of publications that follows is confined to major and easily available studies and memoirs relating to Irish foreign policy.

Bowman, John, *De Valera and the Ulster question, 1917–1973* (Oxford, 1982).

Brennan, Robert, *Ireland standing firm* (Dublin, 2002).

Connelly, Tony, *Brexit and Ireland* (2nd edn; Dublin, 2018).

Department of Foreign Affairs, 'Challenges and opportunities abroad', White Paper on foreign policy (Dublin, 1996).

Doyle, John, Noel Dorr, Michael Kennedy and Ben Tonra (eds), *Irish foreign policy* (Dublin, 2012).

Dorr, Noel, *Ireland at the United Nations: memories of the early years* (Dublin, 2010).

Dorr, Noel, *A small state at the top table: memories of Ireland on the UN security council, 1981–82* (Dublin, 2011).

Dorr, Noel, *Sunningdale: the search for peace in Northern Ireland* (Dublin, 2017).

Evans, Bryce and Stephen Kelly (eds), *Frank Aiken: nationalist and internationalist* (Dublin, 2014).

Fanning, Ronan, *Fatal path: British government and Irish revolution, 1910–1922* (London, 2013).

Fisk, Robert. *In time of war: Ireland, Ulster and the price of neutrality, 1939–45* (Dublin, 1983).

FitzGerald, Garret, *All in a life: an autobiography* (Dublin, 1991).

FitzGerald, Garret, *Reflections on the Irish state: Ireland since independence* (Dublin, 2002).

Geary, Michael, *An inconvenient wait: Ireland's quest for membership of the EEC, 1957–1973* (Dublin, 2009).

Government of Ireland, *The global island: Ireland's foreign policy for a changing world* (Dublin, 2015).

Harkness, David, *The restless dominion: the Irish Free State and the British Commonwealth* (Dublin, 1969).

Keatinge, Patrick, *The formulation of Irish foreign policy* (Dublin, 1973).

Keatinge, Patrick, *A place among the nations: issues of Irish foreign policy* (Dublin, 1978).

Kelly, Stephen, *'A failed political entity': Charles Haughey and the Northern Ireland question, 1945–1992* (Dublin, 2016).

Kennedy, Michael, *Ireland and the League of Nations: international relations, diplomacy and politics* (Dublin, 1996).

Kennedy, Michael, *Division and consensus: the politics of cross-border relations in Ireland, 1925–1969* (Dublin, 2000).

Kennedy, Michael and Deirdre McMahon (eds), *Obligations and responsibilities: Ireland and the United Nations, 1955–2005* (Dublin, 2005).

Kennedy, Michael and Art Magennis, *Ireland, the United Nations and the Congo* (Dublin, 2014).

Keown, Gerard, *First of the small nations: the beginnings of Irish foreign policy in the interwar years, 1919–1932* (Oxford, 2016).

Keogh, Dermot, *Ireland and Europe, 1919–48: a diplomatic and political history* (revised edn; Dublin, 1988).

Keogh, Dermot, *Ireland and the Vatican: the politics and diplomacy of church–state relations, 1922–60* (Cork, 1995).

Maher, Denis, *The tortuous path: the course of Ireland's entry into the EEC, 1948–73* (Dublin, 1986).

Mansergh, Nicholas, *The unresolved question: the Anglo-Irish settlement and its undoing, 1912–72* (London and New Haven, 1991).

McCabe, Ian, *A diplomatic history of Ireland 1948–49: the republic, the Commonwealth and NATO* (Dublin, 1991).

McMahon, Deirdre, *Republicans and imperialists: Anglo-Irish relations in the 1930s* (New Haven, 1984).

O'Driscoll Mervyn, Dermot Keogh and Jérôme aan de Wiel (eds), *Ireland through European eyes: Western Europe, the EEC and Ireland, 1945–1973* (Cork, 2013).

O'Halpin, Eunan, *Defending Ireland: the Irish state and its enemies since 1922* (Oxford, 1999).

O'Malley, Kate, *Ireland, India and empire. Indo-Irish radical connections, 1919–1964* (Manchester, 2008).

O'Shea, Helen, *Ireland and the end of the British Empire: the republic and its role in the Cyprus Emergency* (London, 2014).

O'Sullivan, Kevin, *Ireland, Africa and the end of empire: small state identity in the Cold War* (Manchester, 2012).

Skelly, Joseph Morrison, *Irish diplomacy at the United Nations: national interests and the international order* (Dublin, 1997).

Sharp, Paul, *Irish foreign policy and the European Community* (Aldershot, 1990).

Sloan, Geoffrey, *The geopolitics of Anglo-Irish relations in the twentieth century* (London, 1997).

Wilson, Andrew J., *Irish America and the Ulster conflict, 1968–95* (Washington, DC, 1995).

Wright, Frank, *Northern Ireland: a comparative analysis* (Dublin, 1987).

Tonra, Ben, *The Europeanisation of national foreign policy: Dutch, Danish and Irish foreign policy in the European Union* (Aldershot, 2001).

Wylie, Paula, *Ireland and the Cold War: recognition and diplomacy 1949–1963* (Dublin, 2006).

Whelan, Bernadette, *The Marshall Plan and Ireland* (Dublin, 2000).

Williamson, Daniel C., *Anglo-Irish relations in the early troubles, 1969–1972* (London, 2017).

Martin McGuinness and Ian Paisley pictured at the Irish embassy in New York in 2008, with Niall Burgess, the current secretary general of the Department of Foreign Affairs and Trade.

Image credits

During the production process some documents, photographs and illustrations have been retouched or tinted for aesthetic purposes. Every effort has been made to trace the copyright holders of the illustrative items reproduced in this book and to ensure the accuracy of their captions.

Cover

Department of Foreign Affairs and Trade; Cultural Relations Committee of Ireland, DFAT Library Collections. Courtesy of DFAT.

Prelims

iv–v Private collection. Reproduced courtesy of Cormac Louth.
viii National Archives of Ireland; Department of Foreign Affairs collection, DFA/112/47/passport. Courtesy of the Board of the NAI.

Chapter 1: 1919–1922

2 UCD Archives; Papers of Michael MacWhite, IE UCDA P194–737. By kind permission of UCD Archives.
6 Dublin City Library and Archive; Birth of the Republic Collection, 320, BOR F30-03. Courtesy of Dublin City Library and Archive.
7 National Library of Ireland; Irish Large Books Collection, ILB 300 p2 [Item 2]. Reproduced courtesy of the NLI.
8 Irish Defence Forces, Military Archives; Bureau of Military History Contemporary Documents Series, BMH CD 095 6 0600001. Courtesy of the Military Archives.

9 Irish Defence Forces, Military Archives; Bureau of Military History Contemporary Documents Series, BMH CD 095 6 0800001. Courtesy of the Military Archives.

10 National Library of Ireland; Seán T. Ó Ceallaigh Papers, MS 27676/1 (2). Reproduced courtesy of the NLI.

12 National Library of Ireland; Postcard views of Dublin 1916–22 Collection, NPA DOCG 40. Reproduced courtesy of the NLI.

13 Irish Defence Forces, Military Archives; Bureau of Military History Contemporary Documents Series, BMH CD 250 05 0100002. Courtesy of the Military Archives.

14 UCD Archives; Papers of Éamon de Valera, IE UCDA P150-753-4. By kind permission of UCD–OFM Partnership.

15 National Library of Ireland; Seán T. Ó Ceallaigh Papers, MS 27688/5/viii. Reproduced courtesy of the NLI.

16 National Library of Ireland; Art Ó Briain Papers *c.* 1900–*c.*1945, MS 8432/2/8/1/2. Reproduced courtesy of the NLI.

17 National Library of Ireland, National Photographic Archive; Kathleen McKenna-Napoli photographic collection, *Daily Sketch*, London and Manchester, 11 October 1921, NPA MKN33. Reproduced courtesy of the NLI.

18 (top) Irish Defence Forces, Military Archives; Bureau of Military History Contemporary Documents Series, BMH CD 250 5 0500005. Courtesy of the Military Archives.

18 (bottom) National Library of Ireland; Éamonn Duggan Papers, 1913–68, MS 49835/15/8. Reproduced courtesy of the NLI.

19 National Library of Ireland; Michael Collins Papers, relating to his uncle, General Michael Collins, MS 40422/9/28. Reproduced courtesy of the NLI.

20–21 National Archives of Ireland; Dáil Éireann, Comptroller and Auditor General Files Series, DE/3/1/1/273. Courtesy of the Board of the NAI.

23 UCD Archives; Papers of Mary MacSwiney, P48a 303 001. By kind permission of UCD Archives.

24–5 National Library of Ireland, National Photographic Archive; Hogan-Wilson Collection, HOGW 60. Reproduced courtesy of the NLI.

27 Irish Defence Forces, Military Archives; Bureau of Military History Contemporary Documents Series, BMH CD 095 7 0800001. Courtesy of the Military Archives.

28 Department of Foreign Affairs and Trade; Cultural Relations Committee of Ireland, Brochure, DFAT Library Collections. Courtesy of DFAT.

Chapter 2: 1922–1932

32 National Library of Ireland, National Photographic Archive; Kathleen McKenna-Napoli photographic collection, NPA MKN11. Reproduced courtesy of the NLI.

34 Library of Congress, Prints and Photographs Division; National Photo Company Collection, LC-F8-33878. Courtesy of the Library of Congress.

35 National Archives of Ireland; Department of Foreign Affairs collection, DFA Early Series/2/202/22. Courtesy of the Board of the NAI.

36 Library of Congress; Prints and Photographs Division; National Photo Company Collection, LC-F8-37604. Courtesy of the Library of Congress.

37 UCD Archives; Papers of Michael MacWhite, IE UCDA P194-781. By kind permission of UCD Archives.

38 Police Museum, Belfast; 1994.051. Courtesy of the Police Service of Northern Ireland.

39 Hulton Archive/Getty; 3350716, Photo by Firmin/Topical Press Agency. © Getty Images.

40 UCD Archives; Papers of Desmond and Mabel FitzGerald, IE UCDA P80-420-28. By kind permission of UCD Archives.

41 Hulton Archive/Getty; 3267780, Photo by Brooke/Topical Press Agency. © Getty Images.

42–3 UCD Archives; Papers of Kevin O'Higgins, IE UCDA P197-186. By kind permission of UCD Archives.

44 UCD Archives; Papers of Kevin O'Higgins, IE UCDA P197-186. By kind permission of UCD Archives.

45 National Archives of Ireland; Department of Foreign Affairs collection, DFA/112/47. Courtesy of the Board of the NAI.

46 Chicago History Museum; *Chicago Daily News* negatives collection, DN-084734. Courtesy of Chicago History Museum.

47 Getty; Universal Images Group Collection, 959124734, Photo 12/UIG. © Getty Images.

48 National Archives of Ireland; Department of the Taoiseach, S series files, TAOIS 3/S/5731. Courtesy of the Board of the NAI.

49 RTÉ Stills Library; Cashman Collection, 0506/048, Photo by Joseph Cashman. Courtesy of RTÉ Archives.

50 ESB Archives; Shannon Scheme Photographic Collection, PG.SS.PH.326.18. Courtesy of ESB Archives.

51 The Wolfsonian-Florida International University; The Mitchell Wolfson, Jr. Collection, TD1988.34.1, Photo by Bruce White. Courtesy of the Wolfsonian-Florida International University.

52 National Library of Ireland; Prints and Drawings, Gordon Brewster Cartoon Collection, PD 2199TX361, *Evening Herald*, 27 June 1931. Reproduced courtesy of the NLI.

53 Das Bundesarchiv; Fotoagentur Aktuelle-Bilder-Centrale Georg Pahl, Bild 102-08594. Reproduced courtesy of Das Bundesarchiv.

Chapter 3: 1932–1939

56 Alamy; Süddeutsche Zeitung Photo, CPJE2B, SZ Photo/Scherl. © Alamy Stock Photo.

58 National Archives of Ireland; Department of Foreign Affairs collection, DFA/112/47/passport. Courtesy of the Board of the NAI.

60 Private collection. Reproduced courtesy of Claire Dulanty.

62–3 National Library of Ireland; Ephemera Collection, Empire Marketing Board, Industrial Series, EMB/1, poster by Margaret Clarke. Reproduced courtesy of the NLI.

64 Hulton Archive/Getty; 3350724, Photo by Stephenson/Topical Press Agency. © Getty Images.

66 National Library of Ireland; National Photographic Archive, Independent Newspapers (Ireland) Collection, IND H-2056. Reproduced courtesy of the NLI.

67 NUI Galway, James Hardiman Library Archives; Rynne Family Papers, Michael Rynne Papers, P133/4/10/10A. Courtesy of NUI Galway.

68 National Library of Ireland; Seán T. Ó Ceallaigh Papers, MS 27.685/3/1. Reproduced courtesy of the NLI.

69 UCD Archives; Papers of Éamon de Valera, IE UCDA P150-2789-5. By kind permission of UCD–OFM Partnership.

70 UCD Archives; Papers of Éamon de Valera, IE UCDA P150-2816-1. By kind permission of UCD–OFM Partnership.

71 NUI Galway, James Hardiman Library Archives; Rynne Family Papers, Michael Rynne Papers, P133/4/10/10A. Courtesy of NUI Galway.

72 UCD Archives; Papers of Seán Lester, IE UCDA P203-152-1. By kind permission of UCD Archives.

73 (**top**) UCD Archives; Papers of Seán Lester, IE UCDA P203-127. By kind permission of UCD Archives.

73 (**bottom**) National Archives of Ireland; Department of Foreign Affairs collection, DFA 5/305/274. Courtesy of the Board of the NAI.

74 National Archives of Ireland; Department of Foreign Affairs collection, DFA 10/2/57. Courtesy of the Board of the NAI.

75 UCD Archives; Papers of Éamon de Valera, IE UCDA P150-2583. By kind permission of UCD–OFM Partnership.

76 UCD Archives; Papers of Éamon de Valera, IE UCDA P150-2536. By kind permission of UCD–OFM Partnership.

78 Library of Congress, Prints and Photographs Division; Harris and Ewing Collection, LC-H22-D-5265. Courtesy of the Library of Congress.

79 National Library of Ireland; Robert Brennan Papers, MS 49686/31/7. Reproduced courtesy of the NLI.

80–81 Private collection. Reproduced by permission of the family of Caitlín de Bhaldraithe.

82 New York Public Library, Manuscripts and Archives Division; New York World's Fair 1939–40 Records, b11686556, Item ID 1676099. Courtesy of New York Public Library.

83 Private collection. Reproduced by permission of the family of Caitlín de Bhaldraithe.

84 United Nations; UN Photo Library, UN Photo/Evan Schneider 800148. Courtesy of UN News and Media.

Chapter 4: 1939–1948

88 National Archives of Ireland; Department of Foreign Affairs collection, DFA 4/241/89. Courtesy of the Board of the NAI.

90 Alamy; Trinity Mirror/Mirrorpix, ERT9AY, Photo by Mirrorpix. © Alamy Stock Photo.

92–3 National Archives of Ireland; Department of the Taoiseach, S series files, TAOIS S/114455 A1 (1–2). Courtesy of the Board of the NAI.

94 National Archives of Ireland; Department of Foreign Affairs collection, DFA 1/4/751. Courtesy of the Board of the NAI.

96 Irish Defence Forces, Military Archives; Air Corps Vertical Aerial Photographs Collection, IE-MA-ACVN-P2-L10-01092. Courtesy of the Military Archives.

97 UCD Archives; Papers of Daniel Bryan, IE UCDA P 71-479-1. By kind permission of UCD Archives.

98 Irish Defence Forces, Military Archives; Hanley Collection/Emergency, MA 90-87. Courtesy of the Military Archives.

99 Dublin City Library and Archive; North Strand Bombing, 1941, NSB06 North Strand Road, Photo by H. McCrae. Courtesy of Dublin City Library and Archive.

100 National Archives of Ireland; Department of Foreign Affairs collection, Legal Adviser's miscellaneous papers. Courtesy of the Board of the NAI.

105 NUI Galway, James Hardiman Library Archives; Rynne Family Papers, Michael Rynne Papers, P 133/4/10/10A. Courtesy of NUI Galway.

106 NUI Galway, James Hardiman Library Archives; Rynne Family Papers, Michael Rynne Papers, P133/4/10/10A. Courtesy of NUI Galway.

108 National Archives of Ireland; Department of Foreign Affairs collection, DFA 2/24/3/1. Courtesy of the Board of the NAI.

109 National Archives of Ireland; Department of Foreign Affairs collection, DFA 6/419/1/4. Courtesy of the Board of the NAI.

110 National Archives of Ireland; Department of Foreign Affairs collection, DFA 6/419/1/3. Courtesy of the Board of the NAI.

111 National Archives of Ireland; Department of Foreign Affairs collection, DFA 6/419/4/22/2. Courtesy of the Board of the NAI.

112 National Archives of Ireland; Department of Foreign Affairs collection, DFA 6/419/1/7. Courtesy of the Board of the NAI.

114–15 National Archives of Ireland; Department of Foreign Affairs collection, DFA /6/419/4c (1–2). Courtesy of the Board of the NAI.

117 UCD Archives; Archives of the Fianna Fáil party, IE UCDA P176-1206. By kind permission of UCD Archives.

Chapter 5: 1948–1955

120 National Archives of Ireland; Department of Foreign Affairs collection, DFA 5/305/57/148/4. Courtesy of the Board of the NAI.

122 National Archives of Ireland; Department of Foreign Affairs collection, Holy See Embassy, 24/65.Courtesy of the Board of the NAI.

123 European Commission; Audiovisual Services, Photo archive, P-034170/00-01. Photo by Heckly. © Associated Press. Reproduced by permission of the European Commission.

125 National Archives of Ireland; Department of Foreign Affairs collection, DFA Buenos Aires 620/30/3. Courtesy of the Board of the NAI.

126 National Archives of Ireland; Department of Foreign Affairs collection, DFA 5/305/14/86. Courtesy of the Board of the NAI.

127 UCD Archives; Papers of John Hearne, IE UCDA P 291-47-15. By kind permission of UCD Archives.

128 UCD Archives; Papers of Frank Aiken, IE UCDA P104-4878 . By kind permission of UCD Archives.

129 NUI Galway, James Hardiman Library Archives; O'Malley Family Archive, Papers of Mary O'Malley, T4/3/2/3/1353. Courtesy of NUI Galway.

130 UCD Archives; Papers of Éamon de Valera, IE UCDA P150-2969-01. By kind permission of UCD–OFM Partnership.

131 Getty; The LIFE Picture Collection, 50643640, Photo by Larry Burrows. © Getty Images.

132 (top) UCD Archives; Papers of Frank Aiken, IE UCDA P104-4849-2. By kind permission of UCD Archives.

132 (bottom) Hulton Archive/Getty; Independent Newspapers Ireland/NLI Collection, 529089678, Photo by Independent News and Media. © Getty Images.

134 National Library of Australia; Albert Dryer photograph collection, 1914–55, PIC Album 1187, P829/35. Courtesy of the National Library of Australia.

135 Department of Foreign Affairs and Trade, Embassy of Ireland to Australia; Photo by member of embassy staff. Reproduced by permission.

136 National Archives of Ireland; Department of Foreign Affairs collection, DFA 5/317/27. Courtesy of the Board of the NAI.

137 National Archives of Ireland; Department of Foreign Affairs collection, DFA 5/317/30/1. Courtesy of the Board of the NAI.

138 Private collection. Reproduced by permission of the McDonagh Family.

140 (top) National Archives of Ireland; Department of Foreign Affairs collection, 5/317/65/2-MCNWEIN3. Courtesy of the Board of the NAI.

140 (bottom) National Archives of Ireland; Department of Foreign Affairs collection, DFA London Embassy E109/9. Courtesy of the Board of the NAI.

141 Private collection. Reproduced by permission of the McDonagh Family.

142 National Archives of Ireland; Department of Foreign Affairs collection, DFA 10/2/433. Courtesy of the Board of the NAI.

143 National Archives of Ireland; Department of Foreign Affairs collection, DFA 6/410/184. Courtesy of the Board of the NAI.

145 National Museum of Ireland; Museum of Country Life, 'Come Back to Erin' Exhibition, CIE Poster, F:2007.03. Courtesy of the National Museum of Ireland.

146 NUI Galway, James Hardiman Library Archives; Rynne Family Papers, Michael Rynne Papers, P133/4/11/9. Courtesy of NUI Galway.

148 National Archives of Ireland; Department of Foreign Affairs collection, DFA F/132/1/2. Courtesy of the Board of the NAI.

152 National Archives of Ireland; Department of Foreign Affairs collection, DFA 6/402/218. Courtesy of the Board of the NAI.

153 United Nations; UN Photo Library, UN Photo/MB 159499. Courtesy of UN News and Media.

154 National Archives of Ireland; Department of Foreign Affairs collection, DFA 6/433/26/14. Courtesy of the Board of the NAI.

Chapter 6: 1955–1957

158 National Archives of Ireland; Department of Foreign Affairs collection, DFA Washington Embassy D22. Courtesy of the Board of the NAI.

160 National Archives of Ireland; Department of Foreign Affairs collection, DFA 6/417/33/7. Courtesy of the Board of the NAI.

161 United Nations; UN Photo Library, UN Photo/MB 159495. Courtesy of UN News and Media.

162–3 United Nations; UN Photo Library, UN Photo/MB 87885. Courtesy of UN News and Media.

164 Irish Photo Archive; Lensmen Collection, A535-692. © Irish Photo Archive.

165 Irish Photo Archive; Lensmen Collection, A535-694. © Irish Photo Archive.

166 National Archives of Ireland; Department of Foreign Affairs collection, DFA Washington Embassy D22. Courtesy of the Board of the NAI.

168 Private collection. Reproduced by permission of the McDonagh Family.

169 UCD Archives; Papers of Frank Aiken, IE UCDA P104-8216-8. By kind permission of UCD Archives.

170–71 National Library of Ireland; Seán T. Ó Ceallaigh Papers, MS 27688/8 (4). Reproduced courtesy of the NLI.

Chapter 7: 1957–1968

174 UCD Archives; Papers of Frank Aiken, IE UCDA P104-7800-1. By kind permission of UCD Archives.

177 United Nations; UN Photo Library, UN Photo 363129. Courtesy of UN News and Media.

178 Aiken Family; Photo courtesy of the National Museum of Ireland, National Treasures Collection and the Aiken Family.

179 (top) United Nations; UN Photo Library, UN Photo 373387. Courtesy of UN News and Media.

179 (bottom) UCD Archives; Papers of Éamon de Valera, IE UCDA P150-3851. By kind permission of UCD–OFM Partnership.

180 National Archives of Ireland; Department of Foreign Affairs collection, DFA 6/438/21/92. Courtesy of the Board of the NAI.

181 Getty; Bettmann Archive, 515258742. © Getty Images.

183 United Nations; UN Photo Library, UN Photo/YES 383437. Courtesy of UN News and Media.

184 United Nations/The McDonagh Family; UN Photo Library, UN Photo/MB 378550. Courtesy of UN News and Media and the McDonagh Family.

185 United Nations; UN Photo Library, UN Photo 143452, Photo by Yutaka Nagata. Courtesy of UN News and Media.

186 Irish Defence Forces. Courtesy of Department of Defence.

187 Irish Defence Forces, Military Archives; Bureau of Military History, unnumbered. Courtesy of the Military Archives.

188 (top) United Nations; UN Photo Library, UN Photo/BZ 184402. Courtesy of UN News and Media.

188 (bottom) Irish Defence Forces, Military Archives; Private Collection Lt General Sean McKeown, MA PRCN 1. Courtesy of the Military Archives.

189 United Nations; UN Photo Library, UN Photo 366859. Courtesy of UN News and Media.

190 United Nations; UN Photo Library, UN Photo/BZ 52052. Courtesy of UN News and Media.

191 National Archives of Ireland; Department of Foreign Affairs collection, DFA 5/313/38/B. Courtesy of the Board of the NAI.

192 National Archives of Ireland; Department of Foreign Affairs collection, DFA Rome Embassy 555 D (II) 5. Courtesy of the Board of the NAI.

193 (top) UCD Archives; Papers of Frank Aiken, IE UCDA P104-8264-2r. By kind permission of UCD Archives.

193 (bottom) Private collection. Reproduced by permission of Orla O'Hanrahan.

195 *Time* Magazine; July 1963. © Time Inc.

196 Córas Tráchtala Poster; 1964 Irish Export Fashion Fair. Image courtesy of Brian MacMahon/Brand New Retro.

197 National Archives of Ireland; Department of Foreign Affairs collection, DFA Rome Embassy 555 (J) 13. Courtesy of the Board of the NAI.

198–9 National Archives of Ireland; Department of the Taoiseach, S series files, TSCH/3/S17401C63. Courtesy of the Board of the NAI.

200 John F. Kennedy Presidential Library and Museum; White House Photographs, KN-C29378, Photo by Robert L. Knudsen. Courtesy of John F. Kennedy Presidential Library and Museum.

201 Private collection. Reproduced by permission of Orla O'Hanrahan.

202 (top) Irish Defence Forces, Military Archives; President John F. Kennedy Visit 1963, Cadet School Digital Collection, Item 3, Photo by Cpl P. Fogarty retd. Courtesy of the Military Archives.

202 (bottom) Private collection. Reproduced by permission of Orla O'Hanrahan.

203 National Archives of Ireland; Department of Foreign Affairs collection, DFA Ottawa Embassy DI/2/IA. Courtesy of the Board of the NAI.

204 Private collection. Reproduced by permission of Orla O'Hanrahan.

205 UCD Archives; Papers of Frank Aiken, IE UCDA P104-6942-2r. By kind permission of UCD Archives.

207 Getty; Popperfoto Collection, 687082811, Photo by Rolls Press/Popperfoto. © Getty Images.

Chapter 8: 1968–1973

212 Public Record Office of Northern Ireland; Northern Ireland Government Information Service, Photographs, NI Government and Politicians, INF/7/A/5/110. Courtesy of PRONI.

214 United Nations; UN Photo Library, UN Photo/Teddy Chen 232632. Courtesy of UN News and Media.

217 Alamy; Keystone Pictures USA, E10RB6. © Alamy Stock Photo.

218 Dublin City Library and Archive; Dublin City Council Photographic Collection, 26217, Photo by William Mooney. Courtesy of Dublin City Library and Archive.

220 European Commission; Audiovisual Services, Photo archive, P-009247/00-1, Photo by Marcelle Jamar. Reproduced by permission of the European Commission.

222 Alamy; Keystone Pictures USA, E0YA25. © Alamy Stock Photo.

223 National Archives of Ireland; Department of Foreign Affairs collection, DFA Paris Embassy 2001/21/122. Courtesy of the Board of the NAI.

224 UCD Archives; Papers of Dr Patrick Hillery, IE UCDA P205-182-2. By kind permission of UCD Archives.

225 UCD Archives; Archives of the Fianna Fáil party, IE UCDA P176-1252. By kind permission of UCD Archives.

226 Private Collection. Reproduced by permission of Michael Kennedy.

228 UCD Archives; Papers of Dr Patrick Hillery, IE UCDA P205-178-7-10-1. By kind permission of UCD Archives.

229 Irish Photo Archive; Lensmen Collection, E16-960. © Irish Photo Archive.

230 Irish Photo Archive; Lensmen Collection, D85-772. © Irish Photo Archive.

233 Dublin City Library and Archive; Dublin City Council Photographic Collection, 30628, Photo by William Mooney. Courtesy of Dublin City Library and Archive.

234 United Nations; UN Photo Library, UN Photo 129818, Photo by J. Riedel. Courtesy of UN News and Media.

235 Private Collection. Reproduced by permission of Donal Denham.

236 Department of Foreign Affairs and Trade; Irish Aid. Courtesy of DFAT.

Chapter 9: 1973–1985

240 European Commission; Audiovisual Services, Photo archive, P-001964/08-10, Photo by Christian Lambiotte. Reproduced by permission of the European Commission.

242 Private collection. Reproduced by permission of Marie Cross.

244 European Commission; Audiovisual Services, Photo archive, P-003879/06-21. Reproduced by permission of the European Commission.

245 European Commission; Audiovisual Services, Photo archive, P-001963/02-19. Reproduced by permission of the European Commission.

246 National Archives of Ireland; 2017/11/222. Courtesy of the Board of the NAI.

247 (top) UCD Archives; Papers of Garret FitzGerald, IE UCDA GFG05. By kind permission of UCD Archives.

247 (bottom) Private Collection. Reproduced by permission of the Holmes Family.

248 Alamy; Trinity Mirror/Mirrorpix, B3NKBC, Photo by Mirrorpix. © Alamy Stock Photo.

250 UCD Archives; Papers of Garret FitzGerald, IE UCDA P215-68-2. By kind permission of UCD Archives.

251 UCD Archives; Papers of Garret FitzGerald , IE UCDA GFG003. By kind permission of UCD Archives.

252 RTÉ Stills Library; Item 0695/041. Courtesy of RTÉ Archives.

254 UCD Archives; Papers of Dr Patrick Hillery, IE UCDA P205-187-1. By kind permission of UCD Archives.

255 (top) European Commission; Audiovisual Services, Photo archive, P-001983/069H. Reproduced by permission of the European Commission.

255 (bottom) Private Collection. Reproduced by permission of Orla O'Hanrahan.

257 United Nations; UN Photo Library, UN Photo 263326, Photo by Yutaka Nagata. Courtesy of UN News and Media.

258 United Nations; UN Photo Library, UN Photo 263315, Photo by Yutaka Nagata. Courtesy of UN News and Media.

260 Private Collection. Reproduced by permission of the Holmes Family.

261 UCD Archives; Papers of Dr Patrick Hillery, IE UCDA P205-1706-29. By kind permission of UCD Archives.

262 United Nations/The McDonagh Family; UN Photo Library, UN Photo 267498, Photo by Yutaka Nagata. Courtesy of UN News and Media and the McDonagh Family.

263 UCD Archives; Papers of Garret FitzGerald, IE UCDA GFG001. By kind permission of UCD Archives.

264 Private Collection. Reproduced by permission of Noel Dorr.

265 Hulton Archive/Getty; Independent Newspapers Ireland/NLI Collection, 540622878, Photo by Matt Walsh/Independent News and Media. © Getty Images.

266 (top) Alamy; Trinity Mirror/Mirrorpix, B4WKWN, Photo by Mirrorpix. © Alamy Stock Photo.

266 (bottom) Private Collection. Reproduced by permission of Michael Lillis.

267 UCD Archives; Papers of Dr Patrick Hillery , IE UCDA P205-189-8. By kind permission of UCD Archives.

Chapter 10: 1985–1998

272 Irish Photo Archive; Lensmen Collection, R99-666. © Irish Photo Archive.

274 Private Collection. Reproduced by permission of Niall Holohan.

275 National Archives of Ireland; Department of Foreign Affairs collection, DFA 2017/14/21. Courtesy of the Board of the NAI.

277 Private Collection. Reproduced by permission of Marie Cross.

280 Alamy; Allstar Picture Library, BHTKF3. © Alamy Stock Photo.

281 Alamy; G446AT. © Alamy Stock Photo.

285 National Archives of Ireland; Department of Foreign Affairs collection, DFA 13/2009/132/75. Courtesy of the Board of the NAI.

Chapter 11: 1998–2019

288 United Nations; UN Photo Library, UN Photo 84177, Photo by Andrea Brizzi. Courtesy of UN News and Media.

290 United Nations; UN Photo Library, UN Photo 686365, Photo by Eskinder Debebe. Courtesy of UN News and Media.

291 United Nations; UN Photo Library, UN Photo 157878, Photo by Tara Engberg. Courtesy of UN News and Media.

293 Irish Defence Forces, Military Archives; KFOR Deployment, IE MA 55-79. Courtesy of the Military Archives.

294 European Commission; Audiovisual Services, Photo archive, P-010383/00-23, Photo by Jan van de Vel. Reproduced by permission of the European Commission.

295 Department of Foreign Affairs and Trade; Secretary General's Office, Iveagh House. Courtesy of Phil Behan/DFAT/The Gallagher Family.

296–7 Department of Foreign Affairs and Trade. Courtesy of DFAT.

298 Department of Foreign Affairs and Trade. Courtesy of DFAT.

299 Private Collection. Reproduced by permission of Niall Burgess.

300 Alamy; GARNHK. © Alamy Stock Photo.

301 Getty; AFP/Adalberto Roque, 84881985. © Getty Images.

302 European Commission; Audiovisual Services, Photo archive, P-009167/00-24, Photo by Mike St Maur Sheil. Reproduced by permission of the European Commission.

303 Department of Foreign Affairs and Trade. Photo by Ray Attard. Courtesy of DFAT.

304 Department of Foreign Affairs and Trade. Courtesy of DFAT.

305 Department of Foreign Affairs and Trade. Photo by Maxwell Photography. Courtesy of DFAT.

306 Department of Foreign Affairs and Trade. Photo by Maxwell Photography. Courtesy of DFAT.

307 Vatican Media; Eventi 2014, 00688_11112014. Reproduced by permission.

308 (top) Private Collection. Reproduced by permission of Rory Montgomery.

308 (bottom) Fáilte Ireland, Ireland's content pool; ID 025BBDED-D440-4AD0-A605A161BF48BAF3, Photo by Peter Grogan. Courtesy of Fáilte Ireland.

311 Department of Foreign Affairs and Trade. Photo by Maxwell Photography. Courtesy of DFAT.

312–13 Department of Foreign Affairs and Trade. Photo by Maxwell Photography. Courtesy of DFAT.

314 Department of Foreign Affairs and Trade. Photo by Paul McErlane. Courtesy of DFAT.

316 Private Collection. Reproduced by permission of Niall Burgess.

317 (top) United Nations; UN Photo Library, UN Photo 631936, Photo by Evan Schneider. Courtesy of UN News and Media.

317 (bottom) Department of Foreign Affairs and Trade. Courtesy of DFAT.

318–19 Department of Foreign Affairs and Trade. Photo by Julien Behal. Courtesy of DFAT.

320 Department of Foreign Affairs and Trade. Courtesy of DFAT.

321 (top) Irish Defence Forces. Courtesy of Department of Defence.

321 (bottom) Department of Foreign Affairs and Trade; Photo by Julien Behal. Courtesy of DFAT.

322–3 Department of Foreign Affairs and Trade. Courtesy of DFAT.

324 Department of Foreign Affairs and Trade. Courtesy of DFAT.

Endmatter

326 National Library of Ireland; Seán T. Ó Ceallaigh Papers, MS 27688/8 (3). Reproduced courtesy of the NLI.

338 Royal Irish Academy; Illustration © Paula McGloin. Courtesy of the RIA and Paula McGloin.

343. Photograph © John Minihan; reproduced with permission.

Index

B

Baldonnell Aerodrome, Dublin, 186
Baldwin, Stanley, 41
Balfour Declaration (1926), 41, 44
Ballywristeen, Co. Waterford, 98
Ban Ki-Moon, 317
Bangladesh, 209, 232
Barnier, Michel, 318–20
Barrington, Ted, 262
Barry, Peter, 262, 330
Barton, Robert, 18
Battle of Britain (1940), 90, 99
Battle of the Atlantic (Second World War), 91, 99
Battle of the Boyne (1690), 299
Beckett, Samuel, 269
Behan, John, 288–9
Beijing, 267
Beirut, 258
Belfast, 107, 131, 213, 214–15, 218, 262–3, 266, 279–80, 314
Belfast Agreement, *see* Good Friday Agreement
Belgium, 16, 47, 110, 143, 221, 224, 227, 240–41, 303
Berehaven, 77; *see also* Treaty Ports
Bergen-Belsen, 101
Berlin, 17, 47, 49–50, 52–3, 72–5, 88–9, 91–5, 98, 100–101, 111, 193
Berne, 91, 95, 113
Bewley, Charles, 26, 72–5, 91
Biafra, 231
Biggar, Francis, 220–21
Binchy, Daniel, 53
Birkenau, 101
Birmingham Six, 279
Blacksod Bay, Co. Mayo, 102
Blair, Tony, 282, 284–5
Blaney, Neil, 215
Bloody Sunday (1972), 218
Boland, Frederick, 90, 106–7, 113–16, 123, 136, 147, 148–9, 151–3, 161, 162–3, 166, 178, 181, 185, 331

Boland, Harry, 13–15, 22
Boland, Kevin, 186
Bolger, Caroline, 266
Bonn, 147, 193
Bono, 306
Book of Kells, 306–7
Boothe Luce, Clare, 123
Bord Fáilte, 144–6; *see also* Fáilte Ireland
Bosnia and Herzegovina, 292
Boston, 14, 28, 50, 65, 155, 253
Boundary Commission, 22, 37–41, 213
Boyne Visitor Centre, 299
Brandt, Willy, 193
Brazil, 306, 311
Brennan, Charles, 166
Brennan, Claire, 137
Brennan, Edward, 247
Brennan, Joseph D., 137, 166
Brennan, Maeve, 78
Brennan, Patrick, 78
Brennan, Robert, 11, 16, 22–3, 78, 97, 101, 102, 104, 106–7
Brennan, Tony, 264
Brexit, 155, 303–4, 314–315, 320
Briand, Aristide, 47
Brisbane, 135
Britain, 3–22, 33, 34, 37–46, 50, 57–61, 64, 67, 75–7, 89–100, 104–5, 107, 116, 123, 128–30, 133, 138–41, 143, 146, 147–9, 150–52, 160, 163–5, 167, 181, 187, 191–4, 203, 214–19, 221–2, 228, 229, 234, 242, 243–4, 246, 247, 248–66, 273, 274, 278–85, 300, 304, 311–15, 320
British Empire, 4, 17, 22, 34, 61–3, 128, 137
Brooke, Peter, 280
Brussels, 16, 47, 191, 221, 224, 227, 240–41, 303
Buenos Aires, 111–13, 124
Bulfin, Eamon, 16
Burgess, Niall, 331, 343
Burke, Ray, 330
Bush, George, Snr, 263
Byrne, Thomas, 200
Byrne Nason, Geraldine, 84

C

L

Labour Party, 116, 121–2, 227, 241, 256, 259, 317
Lagos, 154, 191
Land Acts, 59
Lawless, Gerard, 234
League of Nations, 3, 26, 34–7, 47, 49, 50, 51–2, 58, 61–75, 91, 113, 159, 163, 176, 233–4
Lebanon, 176, 181, 246, 248, 258, 278
Lemass, Seán, 78, 106–7, 146, 186, 189–96, 200, 212–14, 221, 228
Lenihan, Brian, 228, 255, 272–3, 329, 330
Lesotho, 232
Lester, Seán, 26, 61–5, 72, 73, 91
Liberia, 292
Libya, 274, 310
Lie, Trygve, 113
Liebherr, Hans, 228
Lillis, Michael, 258, 262–3, 264, 266
Limerick, 303
Lisbon, 95, 111
Lisbon Treaty (2007), 294–8
Liverpool, 129–30
Livni, Tzipi, 298
Lloyd George, David, 17
local staff, 209, 235
Lomé Convention, 244, 245
London, 15, 17–22, 41–4, 46, 50, 58–61, 91–5, 100, 104, 139–41, 143, 147–9, 151, 248, 254–6, 259, 281, 282
Lough Swilly, 77; see also Treaty Ports
Lusaka, 235
Luxembourg, 146, 227, 243, 255
Lynch, Bridget, 18
Lynch, Diarmaid, 13
Lynch, Fionán, 18
Lynch, Jack, 194, 206–7, 214–18, 224–9, 241, 253–4, 256
Lynch, Máirín, 206–7
Lyons, Alice, 18
Lyons, Ellie, 18

M

McAleese, Martin, 311
McAleese, Mary, 311
Macaulay, William J.B., 66
MacBride, Seán, 121–7, 130–33, 136, 137, 141, 234, 329
McCann, Hugh, 78, 80–81, 331
McCartan, Patrick, 13, 16
McCarthy, Justin, 176–7
McCauley, Leo, 72, 136
McDonagh, Bobby, 141
McDonagh, Philip, 141
McDonagh, Robert, 141, 184–5, 216, 262, 331
MacDonald, Malcolm, 64
MacDonald, Ramsay, 38–9
McEntee, Helen, 324
MacEntee (Mhac an tSaoi), Máire, 136
MacEoin, Seán, 182, 188
McGilligan, Patrick, 49, 52, 329
McGrath, Joseph, 18
McGuinness, Máiread, 318–20
Mackenzie King, William Lyon, 127
MacKernan, Pádraig, 262, 263, 331
McLaglen, Victor, 133
McLaughlin, Dermot, 278
MacNeill, Eoin, 35, 41
McNeill, James, 66, 123–4
McNeill, Josephine, 123–4, 140–41
McQuaid, John Charles, 121
MacSwiney, Marquis, 32–3, 35
MacSwiney, Mary, 22
MacWhite, Michael, 2–3, 26, 34–5, 37, 65, 106–7, 111
Maas, Heiko, 321
Maastricht Treaty, 276, 277
Madigan, Emma, 306–7
Madigan, Josepha, 324
Madrid, 17, 22, 67–9, 73, 95, 100, 111, 135
Maffey, John, 91
Magee, Roy, 281
Major, John, 280–82
Maldives, 209